THE HIST(

A Concise History of Galicia

SHARIF GEMIE

UNIVERSITY OF WALES PRESS
CARDIFF 2006

Published by the University of Wales Press

University of Wales Press
10 Columbus Walk
Brigantine Place
Cardiff
CF10 4UP

www.wales.ac.uk/press

ISBN-10 0-7083-1989-0 hardback
ISBN-10 0-7083-1988-2 paperback

ISBN-13 978-0-7083-1989-5 hardback
ISBN-13 978-0-7083-1988-8 paperback

British Library Cataloguing-in-Publication Data.
A catalogue record for this book is available from the British Library.

Printed in Great Britain by Antony Rowe Ltd, Chippenham, Wiltshire

THE HISTORIES OF EUROPE

A Concise History of Galicia

Series Editor
Ned Thomas
Mercator Centre, University of Wales, Aberystwyth

For series information, please visit the University of Wales website:
www.wales.ac.uk/press

To Ursula

Contents

Acknowledgements

Although only one person is listed as the author of this work it is, like most books, actually a collective work. I would like to thank all those people who have helped me in my research and writing, and in particular to express my gratitude to the following:

Patricia, *mi compañera* and guide, who has given me invaluable help throughout this project: 'ce soleil-là . . .'; Adrian Price, for the original suggestion that I consider researching this topic; Ashley Drake, director of UWP, for his enthusiasm and encouragement; Sarah Lewis, commissioning editor of UWP, for her support; the Librería Renacimiento (*www.libreriarenacimiento.com*) for their astonishing ability to find long-out-of-print texts; *os mozos e as mozas* of AS: Carl, Ruth, Richard, Ian, L. Susan and Jon; Roz Tarry, for her amazing emergency translation service; Mariola Mourelo (*www.geocities.com/mariolamourelo*), Silvia Carril Caldelas and Anxela Carril Caldelas, for their helpful comments on modern Galicia (the views expressed in chapters 5 and 6 are my own, and are not necessarily shared by Mariola, Silvia and Anxela); Mariola, for her assistance in providing and locating pictures; Ned Thomas and Elisa Costa-Villaverde, for the care with which they read the first draft manuscript; Fiona Reid, Barry Cunliffe and Ruth Kinna, for their useful critical comments on early drafts of this work.

Introduction

This work has three purposes. Firstly, it aims to provide the general reader, probably new to this subject, with an introduction to the landmarks of Galician history. However, these key points do not exist in some splendid isolation, untouched by debate and challenges. The second aim of this book is to alert the reader to some of the controversies and debates inherent in the processes of nation-building and identity-formation in this corner of Spain, and to point out the connections and interplay between the history of Galicia and wider currents in Spain, Europe and across the Atlantic. Within this wide spectrum of debate, some special attention will be paid to the arguments and analyses of Galician nationalists: this constitutes the third aim. Galician nationalist groups have never dominated Galicia's political cultures. They have rarely acquired the backing of more than a fifth of the population of the region, although – as Galician nationalists would be quick to point out – there have been several important episodes in Galician history which suggest a broader and deeper level of support. Nationalism will be studied here because it is – arguably – the most interesting political current to come out of Galicia.

There are some obvious difficulties in trying to write a work which covers more than two millennia in six chapters. Like any historical work, these challenges can only be resolved by making a selection, by choosing to study particular themes. In this work, the first two chapters provide an overview of Galicia's ancient, medieval and early modern history, the third and fourth chapters study the political crises of the early and mid-twentieth century, while the two final chapters consider some issues in post-1975 Galicia. In adopting this approach to the chronology of Galician history, I am focusing on the recent past as the most relevant to today's readers.

A brief note on terminology: I will be using the terms 'region' and 'land' in this work to refer to Galicia. This is not a response to the claims of Galician nationalism, but merely a stylistic convenience, allowing comparisons between Galicia and Spain to be made easily within the same sentence. I have attempted to use Galego orthography when referring to people or places in Galicia, and Castilian orthography for people and places in the rest of Spain: however, as this work involves a number of English-language studies and makes some reference to France and to Argentina, it has not been possible to be entirely consistent.

A glossary of specialist terms and acronyms is provided.

Glossary

Autonomous Community – the 1978 Spanish constitution redefined Spain as a country formed of different regions. Seventeen regions were recognized: each of these forms an 'autonomous community' within the structures of the Spanish Constitution.

Bloque Nacional Galego (BNG) – created in 1977 as the Bloque Nacional – Popular Galego, this was originally an electoral platform for the UPG, which admitted other similar currents of opinion. In the 1990s it grew into a substantial political force, and it remains the principal voice of Galician nationalism.

Carlism – a revolutionary, reactionary grouping, inspired by a romantic idealization of an older, Catholic and monarchist Spain. Carlists opposed the existing Spanish monarchy, and fought three civil wars in the nineteenth century.

Cortes – the Spanish parliament.

Dereita Galeguista – a right-wing split from the Partido Galeguista, formed in 1935.

Esquerda Galega (EG) – Galician Left. A 'new left' formation, formed in the late 1970s.

Galego – the language of Galicia.

Galeguista – Galego term meaning 'Galician patriot'.

Partido Galeguista (PG) – Galician nationalist party, created in December 1931.

Partido Popular (PP – Popular Party) – created in 1990, as a modernization of the older Alianza Popular of 1977. Spain's principal right-wing party.

Partido Socialista Galego (PSG – Galician Socialist Party) – a social-democratic grouping, created in 1963, which turned to radical nationalism in the late 1960s. This group grew closer to the BNG in the 1980s: uniting the two organizations was a complex process, but was finally achieved in 1993.

Partido Socialista Obrera Español (PSOE – Spanish Socialist Workers Party) – the main socialist party in Spain, created in 1879. The approximate equivalent of the British Labour Party.

Province – today, Spain is divided into fifty provinces, the approximate equivalent to the British county. Each province takes its name from its capital city: thus there is the city of Lugo and the province of Lugo.

Traditionalists – in the late nineteenth century, Carlists grew disillusioned with their repeated failure to bring down the orthodox Spanish monarchy. 'Traditionalism' was their attempt to remodel their movement as a political organization with a distinct political philosophy.

Unión do Povo Galego (UPG – Union of the Galician People) – founded in 1963 as a revolutionary Galician nationalist organization. The UPG was also one of the founding members of the BNG, which was created to fight the 1977 Spanish general elections. The UPG remains an important faction within the BNG.

Xunta – the Galician regional assembly, created in 1981.

1

Celts, Moors and the myth of Saint James: Galicia from prehistory to c.1500

The history of this land starts with a single word: the Roman term 'Gallaecia'. While this probably referred to a specific tribe in north-west Spain, it is derived from the Latin word 'Gaul', which was the Romans' equivalent for the earlier Greek term *Keltoi*, 'the Celts'. There were several Galicias in the Roman world: as well as our Galicia, in Spain, there was another alongside today's German–Polish border, and a third lay in contemporary Turkey. Much of today's France was 'Gallia', and the Spanish word for 'Welsh' is still 'Gales'. For the Romans, there were Gauls – or Celts – to be found everywhere in Europe. But it is often unclear exactly what this term meant. At times it was little more than an insult, and the term 'Gallaecia' might be as scientifically accurate and culturally perceptive as the label 'Taff-land'. Following the destruction of Rome in 390 BC by a Gaulish invasion force, the Romans were terrified of the Gauls, and their later accounts preserve images of fierce giants, lumbering Obelix-like into battle on their creaking carts, screaming insults at the smaller, more disciplined Roman forces, and then gathering their strengths for one massive, furious charge. Such tales make for stirring reading, and for this reason they were often exploited by Roman leaders seeking to build up their own reputations as military leaders. Some of the oppositions which these accounts set up – such as the contrast between rational, Latin thinking and Celtic passion – are still with us today. But these texts do not constitute accurate ethnological descriptions. 'Gaul' and 'Celt' were loaded words in the classical world, and need to be used with care by today's historians.

A second historical problem with the Romans' term 'Gauls' is that it can only be used to frame sets of oppositions. The Romans were defined by what the Gauls were not; they possessed an urban civilization while the Gauls were rural; they worshipped true gods while the Gauls followed mere cults; they were advanced while the Gauls were primitive; and so on. This form of historical thinking, built around simple oppositions, is surprisingly similar to some of the dominant interpretations of Spanish history that form the 'invasionist' thesis, according to which modern Spain was created through a near-constant series of conquests and battles.[1]

Certainly, there were frequent attacks into Spanish territory. One can identify many waves of invaders who reached Galicia: Celts, Romans, Suebes, Visigoths, Moors, Berbers and Asturians. One can even further complicate the historical record by classifying Christians as an eighth invading force. But this perspective reduces history to a set of battles and conflicts: it hides the exchanges and interplay between peoples, and so underestimates – for example – the importance of Roman-Iberian culture. In place of a bloody history of battles, we need something more subtle to understand the complex processes which prefigured the creation of modern Galician identities for, if there is one constant stretching through almost three millennia of Galician history, it is the *absence* of clearly structured political forms.

This chapter will provide an introduction to some of these debates. I will briefly identify some of the most important 'invasions', and evaluate their long-term effects on the development of Galicia. Within this short chapter I cannot provide an in-depth historical study of these processes: interested readers must consult the works listed in the bibliography or the notes for further information. The key issue to be debated in this chapter is whether one can identify some single event as constituting the beginning of Galicia.

Celts and castles

This corner of north-west Spain has been inhabited for a long time. Before the Celts, a prehistoric people settled in this region as the climate grew warmer after the last great Ice Age. We know little about them, beyond a few obvious points. They were not isolated: new people, bringing with them new techniques of food production, arrived by land and by sea into this north-west corner of the peninsula. As their civilizations grew more complex, they put up the enormous standing stones that remain to this day, some twenty thousand of them, still scattered across the surface of Galicia.[2] These people lived in small, itinerant, relatively egalitarian communities, and developed skills in metalworking and then pottery: they traded with the peoples to the north and south.

About two millennia before Christ, this culture began to evolve once more. They now built *castros*, or hill-forts. These were the first permanent settlements in Galicia. They were set in high places, and had multiple walls surrounding dense clumps of circular houses.[3] These were more structured communities, probably ruled by a military elite. The dead were buried, and these graves preserve evidence of a more sophisticated material civilization. Their swords, scabbards and jewellery, dating from the fifth century BC, resemble similar objects in the 'La Tène' style found elsewhere in central Europe: such objects are now considered one of the key signs of a Celtic civilization. The objects in these early Galician graves have the same swirling motifs, the same intricate curves, the same considered beauty in their designs.

Similar evidence of Celtic cultures can be found across the northern and western two-thirds of the Iberian peninsula, but there are some traits which mark out the people of the north-west as different: their *castros*, their use of gold, and the distinctive patterns on their jewellery and pottery. Greek and Roman observers identified all the peoples in the west of the Iberian peninsula as Celts or Gauls, referring to the 'Gallaeci lucense' in the north-west corner, the 'Gallaeci bracari' to the south of the river Minho (in present-day Portugal), the 'Lusitani' in the west, and the 'Celtici' in the south-west. There is, however, one piece missing from this pan-Celtic jigsaw: linguistic evidence. Until about the third century AD, most of the peoples labelled as Celts were non-literate, and so any evidence concerning their languages is indirect and therefore less than certain. In north-west Europe, of course, the evidence for a strongly rooted family of similar Celtic languages is reasonably consistent. The data from Galicia is less clear. There are just a few scattered, unclear inscriptions from funeral inscriptions, and some hints from Roman transcriptions of place names which suggest the use of a Celtic language; certainly nothing that one could term 'literature': no Celtic-language folk tales or poetry.

So, were these people Celts? Those who consider that language is at the heart of cultural identity will probably answer 'no'. This point could be pushed a little further: a Galician tribal chief wielding a La Tène-style sword was probably no more Celtic than a present-day Saudi prince driving a BMW is German. But perhaps this is the wrong question to ask. There was no 'nationality test' in these ancient times; no distinct barrier between the Celtic and the non-Celtic, beyond the Romans' over-schematic distinctions. It is probably more accurate to see the culture of the *castros* as connected to themes of Celtic Europe, but also linked to the indigenous culture of north-west Spain. Rather than proving that there was a Celtic conquest of the region, or a massive Celtic migration, the *castros* instead suggest a fusion of indigenous and Celtic cultures.

The Romans

The Roman occupation of Spain was a slow process, starting in 206 BC on the eastern coast, involving a bloody cycle of battles from 155 BC to 133 BC, pushed forward by Julius Caesar's legions from 61 to 59 BC, and not finishing in Galicia until the victory by Octavian (who later became Emperor Augustus) in 19 BC. The Romans sought to accomplish two aims by taking the north-west. The first was to prevent the region from being used as a base for attacks on Roman settlements. Its occupation would complete the pacification of Spain, and would therefore allow the withdrawal of Roman soldiers. But, secondly, the Romans knew of Galicia's mineral resources, in particular its gold, but also its iron, tin and silver. At one point, Galicia was supplying 7 per cent of Imperial Rome's gold, and some 230 ancient mining-sites have been identified in north-west Spain.[4] Rome's rule meant the region's integration into wider economic structures; Galicia's metalwork and ceramics began to circulate throughout the Empire. Some of its men were conscripted to serve with the Roman legions, while Roman legal norms changed local patterns of land ownership and commercial transactions.

It would be false, however, to consider this period as the military annihilation of Galicia. Roman experts judged that it was impossible to conquer every hill and every wood in the region. The mountains in the present-day eastern half of Galicia posed a particular problem: they provided ideal refuges for brigands and outlaws. Instead, the Roman strategy was more partial. Their legions sought to secure the routes along which gold and other minerals were exported. The principal Roman settlement in present-day Galicia was Lucus Augusti (now Lugo), on the flat plain just west of the mountains, with eighty-five towers and a two-kilometre-long wall, which survives to the present.[5] The Roman presence in the western half of present-day Galicia was less significant.

The new Roman roads served many purposes. They enabled the flow of trade, but they also embedded the threat of military force, which allowed Roman rulers to collect taxes in this region. The roads connected settlements to form a new urban network: Bracara Augusta, on the Atlantic coast, in present-day Portugal; Asturica Augusta, to the east of present-day Galicia; Lucus Augusti, in the north-east of the current Galicia; and Iria Flavia (now Padrón), on the western coast, which later became the main Christian centre in Galicia. These were real urban settlements, housing administrative and economic specialisms distinct from the surrounding countryside.[6]

While the first Galician languages were replaced by Latin dialects, there is evidence of cultural and social continuities during the Roman period. One study of eighty-eight place names from the sixth century finds that fifty-one of them (58 per cent) were pre-Roman.[7] The *castros* themselves survived into the Roman period and after: significantly, however, their architecture began to change. They began to incorporate straight roads, planned quarters and even rectangular houses. Pre-Christian religions survived among the mass of the population. Above all, indigenous elites often survived from the *castro* period, now living in Roman-style villas, adopting the Latin language and Roman decorations. Landless labourers worked on their nearby estates.

Christianity did not arrive in Galicia until about AD 200, later than in other parts of Spain, and it developed only slowly and superficially over the next two centuries. Galician religious beliefs did, however, attract the Church's attention. Priscillianism thrived there, a heresy about which extremely little is known. Its contents can be guessed at only by studying its orthodox critics. It appears to have been ascetic and critical of the established Church, perhaps more rooted in the belief systems of the countryside. It was condemned at the Church's Council of Toledo in 400.[8]

Nineteenth-century historians would have described these processes as three invasions: by Celts, Romans and Christians. In each case, there were certainly episodes of violence, but one should not consider these moments as simple confrontations or as the brutal imposition of alien power-structures on to a settled polity. What is clear is that these episodes did not produce strong political authorities in the region, and that there was often a lack of any clear sense of 'us' and 'them'. While the term 'Galicia' was used by the Romans as an administrative shorthand for north-west Spain, neither its boundaries nor its significance were clear. Instead, this early period is marked by adaptations and fusions, by shifting developments as old local elites changed within new structures of power.

The Suebes

In the late third century the Roman *limes*, the militarized line of forts, roads, walls and ditches that stretched from the Danube to the Rhine, began to fail. It was never intended to be an impregnable barrier, but was something more akin to a military superhighway for the Roman army, enabling the Imperial forces to act quickly to prevent the entry of hostile forces. Its collapse ended the first European attempt to embody a clear contrast between 'them' and 'us' in a physical form. Local elites across Europe turned from consciously adapting to Roman norms to deliberately reviving and reinventing older pasts.[9] New vernacular spoken languages evolved, drawn from Latin, but also incorporating other influences. The history of the next six or seven centuries is poorly documented, and therefore less clear than the Roman epoch; yet, paradoxically, it is also this period that nationalist historians from across Europe often choose as the birthplace for so many modern nationalities.

In this epoch of Imperial decline, two tribes crossed from central Europe down to the south-west. The Suebes, a tribe probably originating from present-day north-west Germany, crossed the *limes* in 406, and by 411 were present in Galicia, making the southern town of Braga their capital. There were approximately thirty thousand of them: a large number, perhaps, but not so many that they could not be accommodated within the region.[10] They were followed by the Visigoths, in still larger numbers, who settled across the peninsula. The Visigoths made use of Latin for their law codes and perhaps also for their daily speech, and they followed a heterodox form of Christianity, Arianism. These features have led one prominent historian to observe that, paradoxically, it was these 'barbarians' who implemented the final, true 'romanization' of Spain.[11]

Less is known of the Suebes. In the first decades that they were present in Galicia, they appear to have been a peaceful people. Then in 429, their leaders adopted Christianity, perhaps in an attempt to weld together an alliance with the indigenous peoples. A series of battles followed, as the Suebe leaders tried to expand their power southwards and eastwards into the areas of Spain controlled by the Visigoths. They were defeated in 456, and the Visigoths then took Braga. Following this, the Suebe leaders converted to the Visigoths' Arian form of Christianity. In effect, they also accepted religious guidance from Toledo, the Visigoth capital in the centre of Spain.

The great twentieth-century Galician nationalist, Alfonso R. Castelao, discusses the Suebes in his lyrical text, *Sempre en Galiza*, written in exile in the 1940s. He claims that this group created 'the first form of State' in Spain.[12] Why did Castelao value these largely illiterate tribes, with their ineffective leaders, so highly? In part, he is following two long-standing Spanish prejudices: a condemnation of the influence of the Roman Empire, which was frequently seen as anti-Christian, but also a condemnation of the subsequent Muslim domination of the peninsula (to be discussed below).[13] Given these two unacceptable historical precedents, nationalist historians, whether Spanish or Galician, were obliged to look to the period between the fourth and the eighth century for evidence of the birth of nationhood. Moreover, there are some peculiarities about the Suebian period, which fascinated Castelao. It is noticeable that, for example, no 'Suebia' was founded: the new elites continued to talk of 'Gallaecia', and to claim power over an area considerably larger than the present-day Galicia.[14] For Galician nationalists such as Castelao, the Suebes are important, as it was during their rule that a Galician territory was marked out as sharply distinct from the rest of Spain. This new power certainly did not constitute a modern nation, but – equally – 'Gallaecia' was now more than a mere administrative subdivision. There are some important flaws in such arguments, to which I will return later.

During this confused period, another new force appeared in Galician history. In the fifth and sixth centuries migrants left from the western regions of the British Isles: probably from present-day Wales or Cornwall. It seems likely that they were fleeing from advancing Saxon forces, but it is possible that it was pressure by incomers from present-day Ireland that pushed them to leave.[15] Most sailed to western France, and so contributed to the region now known as Brittany. Some, however, travelled further south to Galicia, in which there is still a village of Bretoña (located in today's province of Lugo). It is difficult to be certain of the long-term importance of this group. It seems likely that they contributed to the development of Christianity in Galicia, for in this period Christian structures were more firmly rooted and better organized in the British Isles than in Spain. We do know that they had their own bishop, who participated in the first Church Council at Braga in 561. One wonders about their linguistic contribution. In the case of Brittany, many have argued the newcomers from the Isles strongly affected the development of a local Celtic language. In Galicia, they seem to have contributed little to Galego, the regional language which developed during the medieval period.

During the Visigoths' domination of Spain, the old Roman towns decayed.[16] The new elite stayed in the old Roman villas, and used slave labour on their estates. In the 580s their king and bishops converted from Arianism to the official Christianity of the Roman Church. In 672, the Visigoth King Wamba was consecrated – the first western monarch to go through this ceremony, and therefore to receive the Church's explicit approval. Towns in the centre and south – Toledo and Seville – became centres of Christian learning and worship. More worryingly, these new Christian rulers initiated an official policy of anti-Semitism, seeing Jews as an obstacle to the unity of their kingdom. Forty discriminatory laws were passed between 681 and 694: one of the last demanded that all remaining Jews become slaves. The passing of these laws did not mean that all the peoples of Spain followed the Visigoths' religious policies. Folk beliefs, paganism, popular cults based on woods, rivers and mountains, continued for centuries afterwards. Furthermore, the official anti-Semitism of the Germanic ruling class attracted little popular support.

These Germanic tribes left few permanent changes within Spain; their rule was chaotic, without clear guiding principles. Rather than providing directions for the whole of a society, they were military castes who converted themselves into landowning aristocracies, small groups of linked families who formed elites, exploiting the rest. One sign of the shallowness of their presence can be gained by examining the linguistic record: it has been estimated that only about ninety words derived from the Visigoth languages survive in modern Spanish.[17]

Whether the Visigoths would ever have been able to create a stable, unified and coherent polity is an open question, as is the position of Galicia within their rule. Their domination of Spain, however, was short-lived.

The Moors

In 711 a new invading force entered Spain, this time from the south. These were Muslims, or 'Moors': Arabs from the Middle East and newly converted Berber tribes from North Africa. Compared to the previous incursions by Romans and Visigoths, the Moors moved quickly. Lugo was conquered in 714, and the Moors had taken almost the whole of Spain by 720. During this process, there were few dramatic or intense military confrontations. Visigoth rule simply fell apart; the Moors were better equipped and better organized. They were also, in many ways, more civilized. Their medical and scientific knowledge was far in advance of the Visigoths' primitive imitations of Roman culture. In the new Muslim polity of Al-Andalus, the Visigoths' anti-Semitic legislation was withdrawn. Most of the old elements of Spanish society stayed in place. Such groups became known as 'Mozarabes': Jews, Christians and others who accepted Muslim rule. Islamic scholars and politicians debated the status of this new population, who lived within an Islamic legal framework, but who were not Muslims. They devised the concept of the *dar al-'ahd*, the 'land of the pact', to regularize their status.[18] While Arabic became the language of culture and learning, a Mozarabic dialect, derived from Latin, also evolved.[19] In the south of Spain, in particular in the cities of Córdoba and Granada, there was a unique cycle of debate and study, in which Christians, Muslims and Jews all participated.

One enclave alone resisted the Muslims: Asturias, the mountainous region immediately to the east of present-day Galicia. A document from 911, which may be fraudulent, suggests that in 718 Pelayo, a local noble, was elected by the remaining Visigoth and Asturian nobility as the king of this tiny kingdom. Pelayo appears to have led an armed force against an advancing Moorish unit at the battle of Covadonga, and thus prevented the Moorish domination of Asturias.[20] The Arabs left Galicia for the Berbers to conquer. They probably arrived shortly after 714. It seems that they found the region's climate too cold and wet, its mountains too barren and its people too hostile, and that they left after a few decades. Following their withdrawal, Galicia slowly came under the domination of the Christian monarch in Asturias, Alfonso I (739–57).

The king's court in Asturias during this period must have been a strange place. This northern corner of Spain, protected by its mountains from invading forces, was also isolated from cultural and technological innovations. Romans, Visigoths and Christians had only had the most superficial effects on these peoples. Its capital at Cangas de Onis, while functioning as a ceremonial centre, was little more than a hillside village. The new kingdom had no true towns, minted no coins until the tenth century, and conducted no long-distance trade. In other words, Asturias was probably the most backward region in Spain in the eighth century. Arab chroniclers in the south did not comment on its existence, and when Charlemagne led a Christian army into Spain in 778, he appears not to have known of the Asturian kingdom.[21] Most Visigoth nobles and Christian priests continued to live in Al-Andalus. Only those who could not compromise took refuge in the far-away court in Asturias. In some cases, these were entire ecclesiastical communities: priests, faithful Catholics, servants and dependants would travel in groups, led by their bishops, carrying their possessions and their books up to the north-west.[22] For some decades, there was probably a type of ecclesiastical overpopulation in this little kingdom, overmanned with refugee bishops and priests.

Initially, the future looked bleak for this tiny community. Muslim forces crossed the Pyrenees and reached past Bordeaux, only to be defeated at Poitiers, in western France, in 732. Following this setback the Moors retreated, pulling back their forces from north-western Spain to leave a 'march', a type of lengthy no man's land, between their settlements and the kingdom of those they saw as 'the mountain folk'. This was not exactly a declaration of peace: raids and fights continued intermittently along this unclear borderline. But, equally, this was not outright war. The Muslim rulers of Al-Andalus grudgingly accepted the presence of the new kingdom. The new Christian monarchs were then faced with an unheard-of task: they had to demonstrate to their peoples that they, rather than the victorious Moors, were the legitimate rulers. Their main strategy for this was to prove that they were the 'authentic inheritors of the collapsed Spanish-Gothic kingdom of Toledo'.[23]

At this stage, the first priority of these new monarchs was to build up a permanent and secure base. Securing Galicia, the region on their western flank, was an obvious first step. However, it was not certain that the Galicians would accept rule from Asturias. Local Galician chieftains and notables resisted vigorously in the 760s, fearing that the new monarchy would reduce their privileges.

Significantly, no single leader emerged to represent their interests: these Galician elites were fragmented, with little sense of political unity. 'At the beginning of the ninth century, the Galician aristocracy was little more than an unstable group of rich and powerful men', observes Baliñas; 'this land-owning aristocracy needed the Asturian monarch to turn them into a nobility.'[24] However, the people of Galicia feared further incursions by the Muslims, and they had seen that their local chiefs were unable to defend them. If the kingdom of Asturias could provide protection, then its rule was to be welcomed. During the reign of Alfonso II (791–842), Galicia was gradually incorporated into the new kingdom; henceforth, it was ruled by a count appointed by the king.

The myth of Saint James

Securing the region of Galicia was merely the first step within a bigger project. One could summarize the tasks that faced the new Asturian kingdom as:

1. the defence of its existing territory from Muslim attacks;
2. the consolidation of its government;
3. the construction of its political legitimacy;
4. the assertion of its military power against Al-Andalus.

Religious ideas and arguments were of crucial importance to this kingdom and, eventually, permanently changed the nature of Galician society. While at this stage it was impossible to plan any definitive military victory against the Muslims, it was possible to *imagine* a new Spain. In the 780s a monk exiled in Asturias, Beato de Liébana, wrote a hymn, *O Dei Verbum*.[25] This visionary work contained images somewhat similar to those of Blake's 'Jerusalem': it imagined a Spain that had been visited by the apostle Saint James and that, one day, would be cleansed of the Muslim presence. The idea that Saint James had left the Holy Land and travelled across the Mediterranean had been suggested by some previous Christian writers but, it must be noted, there is no biblical support for this idea. Some of the implications of Beato's thinking are revealed in another text by him: an essay, *In Apocalypsim*, written in 776. Here, Beato equates the new Muslim power with the Antichrist, and portrays their capital in Córdoba as the new Babylon.

These arguments did not gain any immediate resonance. In effect, Beato was appealing to Rome to recognize the strange new kingdom of Asturias in place of the still pre-eminent Christian centre in Spain, Toledo. His visionary ideas of Saint James's presence in Spain were not based on any scriptural authority, nor did they correspond to any local cult or religious tradition. What these texts do demonstrate, however, is the speed with which the contest between Al-Andalus and Asturias was set, firstly in religious terms, but also, more importantly, in intransigent and absolute terms. In this new militant vision, being a Christian meant fighting to dominate the territories of Al-Andalus. The priority of these new militants was to establish a Christian state: their fight therefore also meant a refusal of the tolerance practised by the Muslim rulers of Al-Andalus. Once this framework had become an official ideology, there could be no compromise between the two powers. This would be a fight to the finish.

Such ideas formed the ideal of the Reconquista or 'Reconquest' of Spain. One can raise many doubts about the term, above all about the claim to be implementing a 'return' to some previous society. Had those territories controlled by the Muslims ever previously been, in any real sense, 'Christian'? Had there ever been any effective Visigoth government in Spain? To what extent were the Asturian kings really the legitimate inheritors of the previous Visigoth monarchs? Medieval historians have also questioned whether the Reconquista was, in practice, so very different from political developments across Europe, in which monarchies were taking the first steps to unify their territories and to develop more efficient forms of government.[26] Often, what were dressed up as the acts of a pious Christian Crusader were nothing more than an attempt to grab land. Lastly, it must be remembered that Christians, Jews and Muslims all learnt another lesson during these centuries: the art of living together, of *convivencia*, an ideal of tolerance and mutual respect which continued to be respected by many people from all sides, even during the most savage moments of the Reconquista. In other words, we need to keep the ideas of the Reconquista in context: they provided a useful ideological cover for the development of the Spanish monarchy and aristocracy, but they were never an accurate representation of the world-view of the majority of the peninsula's inhabitants.

Within the moralistic logic of the Reconquista, debates or arguments concerning the status of the Catholic monarchs were simply not permitted. These new rulers wanted, above all, the *appearance* of a restoration, in order to justify their rule. Under their leadership, historical debate produced ideas concerning the 'essence' of Spain, in which a contrast was drawn between the rich, fertile lands of the south and east, swiftly conquered by Romans and Moors, and the tough, honest peoples of the north and west, less advanced, perhaps, but loyal, uncontaminated by foreign influences and more ready to fight for their ideals.[27]

At some point in the early ninth century, during the reign of Alfonso II, a strange rumour from Galicia reached the Asturian court.[28] A claim, perhaps no more than a tale, was circulating that the tomb of Saint James had been found near the religious centre of Iria, far away in the more backward, wooded western half of Galicia. Certainly, there was an old stone tomb, but did it really contain the body of Saint James? There was reason to be sceptical, and successive archaeological excavations have done nothing to dispel these doubts. How had Saint James's body come to have been buried in faraway Galicia? A legend spoke of its transportation in a boat made of stone. If it was Saint James, then why were there no Latin inscriptions on the tomb? Why were there so few signs of a Roman presence in the surrounding areas? Why was there no evidence of Christianity in this part of Galicia in the first century? The papacy was suspicious of the claim. In 1154 the Pope still commanded Spanish Christians to accept Toledo as their centre, and the shrine was not officially recognized by the papacy until 1884. Even the militants of the Reconquista in Asturias were less than enthusiastic. They tended to see Oviedo, the principal town in Asturias, as their religious centre, and had no wish to see it challenged by a new site.[29]

On the other hand, Asturian monarchs could see some advantages in the spread of the legend. Potentially, it reinforced their claim to represent a Christian Spain, faced with a Muslim enemy. A prominent shrine would challenge Moorish-dominated Toledo, and would integrate the north-west into the structures and beliefs of Christian Europe. This new centre could even serve to unite the small kingdom: the development of a shrine in Galicia would dampen the lingering resentment of Asturian rule by some Galician aristocrats. Alfonso III (866–910), who was born in Lugo and felt some real sympathy for his native region, sponsored the construction of a new church at the shrine in 899, which became known as Santiago de

Compostela. The first term is derived from the Spanish form of Saint James. The second term has two possible derivations: it may come from *campus stellae*, meaning the 'field of stars', or from *compostum*, 'burial ground'.[30]

To the surprise of many, the shrine became a prominent international centre for European Christianity. This was partly due to the publicity given to it by the monks at the monastery at Cluny, north of the French city Lyon. In the tenth century their monastery was the centre of a powerful religious organization, which included more than a thousand monasteries and a highly committed body of men, dedicated to the restoration of a Latin culture to serve a newly assertive Christian Church. Their new thinking resembled the new political culture of the Reconquista: the Cluny monks were also deeply hostile to the Islamic forces in the Middle East, the Mediterranean and southern Europe. An integral part of their Christian Renaissance was a new anti-Islamic assertiveness, most prominently displayed in the Crusades.[31]

The Cluny monks sponsored many of the characteristically medieval Christian cults of holy relics, which were seen as permitting direct, physical access to the holy and the sacred. Good Christians were encouraged to visit such relics, and hence the medieval tradition of the pilgrimage became popularized. The experience of the discomfort and danger of the pilgrimage would draw the pilgrim closer to the suffering figure of Christ: they would act 'in imitation of Christ'. In 950–1 Godescalc, the bishop of Puy, in the centre of France, walked to the Galician shrine near Iria.[32] He started a tradition which has lasted to the present day. For the monks of Cluny, these routes were also channels for their influence: the architecture of the buildings along the routes, the songs and the texts generated by the pilgrimage all demonstrate how successful they were in managing and exploiting this movement.

The shrine's location, close to the most westerly point in continental Europe, added to its attraction. Jerusalem was controlled by Muslims, and access to Rome was made difficult by the Alps and by the series of wars and conflicts in northern Italy, but during the twelfth century, Galicia was at once located in a mysterious, semi-legendary place, and yet accessible and relatively safe. Moreover, Santiago de Compostela appeared to house the only grave of an apostle located to the north of Rome.

In 997 the shrine was attacked by an experienced Muslim leader,

Almanzar.[33] Following arguments about the payment of tribute from the Christian monarchy to the Muslim caliphate, Almanzar was sent to demonstrate the Muslims' power. He left from Córdoba in July 997, collecting soldiers (including Christian warriors) from across Spain. He first attacked and burnt Iria, and then turned to Santiago in August. His troops were virtually unopposed. They spent a week levelling the site, and took away much gold and fine cloth, indications of how rich the shrine had become. They even took the church bells, which were placed in a mosque in Córdoba.

At first sight, this attack might seem to mark the end of Santiago. However, there were other lessons to be learnt from the episode. Firstly, paradoxically, Almanzar's attack had demonstrated the shrine's worth: even the Muslims considered it an important place. Secondly, the followers of the new Christian monarchy had been shown what could happen when they argued among themselves. Instead of ending the shrine's development, Almanzar started a new chapter in its history.

The rise of Santiago de Compostela

Archbishop Diego Gelmírez (1067–1140) worked hard to revive and to promote the shrine's status. A second church was built at the site, a true cathedral: its main structure was finished in 1075, and then developed further, until its final completion in the sixteenth century. Four other cathedrals were built in Galicia between 1075 and 1218. In 1080 the date of Saint James's feast day was changed, from 30 December to 25 July: the new date was obviously far more convenient for pilgrims, for it was easier to travel during the summer months. Shortly after 1095, Santiago replaced Iria as the centre for the archbishop of Galicia, who also became the feudal seigneur of the city. Gelmírez was in contact with monks at Cluny, but also visited Rome in 1104, and obtained the Pope's toleration for the new shrine.[34] He laid the foundations of the city's financial prosperity by establishing a specific tax, the *Voto de Santiago*, to be paid in kind by farmers across reconquered Spain to the city. To some extent, Gelmírez's successes seem to have brought with them new problems. Many of Santiago's citizens clearly resented the dues that they had to pay him, and there were two confused urban revolts, in 1117 and 1136, in which the city's most commercially active sectors, its artisans and merchants, appealed to the monarchy to limit the archbishop's powers.[35]

The cult of Santiago reached its peak in the eleventh and twelfth centuries. Pilgrims from across Europe walked thirty or forty kilometres a day, for journeys lasting fifteen weeks or more. They travelled along routes that branched out like capillaries across northern Europe, drawing closer as they crossed the passes of the Pyrenees, and then following an increasingly secure route westwards, into the growing kingdom of Asturias-León. The pilgrims became easily recognizable figures. A fifteenth- or sixteenth-century song, the *Jacobslied*, sung by German pilgrims, describes their appearance. Pilgrims wore wide hats and leather coats to protect them from the rain, snow and winds. They carried sticks and bags, and they travelled across Switzerland, through French territories, before crossing the high, cold passes of the Pyrenees.[36] Another symbol that rapidly became associated with the pilgrimage was the scallop shell. Having reached Santiago de Compostela, many then walked on, westwards, to Padrón, the point at which Saint James's body was said to have been landed on the Galician shore. They then took back scallop shells to demonstrate that they had reached the Atlantic shoreline. As pilgrimages evolved, the scallop came to symbolize the entire journey. Even today in Santiago, one can still see groups of earnest-looking teenagers, with plastic scallop shells stuck to their hats, bursting into song as they reach the city walls.

The pilgrimage route became commercially important. Networks of innkeepers, artisans, guides, priests and monks developed alongside the roads. The Obradeiro square, in front of the cathedral, became an important market. Hospitals, hostels, churches, bridges and roads were built along the route, and – it must be noted – brothels were opened as well. In turn, bandits also preyed on the travellers; in 1175 the Order of Santiago was created to protect pilgrims from such attacks.[37] Systems of control were introduced to regulate the varied streams of travellers. Local priests would issue pilgrims with a type of passport, which would allow pilgrims access to accommodation along the way and exemption from tolls. On arriving at Santiago de Compostela, they would then be given a certificate to demonstrate that they had completed the pilgrimage, a practice which continues to this day. When they returned to their own towns and cities, they would often then join local confraternities of Saint-James, devoted to charitable activities.

One point needs to be stressed about these journeys: they brought together different nationalities, different classes and people fired by different emotions. Pierre Barret and Jean-Noël Gurgand neatly illustrate this variety by listing the different spellings for the settlement of 'Castrogeriz', an important point on the pilgrimage route between Burgos and León. Most French writers spelt it as 'Quatre-Souris' (four mice), though a few also wrote 'Castro Siris'. Germans visited the settlement of 'Castre Sorig', while Italians passed through 'Castel Soriz'.[38] Among the pilgrims were Albigensian and Protestant heretics, disguising themselves to escape the authorities' notice, and convicted criminals who had been punished by being required to follow the pilgrimage.[39] Others were little more than tourists. One thinks of the Wife of Bath in Chaucer's 'General Prologue' to his *Canterbury Tales*, who had visited Santiago de Compostela, but who is presented more as a globe-trotting sightseer than a seeker after religious truth.[40] It seems likely that the majority of pilgrims were men, but probably a third, maybe even more, were women.[41]

Many impulses inspired people to travel to Santiago. However, as Francisco Márquez observes, in a single, devastating line, 'no one ever travelled to Compostela in search of knowledge'.[42] Despite Archbishop Gelmírez's best efforts, Santiago was not a centre of learning, and the level of training for its priests and clerics remained appallingly low. Instead, the shrine was a centre of characteristically medieval piety, based on faith, stories of miracles and the simple, sentimental resonance of place. As the pilgrims walked, sheltered and then gathered together in the city, they talked among themselves. Some were musicians, and it is clear that the pilgrimage stimulated the transmission and development of musical forms, as hymns and other types of religious music were performed in Santiago. English, German, Bohemian and Provençal players swapped tunes, Breton lays were translated into the languages of Europe, and troubadour lyric poetry circulated. For a while, the *Chanson de Roland*, arguably the first example of French-language poetry, was the most popular song among them.[43] But, above all, because of these exchanges, the regional language of Galego developed into a respected, prestigious language, suitable for religious songs, and known to musicians, poets and Christians across Europe. It also became a standard language for administration within Galicia: an analysis of 2,363 documents in Ourense from the tenth to the sixteenth centuries reveals that 1,611 of them were written in Galego, 642 in Latin and 110 in Castilian.[44]

It is difficult to provide reliable estimates for the number of people who made the journey and, of course, numbers ebbed and flowed over the centuries. Edwin Mullins suggests that perhaps half a million pilgrims travelled to Santiago de Compostela each year during the eleventh and twelfth centuries.[45] In the early eighteenth century Louis XIV introduced measures to restrict the numbers travelling: before his laws, the French authorities estimated that some thirty thousand pilgrims left France for Santiago de Compostela each year.[46] In 1962 the Galician writer Alvaro Cunqueiro travelled along the old pilgrim road through the mountains of eastern Galicia, and found that the local people had seen only one pilgrim in the last two years.[47] But as the now-ageing Francoist regime attempted to develop tourism, people came to the city by other paths. In 1965 there were some two and a half million visitors.[48] The shrine became dramatically more popular following Pope John Paul II's visit in 1989, and the cathedral claimed three million visitors in 2003: it now counts every visitor through its doors as if they were a faithful pilgrim, which seems an unlikely claim.[49]

One by-product of the shrine's importance was the writing of travel guides. *The Pilgrim's Guide to Santiago de Compostela* is probably the most famous of these, described by Márquez as 'the first Baedeker in the history of the West'.[50] Some twelve copies of this work survive, dating from the mid twelfth century, when the shrine's prestige was at its height.[51] *The Pilgrim's Guide* is an intriguing mixture of practical information, warnings, prejudices (particularly about the Basques) and detailed description of the cathedral. Curiously, it says little about Spain. It focuses on the links between the monks of Cluny and the shrine of Santiago, suggesting a form of French monastic imperialism.[52] It does, however, include a single paragraph which describes the region of Galicia: this passage is well worth quoting in full:

> This is wooded and has rivers and is well-provided with meadows and excellent orchards, with equally good fruits and very clear springs; there are few cities, towns or cornfields. It is short of wheaten bread and wine, bountiful in rye bread and cider, well-stocked with cattle and horses, milk and honey, ocean fish both gigantic and small, and wealthy in gold, silver, fabrics, and furs of forest animals and other riches, as well as Saracen [that is, Moorish] treasures. The Galicians, in truth more than all the other uncultivated Spanish peoples, are those who most closely resemble our French race by their manners, but they are alleged to be irascible and very litigious.[53]

One important point can be gained from this brief description: for perhaps the first time, Galicia is imagined as a single unity, with identifiable characteristics that make it different from the surrounding areas.

The rites and rhythms of the pilgrimage had created an important cultural process. In simple terms, the pilgrims put Santiago – and Galicia – on the map. In the words of one song:

> James honoured Spain
> And Galicia, and made
> That faithless people
> The church of Christ[54]

But, more than this, the pilgrims initiated a series of exchanges. By attracting crowds of foreigners into the region, year after year, pilgrimages stressed the difference between the visitors and natives. This dynamic suggested a clear, sharp contrast. Of course, not all the people of Galicia were directly affected by the pilgrimages, but many were: the pilgrimages were of central economic, political, cultural and religious importance to the region. For this reason, these journeys can be cited as the beginning of a self-awareness within the region.

Galicia and late medieval Castile

We can see some results of these processes by looking briefly at the court culture of Alfonso X, also known as 'the Wise' (1252–84). Following a prolonged series of military advances, stretching from the late eleventh century to the early thirteen century, Alfonso X was not the ruler of a tiny Asturian kingdom, but a monarch who commanded most of the peninsula, with the exceptions of the duchy of Portugal to the west, the kingdoms of Catalonia and Aragon to the north-east, and the Arab kingdom of Granada in the south-east corner of Spain, the last remnant of Al-Andalus. After the taking of the southern port of Cádiz in 1263, a long period of peace followed, with the kingdom of Granada surviving as a Moorish vassal-kingdom that paid tribute to Alfonso. During these decades, Alfonso X consolidated his rule.[55] In the eighth century, Galicia had been a vital component of the tiny Asturian kingdom. By the thirteenth century, it had returned to its familiar peripheral status. The centres of the new kingdom were the regions of Old and New Castile (a term derived from the word for 'castle'), in the north and centre of the peninsula.

Alfonso X, a learned man, acted to standardize competing and erratic linguistic norms. He devised a correct form of *castellano*, the language of the Castiles, in 1276.[56] Henceforth, this would be the official language for law, science and history. Alfonso X was also a poet and a musician. He edited (rather than actually authored) the collection of four hundred and twenty songs known as the *Cantigas de Santa Maria*, a prestigious anthology of dance tunes, hymns and lyrics, which incorporate both Arab and southern French, Occitan troubadour influences. Significantly, the language used for most of these works was a form of Galego. Perhaps, as Mary O'Neill observes, this tongue was seen as more accessible, as it was more akin to other west European languages. An indication of the cosmopolitan nature of court culture during this period can be gained by considering the court of Fernando III, successor to Alfonso X. He employed twenty-six paid musicians: thirteen Moors (of whom two were women), one Jew and twelve Christians.[57] The presence of this range of musicians at his court is a reminder of the lasting strength of the ideal of *convivencia* within the peninsula.

In other words, while Galicia was clearly at the periphery of the Spanish kingdom in the thirteenth century, Galego retained a certain prestige within particular cultural fields, particularly in lyric poetry of a religious nature. But even here, Galego was being pushed back by Castilian. A collection of poems entitled the *Cancionero de Baena*, from the late fourteenth century, begins with works in Galego but, significantly, ends with Castilian verse.[58]

Galicia and the new Saint James

In the twelfth century the duchy of Portugal rebelled against the Spanish Crown, and became an independent kingdom. Many Galician nobles settled in the new kingdom: arguably, it took with it the most dynamic and aggressive of Galicia's warriors. The lands to the north of the river Minho now formed a new, smaller region; its frontiers are those of today's Galicia. The two lands retained many links: aristocratic families from both areas were closely connected, and during the political and military crisis of the 1480s, many Galician nobles sided with the Portuguese, against the Spanish king.

Even today, it is still clear that the Galician and Portuguese languages are similar, a point to be discussed in chapter 6.

In 1492, the last Moors were driven from Granada. What part would Galicia play in this new Spanish, Catholic kingdom? It had become a region dominated by the Church, with a powerful ecclesiastical aristocracy as its ruling class. The Cistercian Order, in particular, sponsored the construction or reconstruction of fourteen great monasteries in the region between 1142 and 1225.[59] They were also the biggest landowners of the region. In the fifteenth century a system of contracted tenancies (*foros*) became the dominant form of land-holdings. Under this arrangement, landowners continued to receive both rents and feudal dues from tenants and peasants, while returning almost nothing to the rural people. Secular aristocrats attempted to extract ever-greater amounts from their peasants. This arrangement aroused much discontent, culminating in the series of battles – indeed, a virtual civil war – that broke out in Galicia from 1467–69, known as the Great War of the Confraternities. Here, religious confraternities provided the structures of solidarity that united peasants, urban citizens, lesser nobles and some members of the clergy against the feudal exactions by the elite of secular nobles. Approximately eighty thousand men were organized in this fashion: during the war they destroyed some one hundred and thirty aristocratic castles and forts.[60] The revolt was finally ended by the intervention of the Crown's soldiers, who used the new arquebuses against the rebels' improvised armies.

The secular aristocracy, like aristocrats across Europe, were then faced with the loss of their independence from the Crown. Administrative and bureaucratic structures were developed from the centre; aristocrats were slowly incorporated into them as officers or bureaucrats. One result of this process was the growing prestige of the Castilian language in Galicia. By the late fifteenth century it had become not just the official language of administration, but also the dominant written language, while Galego was relegated to the status of an oral language.

And what of Saint James in this new Spain? During the twelfth century, a new image of Saint James evolved: the *matamoros*, the Moor-slayer. The Apostle was now depicted with sword in hand, riding over the corpses of slain Muslims. This was a profound shift in forms of representation. It drew Saint James and the city of Santiago away from popular religious culture, and it turned the Apostle into an instrument of propaganda for the new Spanish state.[61]

As the Reconquista extended its territory, the older Christian sites came into Spanish control. In 1085 Toledo was taken, and it began to compete in popularity with Santiago. By the fourteenth century, civil calm had returned to north Italy, and the papacy was working hard to reassert the primacy of Rome as a pilgrimage site. In particular, the Pope offered the sale of indulgences: certificates which were often presented as offering the buyer absolution from sins. The rise of these sites meant a relative decline in Santiago's importance. Compared to Renaissance Rome, Santiago looked like a small, muddy town.

More significant, however, was a change in sensibility in the fourteenth and fifteenth centuries, as new humanist ideas began to circulate. Such thinkers began to look with critical eyes at the established patterns of medieval Christianity. There had, of course, always been sceptics about Santiago and its pilgrims. One popular pun asserted that good women set off on the journey as *romeras* (pilgrims) and came back as *rameras* (whores).[62] Critics had also questioned the veracity of some relics: Chaucer was not alone in suspecting that some were nothing more than pigs' bones.[63] But the new humanists also suggested a more profound critique: the pilgrim's simple, naive desire to touch the sacred was now seen as the expression of a crude and misplaced religiosity. For the humanists, true spirituality was an inner, mental quality. It could not be touched; it had to be thought. Correspondingly, the key focus of devotion evolved from the relic to the picture.[64]

Saint James, *Matamoros*, did not simply disappear. According to legend, he reappeared twelve times, with sword in hand, between 1518 and 1817, although – curiously – he neglected to save the Spanish Armada in 1588.[65] Foreign mercenaries fighting for Spain in Italy in 1500 were instructed to shout 'Santiago, España!' as they went into battle, and the same words were shouted by Pizarro's few dozen soldiers as they charged thousands of Incas in Cajamarca in November 1532.[66] When Spanish troops were sent to fight in Iraq in the summer of 2003, they wore small patches representing Saint James on their uniforms. 'It would be difficult to come up with any symbol more offensive to the Shia population than this cross', noted one Spanish journalist.[67] In practice, however, the figure of Mary, the mother of Christ, came to replace the older warrior figure within Spanish religious culture.

Conclusion

When was Galicia? As Patrick Geary has noted, the years between 400 and 1000 appear as 'the fulcrum of political discourse across much of Europe', for it is in these centuries that nationalists tend to locate the origins of their respective myths of nationhood.[68] In this respect, Galician nationalists are not so very different: they, too, tend to imagine a golden age following the collapse of the Roman Empire, when Galicia was independent and proud. The weaknesses in this argument are obvious. Firstly, these are centuries from which there is little reliable documentation. It is simply impossible to *prove* that Galician nationhood was born during these years. But, secondly, the documentation that is available strongly suggests a different type of political evolution. The region of Galicia is marked by shifting, shallow and ephemeral political structures, overlapping structures of rule, and the absence of clear political centres. This pattern is constantly repeated: while one can find evidence for the presence of Celts, Romans, Suebes and Visigoths in the region, in each case there are qualifications. None of these groups 'mastered' the region; none of them took control of its evolution. In place of bloody battles, it seems more accurate to think of their presences in this land as initiating exchanges, squabbles and interchanges; movements within elites, rather than the rise and fall of great kingdoms.

However, Christianity presented a different challenge to Galicia. Unlike the previous 'invasions', this was a cultural form that grew rooted in the region. From the existence of Priscillianism to the structures for the reception of pilgrims, Christianity was a force which did not simply 'change' Galicia, but that, rather, gave Galicians the cultural and social instruments by which they transformed their region. It is no coincidence that Galego becomes a European language as a result of Christianity, or that its greatest city achieves prominence through the rituals of pilgrimage, or that 25 July – Saint James's day – is now the national day of Galicia.

When was Galicia? Maybe we can see that moment in the early ninth century, when those extraordinary rumours began to circulate about the tomb near Iria, as marking the beginning of a process. The discovery of the tomb did not, of course, constitute the beginning of any modern form of nationalism. But the wonder that people felt as they looked at that inexplicable tomb revealed a set of forces, a glimmer of a possibility.

Notes

[1] See the critical commentary provided by Fernando Wulff, *Las esencias patrias: historiografía e historia antigua en la construcción de la identitad española* (Barcelona: Crítica, 2003).

[2] Ramón Villares, *Historia de Galicia* (Vigo: Galaxia, 2004), p.28.

[3] Information in these paragraphs is drawn from Majolie Lenerz-De Wilde, 'The Celts in Spain', in Miranda J. Green (ed.), *The Celtic World* (London: Routledge, 1995), pp. 533–51, and Barry Cunliffe, *Facing the Ocean: The Atlantic and its Peoples, 8000 BC–AD 1500* (Oxford: OUP, 2001), pp. 340–5

[4] Villares, *Historia*, pp. 50–2; Cunliffe, *Facing the Atlantic*, p.377; see also Derek Williams, *The Reach of Rome* (London: Constable, 1996), pp. 230–1.

[5] R. F. J. Jones, 'The Roman occupation of north-west Spain', *Journal of Roman Studies*, 66 (1976), 45–66.

[6] Villares, *Historia*, p. 62.

[7] Ibid., p. 81.

[8] Ibid., *Historia*, pp. 72–6.

[9] Patrick Geary, *The Myth of Nations: The Medieval Origins of Europe* (Princeton: Princeton University Press, 2002), pp. 103–5.

[10] Villares, *Historia*, pp. 76–8.

[11] Pierre Bonnassie, 'La época de los visigodos', in P. Bonnassie, P. Guichard and M.-C. Gerbet (eds), *Las Españas medievales*, trans. Hervàs (Barcelona: Crítica, 2001), pp. 9–48 (pp. 47–8).

[12] Alfonso R. Castelao, *Sempre en Galicia* (Buenos Aires: Galicia, 1976), p.36.

[13] See Wulff, *Las esencias patrias*.

[14] Carlos Baliñas Pérez, *Gallegos del año mil* (A Coruña: Fundación Pedro Barrié de la Maza, 1998), p.41.

[15] Norman Davies, *The Isles: A History* (London: Macmillan, 1999), pp. 207–8; Villares, *Historia*, pp. 99–101.

[16] Information in the following paragraphs is drawn from Bonnassie, 'La época de los visigodos'.

[17] Philippe Wolf, *Western Languages AD 100–1500*, trans. Frances Partridge (London: Phoenix, 2003), p. 63.

[18] Eduardo Manzano Moreno, 'The creation of a medieval frontier: Islam and Christianity in the Iberian Peninsula, eighth to eleventh century', in D. Power and N. Standen (eds), *Frontiers in Question* (Houndsmill: Macmillan, 1999), pp. 32–54.

[19] Wolf, *Western Languages,* pp.131–32.

[20] Marie-Claude Gerbet, 'Los Espanoles de la "Frontera"' in P. Bonnassie, P. Guichard and M.-C. Gerbet (eds), *Las Españas medievales*, trans. B. Hervàs (Barcelona: Crítica, 2001), pp. 189–247; Roger Collins, *The Arab Conquest of Spain, 710–797* (Oxford: Blackwell, 1994), pp. 142–9.

[21] Collins, *Arab Conquest*, pp. 163–4.

[22] Baliñas, *Gallegos*, pp. 44–5.

[23] Ibid,, p. 58.

[24] Ibid., p. 94.

[25] My analysis of this theme is drawn largely from Francisco Márquez Villanueva, *Santiago: tragectoria de un mito* (Barcelona: Bellaterra, 2004), pp. 53–8.

[26] See Manzano Moreno, 'The creation of a medieval frontier'.

[27] See Wulff, *Esencias patrias*, pp. 37–50.

[28] The information in this section is drawn from Márquez, *Santiago*, pp. 38–47.

[29] Ibid., 146–9.

[30] Ibid., pp. 149, 38.

[31] Ibid., pp. 79–83.

[32] Pierre Barret and Jean-Noël Gurgand, *Priez pour nous à Compostelle* (Paris: Hachette, 1978), p. 25.

[33] The information in this paragraph is drawn largely from María Isabel Pérez de Tudela y Velasco, 'Guerra, violencia y terror: la destrucción de Santiago de Compostela', *La España medieval*, 21 (1998), 9–28.

[34] Márquez, *Santiago*, p.242.

[35] Carmen Pallares and E. Portela, 'Les revueltas compostelanas del siglo XII: un episodio en el nacimiento de la sociedad feudal', in Ramon Villares Paz (ed.), *La Ciudad y el mundo urbano en la historia de Galicia* (Santiago de Compostela: Torculo, n.d.), pp. 89–105.

[36] Information taken from the libretto for the CD *¡Santiago! – Música e Peregrinacións na Europea do Renacemento*, performed by Resonet (Clave Records, 2001).

[37] Barret and Gurgand, *Priez pour nous*, pp. 100–3, 154–61.

[38] Ibid., p. 123.

[39] Márquez, *Santiago*, p.84.

[40] Geoffrey Chaucer, *The General Prologue to the Canterbury Tales*, ed. James Winny (Cambridge: Cambridge University Press, 1965), p. 65.

[41] Márquez, *Santiago*, p. 95.

[42] Ibid., p. 114.

[43] Ibid., pp. 114–18; Wolf, *Western Languages*, pp. 105–9.

[44] Villares, *Historia*, p. 169.

[45] Edwin Mullins, *The Pilgrimage to Santiago* (Oxford: Signal Books, 2001), p. 3.

[46] Márquez, *Santiago*, p. 96.

[47] Alvaro Cunqueiro, *El pasajero en Galicia* (Barcelona: Tusquets, 2002), p. 84.

[48] Barret and Gurgrand, *Priez pour nous*, p. 253.

[49] Xerardo Estévez, 'Xacobeo 2004', *El País*, 15 May 2004.

[50] Márquez, *Santiago*, pp. 169–70.

[51] Annie Shaver-Crandell and Paula Gerson, 'Introduction' to their *Pilgrim's Guide to Santiago de Compostela: A Gazetteer* (London: Harvey-Miller, 1995), pp. 24–5.

[52] Márquez, *Santiago*, pp. 173–8.

[53] Shaver-Crandell and Gerson, *Pilgrim's Guide*, p. 74.

[54] Magister Gauterius de Castello Rainardi, 'Regi perhennis gloria', on the CD *Donnersöhne*, by Sequentia (Deutsche Harmonia Mundi, RD 77199).

[55] Manuel González Jiménez, 'Frontier and settlement in the kingdom of Castile (1085–1350)', in R. Bartlett and A. McKay (eds), *Medieval Frontier Societies* (Oxford: Clarendon, 1989), pp. 49–74.

[56] Wolff, *Western Languages*, pp. 134–6.

[57] Mary O'Neill, 'Oral and literate processes in Galician–Portuguese song', *Galician Review*, 3–4 (1999–2000), pp. 8–18.

[58] Wolff, *Western Languages*, p. 160.

[59] Villares, *Historia*, p. 122.

[60] Ibid., pp. 162–4.

[61] Márquez, *Santiago*, p. 201.

[62] Ibid., p. 277.

[63] Chaucer, *General Prologue*, p. 73.

[64] Márquez, *Santiago*, p.273.

[65] Ibid., pp. 284–5.

[66] Henry Kamen, *Spain's Road to Empire: The Making of a World Power, 1492–1763* (London: Penguin, 2003), pp. 107, 332.

[67] *Guardian*, 25 July 2003.

[68] Geary, *The Myth of Nations*, p. 7.

2

Exclusion and decline: Galicia in Catholic Spain, from the sixteenth to the nineteenth century

In 1469 Queen Isabella of Castile married King Fernando of Aragon. Their union led to the creation of a united Catholic monarchy, which soon ruled the largest part of the Iberian peninsula. Castile, the kingdom in central Spain, was joined with Aragon, a newly formed kingdom in the peninsula's north and east regions. This marriage implied a geographic choice: the new dynasty looked eastwards, to the Mediterranean, and away from the Atlantic. In the ninth century, the region of Galicia had been a valuable asset to the tiny Asturian monarchy. In the sixteenth century, Galicia appeared in a different light: it was of little importance, a marginal, forgotten land within the new Catholic kingdom.

This chapter will consider the structures and processes that shaped the development of Galicia within the new Spain. I will first discuss forms of rule and political domination, classes such as the aristocracy and changes such as urbanization, before turning to the experience of ordinary Galicians. As in the last chapter, my intention is to present the reader with a concise evaluation of the most important developments; readers seeking more detailed analyses and descriptions should consult the works recommended in the notes and the bibliography.

After the Reconquista: a new Spain

The dynamic of the Reconquista continued into the fifteenth century and beyond. Religion was vital to this new dynasty. In 1473 the Spanish Inquisition was introduced, with its first aim being to police Catholics within the new monarchy, ensuring that their faith was not influenced by the rival Muslim or Jewish religions. Its methods were often brutal: some seven hundred Christian converts, judged to be heretics, were publicly burned in Seville between 1478 and 1486. The infamous Tomás de Torquemada (1420–98) was responsible for another two thousand being burned or executed before 1498.[1] The same religious fervour inspired the Spanish warriors who fought in the last phases of the Reconquista: they wore red Crusader crosses on their uniforms. When the southern, Moorish city of Málaga was captured in 1487, its entire population of fifteen thousand people were seized as slaves.[2] Granada, the last Moorish stronghold in Spain, was conquered in 1492. Promises were made to respect the defeated Moors' religion but, predictably, these were not honoured.

In the first decades of the victorious new Spanish monarchy, the Inquisition policed those who had converted from Islam to Christianity, always alert to any survival or revival of non-Catholic practices in this new Spain. In the mid sixteenth century it widened its concerns, acting against heresy, vice, Protestantism and Judaism. The ugly concept of *limpieza de sangre*, blood purity, became common: applicants for posts in the civil service were required to prove that they had no Moorish or Jewish ancestors.[3] Yet there was also a surprisingly positive, constructive aspect to the Inquisition's work. One unexpected example is the Inquisition's ruling on witch-craft. This stated that anyone who believed in witchcraft was a heretic, so it prevented any accusations of witchcraft. The result was that Spain was the only European country *not* to suffer witch-hunts in the sixteenth and seventeenth centuries.[4] Perhaps more typically, its religious fervour led to the development of Catholic thought and learning. There was also a second strong argument for the development of education. Because of its empire, Spain needed universities. As well as explorers and soldiers, its colonies required administrators and priests to carry out its political, fiscal and military policies. In 1450 there were six universities in Catholic Spain; by 1600 there were thirty-three. By this later date, no less than 5 per cent of all adult males were graduates; while in Santiago de Compostela in 1635, no less than 52 per cent of all male taxpayers could sign their own names, both astonishingly high figures for sixteenth-century Europe.[5]

As well as being a repressive apparatus, the Inquisition was also part of a wider, pan-European, Catholic Reformation, which aimed to raise standards of religious teaching, to impose a diocesan order and to create a coherent system of religious belief.

Spain's rulers, however, were not only concerned by events within their borders. The dynamic of the Reconquista carried its believers and warriors outside, to create one of the largest empires in history. A common belief grew that the Spaniards were a 'chosen people', sent to rule the world.[6] As the Spanish Empire grew, a whole set of new 'Santiagos' were established across the world: in Brazil, Chile, Cuba, the Dominican Republic, Mexico, Panama, the Philippines and Uruguay. Some were consciously named after the shrine in Galicia, others were more the result of an accident of the calendar: the sites in question were founded on 25 July, Saint James's day.

Galicians were present at the beginning of the empire. There were a dozen Galicians among Magellan's sailors as his ships sailed past the southern tip of the Americas in 1519.[7] In 1588, the 130 ships of the Spanish Armada sailed from A Coruña to attack Britain.[8] There were also merchants in the northern Galician port of A Coruña who were delighted when the Crown permitted the creation of an international spice-trading firm in their city in 1522. Unfortunately for them, the office was closed down a few years later. In practice, the bulk of the trade to the colonies flowed out from the southern port of Cádiz, and the immense quantities of silver obtained in southern America came back along the same route, to circulate across Europe.

In order to regulate colonial expansion, the new monarchy negotiated the Tordesillas Agreement of 1494 with Portugal: an extraordinary document which, with papal blessing, attempted to divide the world into two halves, one to be dominated by Spain, the other by Portugal.[9] The move was unsuccessful. Rivalry continued between the two powers, and – by the seventeenth century – the British and French governments were also attempting to counter Spanish power and to push back the borders of its territories. In 1719 Galicia was raided by British forces, a small episode in a larger international conflict.[10] While the Spanish government attempted to control the export of silver from the new colonies, smuggling boomed, to the extent that a quarter or even a third of the silver that circulated in Europe had probably been transported by smugglers.[11] The vast Spanish Empire was simply too big for Spain to control and exploit, and by the mid seventeenth century the Spanish monarchy's *siglo de oro*, its golden century, had clearly ended.

The Galician aristocracy: from hidalguía *to* caciques

In the late sixteenth century, approximately six or seven million people lived in Spain: of these, some one hundred and thirty thousand were members of noble families.[12] The new Spanish monarchy profoundly changed these aristocrats' lives. Through its wars and conflicts, through its diplomacy and European alliances, it drew these elites into a bigger international context. The monarchy taught them the importance of Catholicism, not simply as an individual religious choice, but also as a guide to diplomacy and politics. It offered ambitious aristocrats the opportunity to achieve wealth, power and glory in southern America and the Caribbean: one thinks of initiatives taken by Hernán Cortes, a minor noble, leading to the Spaniards' celebrated victory over the Mayans in present-day Mexico, or of Francisco Pizarro, conquering the land that would become Peru.[13] But the monarchy also demanded something in return. Aristocrats were no longer independent chieftains, leading their own private armies; they were slowly being transformed into professional military officials, trained in state-run colleges and following royal policies. A university degree was usually the essential first step towards a successful colonial career, even for an aristocrat's son.

The wealthiest and more powerful aristocracy were drawn to the court, where they spent much of the year in close company with the king. Below them, a range of super-rich aristocrats lived on vast estates, mainly in southern Spain. Beneath them were the tens of thousands of minor nobles, or hidalgos.[14] By the mid-eighteenth century, there were approximately eleven thousand of these minor nobles in Galicia.[15] They dominated the region from the sixteenth to the twentieth century.

Their origins are already known to us: they began as warrior leaders, as early as the fifth century. Jealous of their independence, they were suspicious of the new Asturian power, and led a number of futile rebellions against the Asturian kings. More seriously, they retained their familial and cultural links to the Portuguese Crown, and frequently sided with this rival in the conflicts and wars between the Spanish and Portuguese monarchy, as happened in the 1480s. This was a disloyalty which the new Spanish monarchy never forgave. Some Galician nobles were exiled to Granada, in the south-east. Other chose to travel to Madrid to take up residence in the king's court: an expensive option. But there were other, more important, long-term political consequences. From 1520 to 1858 there was no official royal visit to the region.[16] The monarchy devised structures of political representation for Galicia which bypassed the nobility.[17] Its *Juntas de Provincias*, created in 1500, were based on Galicia's cities: initially it included the five cities of Santiago de Compostela, Betanzos, Lugo, Mondoñedo and Our, which were later joined by A Coruña and Tui. This body negotiated with the Crown over taxes and engaged in other tasks, such as organizing conscription, throughout the sixteenth and seventeenth centuries. The Juntas began to decay in the eighteenth century, and became a purely cere-monial institution by the early nineteenth century.

A pattern is emerging: the Galician nobility was formed by nega-tive pressures. These were the people who could not afford to live close to the Crown, who had not emigrated to Portugal, who were not colonists, who were not closely integrated into the state's admin-istrative structures and who were largely unable to afford the appropriate university training for state service. (The outdated facili-ties of the University of Santiago de Compostela were of use only to those planning a career in the Church.) For these reasons, this was an aristocracy which gained few benefits from the empire. Lastly, while these aristocrats were obviously wealthier than their poor tenants, they were not the richest families in Spain.

The aristocracy were the biggest landowners in Galicia. While it is difficult to find reliable estimates of land-holdings, some relevant data exists for the late eighteenth century (see Table 2.1). It can be assumed that most of the territory classified as 'secular' was actually owned by nobles. Secondly, monasteries owned most of the 'ecclesi-astical' lands.

The hidalgos derived less benefit than might be expected from their lands. Their farms were located on the margins of the Spanish kingdom, away from the economically vibrant areas of the Basque country and Catalonia. As nobles, they were bound by a strict socio-cultural code which forbade them from working with their hands; they were therefore little inclined to take an interest in farming, or to sponsor new farming techniques. These poorly managed lands usually failed to be as profitable as those owned by the Church.

Novels give us an insight into aristocratic lifestyles and allow us to see how they may have been regarded in Galician society. Two works in particular, from the late nineteenth century and early twentieth century, present some striking images of the late nineteenth-century

Table 2.1. Distribution of territory in Galicia
in the late eighteenth century[18]

Owner	Percentage of territory
Secular	54.15
Episcopal	21.10
Ecclesiastical	11.89
Royal	8.73
Military orders	2.60
Legal	1.53
Total	94.82

aristocracy. In Alejandro Pérez Lugín's sentimental novel, *La Casa de la Troya* (1925), the Galician nobility is contrasted with the hectic, corrupting modernity of Madrid. The hidalgos live in richly decorated, if old-fashioned, apartments. They uphold conservative, rustic values: their women are grave, profoundly religious and breathtakingly beautiful, providing a fitting cure for the ills of student life in the big city. This is probably the kindest possible interpretation of the Galician nobility that could be presented in a modern Spanish novel. Emilia Pardo Bazán's *Los Pazos de Ulloa* (1886 – 'The Ulloa Château') is a more critical, more typical and – probably –more accurate work. Once again, a contrast is suggested: between a young, delicate and sincere priest from Santiago de Compostela and an old noble family. Here, the nobles proudly live in the greatest set of houses in the parish; they boast of the size, the status of their possessions, but everything is uncared-for, collapsing and decaying. The formal garden has lost its precise lines, there is no glass in many of the windows, and the family archives, their all-important contracts and treaties are scattered, unfiled, across the floors of their rooms. They are rough, violent people, who hunt by day and drink by night, fired solely by a desire to preserve their privileges. Both novelists concur on one point. They depict these nobles as crossing cultures: they normally speak Castilian, but they are also able to understand Galego.

The Galician nobles' defence of their privileges took two important forms. The first concerns land-holdings: a historical topic which most Galician agrarian historians quickly characterize as 'labyrinthine'.[19] The problem starts in the mid-fourteenth century, following the arrival of the Black Death in Galicia, and the consequent labour shortage. At this point, feudal landowners took steps to regularize their possession in the form of contracts, known as *foros*. In the early nineteenth century about ninety per cent of Galicia's farmland was still regulated by *foros* owned by secular or religious aristocrats.[20] Under the *foros*, land-holdings were usually divided into two sections: land which was directly in the possession of the landowner, and land over which he had only indirect control, but from which he could still demand the payment of certain dues, whether in cash or in kind. For tenants, there were some advantages. It was possible to negotiate quite long contracts: at one point in the fourteenth century, the standard *foro* lasted for the life of three kings plus twenty-nine years. Given the nobles' growing lack of interest in farming, longer contracts became increasingly normal, until they became effectively hereditary, giving tenants the sense that their families had acquired ownership of the land that they leased.

There were, however, many drawbacks to the system. Firstly, it grew more complex, an 'irrational mosaic', in the words of Ramón Villares.[21] The area under the landowner's indirect control was often leased out en bloc to a type of sub-landowner, who would then in turn rent it out, in sections, to tenants. (Some historians describe such arrangements as 'sub-*foros*'.) Given Galicia's growing population, there was increasing pressure on the land: in 1500, the region's population was 0.3 million; by 1750 it had reached 1.3 million.[22] Generation by generation, smaller and smaller plots were rented out, often through further sub-leasing arrangements. Even when ambitious and enterprising peasants managed to acquire enough farmland to guarantee their families' livelihood, these plots were often scattered across several parishes. This characteristic patchwork pattern made it difficult to implement any substantial modernization of agriculture.

Once again, it must be stressed that these nobles took very little active interest in agriculture: they are usually described as *rentiers*, meaning that they simply collected rents and dues, without reinvestment in their lands. By the eighteenth and nineteenth centuries, their principal residences were often located in Galicia's small, old, rural towns, so they knew less and less about the estates from which their incomes came. More seriously, their lifestyle still carried with it a certain prestige, and was often imitated by the commercial bourgeoisie who later bought up their land.

The other great contribution of these nobles to the life of the region was *caciquismo* (pronounced 'ka-thee-ki-smo'). This was a telling symbol of the political decay of the Spanish ruling class. It originated as a reaction to the extreme political instability which threatened all Spanish governments during the nineteenth century. Firstly, for much of the nineteenth century, the army functioned almost as an alternative parliament, and was instrumental in making and breaking several governments. Moreover, there was a revolutionary left, represented initially by Republicans, but later also by socialists and anarchists. From 1873 to 1874, following a successful Republican revolt, there was a short-lived republic in Spain. There was also a revolutionary far right, represented by the Carlists, a utopian-reactionary monarchist group which wished to take Spain back to a legendary, pure, decentralized Catholic society, based on responsible nobles and grateful peasants. The Carlists represented a substantial political threat, above all in the north and north-east of Spain. They led three significant rebellions during the nineteenth century.

Under these circumstances, governments felt insecure; every election was dangerous. In 1875 constitutional monarchy returned, supported by two substantial political parties, the Liberals and the Conservatives. In 1890, manhood suffrage was introduced. Yet the substance of this political reform was eradicated by the development of *caciquismo*. This was based on an informal, but effective, agreement between the two main political parties to decide the results of the elections between themselves, rather than risk allowing any expression of Republican or Carlist feeling. The formality of voting was preserved, but voters were directed by *caciques*, or 'bosses', about which party they were to vote for. The classic land of *caciquismo* was Andalucía, where a rich, conservative class of landowners increasingly squeezed a poverty-stricken rural proletariat. Here, the smallest of bribes, or the most pitiful public holiday, was enough to turn voting into a brief, farcical moment of enjoyment. But *caciquismo* also worked extremely well in Galicia. Between 1876 and 1923 there were twenty-one parliamentary elections in Galicia, electing some nine hundred and forty-five deputies. All the elections for rural constituencies, with one debatable exception, were won by candidates supported by *caciques* from either the Liberal or the Conservative parties.[23] In Galicia, *caciquismo* was 'persuasive' rather than intimidatory.[24] There was very little outright violence: when the system worked well, a bribe, a sermon, a speech was enough to persuade the ordinary voter to 'vote properly'. If more forcible persuasion was needed, the local *cacique* was usually able to influence the tax assessment board, and ensure that those who had voted 'badly' would be penalized by a high tax demand. Even in moments of social tension, the simple threat of violence was usually enough to impose conformity.

The restoration of the monarchy in 1875 started the last golden age for the hidalgos. For about five decades, their system seemed near-watertight. They were the wealthiest people in Galicia: in 1875, of the region's sixty richest taxpayers, thirty-eight were nobles.[25] They occupied the key posts in the regional administration; they controlled the mayors, the lawyers, the doctors and the teachers; they employed the *caciques* who fixed the elections; and their family networks and deputies gave them access to central government in Madrid. Their lifestyles and houses were admired by rich merchants; their orders were obeyed by their tenants and villagers.[26]

The Church in Galicia

The one group in Galicia who could challenge the hidalgos was the Church. The founding of the Catholic monarchy in 1469 seemed to promise them much; in 1488 King Fernando and Queen Isabella even went on pilgrimage to the shrine at Santiago de Compostela to pray for victory in their campaign against the Moors in Granada.[27] Following the social struggles of the 1470s, the ecclesiastical nobility seemed to be set to establish their domination over the region. While Table 2.1 shows that the monasteries and bishops owned only about one-third of Galicia's land in the late eighteenth century, this was often the richest and best-farmed land in the region. In the same period, the Church gained about two-thirds of the wealth created by agriculture.[28] However, life within the new Catholic monarchy was to prove difficult for the Galician Church.

The Catholic monarchy took a pragmatic attitude to religion: it used Catholicism, it even exploited it, in a drive to create political unity. Just as with the nobility, the new colonies in Latin America provided great opportunities for ambitious clerics who were willing to serve the Crown. But few Galician priests travelled out from Galicia, down to Cádiz and then on to glory. Instead, Galician clerical culture declined in the new Catholic Spain.

The reasons for this unexpected regression relate to the changes introduced by the Catholic Reformation.[29] Stricter standards were demanded, and the Church in the Galician parishes showed few signs of improvement. Its priests seemed to lack commitment, its buildings were in poor condition, its libraries contained few books and – above all – the people of the countryside seemed to have little clear understanding of Christianity. According to one observer, the rural people were pagans, satanists or Muslims. In some villages, it was rumoured that witchcraft was practiced. The rural people ate and drank in the church during services, they were superstitious and ignorant of Catholic doctrine. The priests themselves, usually from local peasant families, were little better: from 1561 to 1700, 161 Galician priests were prosecuted for crimes ranging from blasphemy to attempting to seduce parishioners during confession.[30] Lastly, in the seventeenth century the Inquisition suspected that Judaism was being practised in secret in Galicia. Once again, Galicia's border position is relevant here: it was easy for Galicians to keep in contact with the Jewish communities in Portugal.

The response by the church authorities to these issues was to attempt to raise standards by better training for priests and better education of parishioners. Bishops were active in encouraging the first printing presses in Galicia. The first was in the town of Monterrei in 1483; a second soon followed in Santiago de Compostela. By the early sixteenth century there were presses in each of the region's six episcopal towns: they largely published works for the Church.[31] In the late sixteenth century seminaries were established in Lugo and Mondoñedo, in the east of the region; Jesuits, Franciscans and Dominicans created new schools, and the University at Santiago de Compostela was reformed. There were even some charitable foundations, which created a handful of schools in the countryside.[32]

There is some evidence that these moves did produce a real effect on popular culture. In 1750, in the province of Ourense, to the south-west of the region, religious names were growing more popular. The most common boys' names were José (or Joseph) and Francisco, which respectively accounted for 14.6 per cent and 10.2 per cent of baptised male children, while the most popular girls' names were María (19.4 per cent) and Josefa (10.9 per cent).[33] New religious confraternities also spread throughout the region. Lastly, the Church in Galicia remained successful in recruiting new priests: to the impoverished peasantry of the region, even the most minor parish priest was still someone with status. Their sons were therefore easy to recruit into the Church. In 1900 there were 33,403 priests in Spain, 1 for every 531 Spaniards. In Galicia, the ratio was 1 priest for every 412 Galegos.[34] Predominantly, these clergy were recruited locally. A study of 63 parishes in Pontevedra province in the early twentieth century shows that 89.5 per cent of the priests were from small rural parishes, and only 10.5 per cent from small towns.[35]

However, the church authorities were not satisfied. Official reports still judged popular religion to be blasphemous and superstitious. One prominent example was the popularity of funeral banquets, a central part of Catholic faith to most ordinary Galician worshippers, but condemned by bishops and clerical officials as debauched and irreligious. Another example of the gap between popular and official Catholicism could be seen in the popular local pilgrimages, organized to commemorate local saints. While many of those who participated were sincere Catholics, these events were often marked by fights between youths from rival villages. Worse still, new fairs and festivals began to spread during the late eighteenth century; these were completely outside the Church's control.

In the late eighteenth century a new challenge faced clerical authorities: this was the weak, shadowy presence of the Spanish Enlightenment. In some European countries – for example, France and Britain – the Enlightenment took the form of a exhilarating new cultural presence, deeply innovative, which gave non-noble scholars a public voice and even a degree of influence on government policy. The Enlightenment, however, was never an eighteenth-century equivalent to the Bolshevik party. Beyond a vague rejection of 'tyranny' and an equally vague optimism that judged that the future would be better that the past, Enlightenment philosophers did not produce any agreed political programme. Their long-term significance is, rather, in changing the nature of European political culture: in giving a platform for secular debate, in establishing the status of non-governmental intellectuals, and in raising the importance of books and journals as instruments for research and discussion. By these means, the Enlightenment permanently changed the nature of politics in Europe. While it was initially non-statist in nature, governments would often listen to Enlightenment ideas and – on occasion – accept reforms or changes to their policies.

Compared with France, it often appears as if there was no significant Enlightenment in Spain. This is a misleading judgement. Charles III (1759–88) was certainly influenced by Enlightenment ideas when he attempted to reform the patchwork administration of early modern Spain, and to move towards some more rationalized and centralized form of rule.[36] While the Spanish network of papers and meeting-houses was certainly far less extensive than that of the French, there were some comparable developments in Spain. In particular, one could look to the network of 'Economic Societies of the Friends of the Nation' as a counterpart to the institutions of the French Enlightenment.

The membership of this network took a specifically Spanish form. Even in France, the 'middle-class intellectual' is at best a semi-fictional character: most who participated in the French Enlightenment were either minor aristocrats, marginalized clerics or would-be aristocrats. In eighteenth-century Spain, the standards of education and the forms of political culture among the middle classes were extremely low, while the aristocracy was – in general – hostile to all forms of intellectual culture. Therefore, the main non-governmental arena for the debate of Enlightenment themes was to be found within the Church.

Many ambitious young men had joined monasteries and religious orders simply because no other career option was available to them: in other words, frequently they had no deep religious faith. Some of them were willing to listen to the new ideas discussed by the Enlightenment. In Galicia they could join one of the region's two 'Economic Societies'. The first was created in Santiago de Compostela in 1784, the second in Lugo in 1785.[37] One can also find some striking models of Enlightenment-inspired activities in the region. For example, there was the Benedictine monk Martín Sarmiento (1695–1772), who published criticisms of colonial policy and debated the status of Galego, opposing its decline. It is possible to argue that this writer was the first Galician nationalist.[38] Pedro Antonio Sánchez (1749–1806) was a secretary to the archbishop of Santiago de Compostela. In the 1780s he wrote a number of extremely original pamphlets, offering what he termed 'new light' on the Galicia economy.[39] He proposed anti-feudal agrarian reforms to end the growing problem of poverty in rural society: his interest in agriculture contrasts dramatically with the hidalgos' apathy. Sánchez certainly was not a Galician nationalist, but one can see in his work a recognition that the Galician economy was different from that of the rest of Spain, and that it would therefore require a specific programme of reform.

Writers such as Sarmiento and Sánchez were brave and original thinkers, and deserve to be remembered as such. However, one must also note their extremely marginalized position. There was no immediate audience for their work: in general, the clergy was hostile to these 'French' ideas, the hidalgos suspicious, and the uneducated, illiterate, Galego-speaking peasantry unable to understand them. During the War of Liberation against Napoleonic rule (1808–14), some of these men had a brief experience of leadership; their ability to argue and debate could gain them respect. But, inevitably, they were swamped by the conservative hidalgos. When insurgent Galicia sent representatives to the Cádiz Cortes in 1812, seventeen of their twenty-five representatives were hidalgos.[40] Predictably, rather than being apostles of decentralization and regional cultures, the Enlightenment's isolated supporters tended to look to central government for support: what other force was available to act against the hidalgos and the conservative Church?

Despite all these issues, the Church remained a formidably powerful institution in early nineteenth-century Galicia. The most significant blow to its authority came from central government. During the 1830s a reforming, liberal government passed some important reforms. For example, in 1833 there was another campaign to rationalize and centralize administration: in Galicia this took the form of reducing the region's seven provinces to the present four (Lugo, Ourense, Pontevedra and A Coruña). In the next year, the tax of corn and wine which Santiago de Compostela claimed was finally abolished, as part of a programme to make taxation uniform across Spain.

The most important of the liberals' reform was the law of *desamortización,* which was passed in September 1835. This transformed the nature of the Church's property: land that had been held 'for eternity' was now placed on the open market, and the money raised was to be taken by the state. Often, common land, held collectively by villages, was treated in the same manner.[41] Some hoped that these land reforms would create an independent, self-sufficient, forward-looking stratum of peasant property-owners. However, while the available data is imprecise, there can be no doubt that the greatest beneficiaries of these reforms in Galicia were the urban, commercial middle class, who bought estates with *foros,* and chose, deliberately, to manage these new estates as if they were old-fashioned *rentier* aristocrats. The Church was further damaged by a general loss of its legitimacy in the countryside. Many peasants now refused to pay tithes and other dues to ecclesiastical landowners.[42]

The survival of the *foros* was an unusual and highly significant aspect of *desamortización* in Galicia. These reforms had been intended to liberalize and modernize Spanish agriculture: their unintended long-term effect was to strengthen the rule of the hidalgos in the Galician countryside.[43]

Ports, towns and villages

During the four centuries from 1500 to 1900, there was a fundamental shift in the region's socio-economic structures. This took the form of a slow movement of wealth, power and people from the old settlements in the east of the region that dated back to the Roman occupation, to new centres on the western and northern coasts. This shift is still continuing today.

The background to these changes was the substantial increase in Galicia's population.

Table 2.2. The population of Galicia, 1752–1900[44]

Year	Population	Galicia / Spain
1752	1,299,312	13.80%
1860	1,799,224	11.47%
1900	1,950,515	10.48%

As the figures in Table 2.2 demonstrate, while Galicia's population was clearly growing, it was not expanding as fast as in other regions in Spain or, indeed, in Europe. Moreover, the distribution of Galicia's population was shifting from east to west, and from the interior to the coast. Even in the sixteenth century a little port like Pontevedra, with only some two thousand households, was developing long-distance fishing for sardines and trading between the Mediterranean and the North Sea. A new caste of merchants, independent of the rural hidalgos, began to run the city.[45] In the early twentieth century, Emilio González López grew up in A Coruña; in his autobiography he records how different this port felt from Galicia's inland settlements. Walking around the docks, he heard conversations about ports in all the continents of the world, from

New York to Barcelona. In 1912, the sinking of the *Titanic* caused real grief in this port, whose people could easily identify with those affected by the disaster.[46]

There are some signs of similar developments along Galicia's coast. In 1787, there were only fifteen towns in Galicia with more than two thousand inhabitants. Nine of these were along the coast; three others were in the western half of the region, and only three were in the conservative eastern interior.[47]

One can see that the history of Galicia's ports would have been very different if the Crown had not insisted on Cádiz's monopoly over the trans-Atlantic colonial trade. From 1573 to 1764 Galicia's external trade was blocked.[48] In the 1760s, however, Charles III pioneered a liberalizing programme. In 1764 A Coruña was granted a licence to run a regular postal service to Havana (in Cuba), which was soon extended to Buenos Aires (in Argentina). For fourteen years the port benefited from this near-monopoly. In 1752, its population was seven and a half thousand; by 1787 it had reached thirteen thousand, half of whom were born outside the city. It had become the third biggest town in Galicia.[49] Its ships crossed the Atlantic, carrying out textiles and metalwork, and bringing back silver and leather.[50] In 1778, the monarchy removed all restrictions on trans-Atlantic trade, and Galicia's ports flourished in their new roles as centres for trans-Atlantic travel: a point to which I will return in the section below.[51]

Aside from the sudden urban growth in the ports, however, Galicia's cities were languishing. In 1860 only three cities had more than ten thousand inhabitants; by 1900 only five.[52] Of course, a city's modernity cannot be measured simply by the size of its population: many small towns can be specialized centres of innovation. This was not the case in Galicia. Towns such as Lugo, Ourense and Santiago de Compostela were 'classic pre-industrial cities: centres of consumption, provincial capitals, market towns'.[53] Even when these cities did grow in size, it was often only by absorbing the surrounding peasant population.

The most surprising aspect of the figures in Table 2.3 is the *increase* in urban-based farmers over the nineteenth century. To their numbers one could also add the aristocratic and bourgeois *rentiers* who depended on agriculture for their incomes, to the point when one wonders whether these towns were much more than big villages. These little settlements provided elegant homes for hidalgos and

Table 2.3. Percentages of the employed population in agricultural work in various Galician towns, 1752–1920[54]

City	1752	1898
Santiago de Compostela	12.5	19.8
Ourense	16.3	19.0
Lugo	13.5	26.3
A Coruña	4.1	–
Ferrol	13.6	
Monforte	27.5	–
Muros	8.1	16.5

priests, centres for a handful of bureaucrats and officials, offices for lawyers and doctors and – in the case of Santiago de Compostela – rooms for students. They had markets and festivals, they were the places where the carriage routes and – after the 1880s – the trains ended, but they were not centres of economic or cultural moderniza-tion. This point is important in relation to *caciquismo*: elsewhere in Spain, cities such as Barcelona, Bilbao, Madrid and Valencia were in the vanguard of pushing back the forces of *caciquismo* and creating independent public spheres of debate and criticism. No such urban centre existed in nineteenth-century Galicia.

What these little towns lacked most was industry. In 1879, Santiago de Compostela was a city with some twenty thousand inhabitants; among them were just ninety-four workers, in eighteen small workshops.[55] Of course, there are some exceptions: one can cite the development of sardine-canning in Vigo as an important step in Galicia's economic history. In 1880 there were six canning factories in the region; by 1902 there were eighty-two.[56] Elsewhere, cigarette- and cigar-factories were established in A Coruña and tanneries were opened in the countryside. But in nearly all these cases, the finance and the control came from outside: Catalan merchants were particularly prominent, but there were also British and Basque investors, and some Spanish state initiatives.[57]

In other words, while it would be wrong to argue that there were *no* economic innovations in Galician society in the eighteenth and nineteenth centuries, it is accurate to conclude that modernization was rare, often superficial, and incapable of changing the region's socio-economic structures. As the great Spanish historian, Manuel Tuñón de Lara, observed, at the end of the nineteenth century

Galicia was the most backward region in Spain.[58] Devices such as the *foros* preserved a conservative rural society throughout the nineteenth century, and well into the twentieth century.

Isidro Dubert has argued that one can almost measure regional archaism by following Galicia's contour-lines: over five hundred metres, in the mountainous areas to the south and east of the region, there were 'geographic fragmentation, difficult communications between settlements and . . . an archaic agriculture'.[59] Again, one must not exaggerate this point. Commercial cattle-rearing and viniculture were developing in areas around Galicia's ports and towns. Even in the conservative interior, the introduction of new crops, such as the potato and maize, were essential for rural families living on their ever-smaller plots. But these crops were not used to develop a modern, cash-based, market-oriented agriculture. Instead, Galicia's farmers grew them for their own families.[60]

Yet, curiously, this backward region was more densely populated than the rest of Spain. In 1877, on average there were thirty-three people per square kilometre in Spain, sixty-three per square kilometre in Galicia.[61] The region's people were scattered in a mass of small villages and hamlets, to the point that in 1920 Galicia contained 40 per cent of all the villages registered on the Spanish census.[62] The mental geography of the country-dwellers was not structured around concentrated central settlements, but knitted into a dense, elaborate spider's web, stretching from the house, through the hamlet, the village, the parish to the market town. Such nebulous patterns worked to restrict communications and – above all – collective identities. One example of this is the manner in which handicrafts developed in the Galician countryside. In most other rural areas, individual villagers develop artisanal specialisms, and therefore become – for example – the local weaver, potter or blacksmith. In the nebulous structures that the Galician lived in, there simply was not a sufficient concentration of the population to permit this, and so a distinctive and unusual pattern of part-time artisans developed, known as *milmaña*, 'a thousand hands'. These people were multi-skilled farmer-artisans, working by themselves for their immediate families and carrying out commissioned work for paying customers.[63] Under these circumstances, rural labourers were unlikely to be able to group together to oppose their priests or *caciques.*[64]

José Maria Cardesin Díaz's ground-breaking research has anatomized the structural tensions within the stultifying structures of the conservative countryside.[65] At first sight, the key division appears to be that between landowners and their tenants, which was mediated by the *foros*. In the nineteenth century, however, due to population pressure and the absence of any counter-authority to limit the landowners' authority, new social sub-groups developed. Indebted peasants were reduced to the position of sharecroppers, who would be allowed to work the landowners' fields in return for splitting the eventual harvest with him: often, landowners would take between a third and a half. Sometimes similar arrangements would also be used for cattle-rearing. At the bottom of the social hierarchy were the *camareiras*, or cottagers. These were usually single women, often mothers, whose husbands had deserted them: a sure sign of social dislocation. If they found work, they would be hired only by the day, often with their children. If they were without work, they depended on the right to glean fields after the harvest, or to make use of the dwindling stock of communal land. In an intensely vulnerable position, they were exploited by their employers. Incidents of seduction and of rape were common. Cardesin cites one study which suggests that a quarter of the households in some parts of Lugo province were in this position.

Yet such subordinate groups were almost invisible to state officials and pioneering sociological surveys. Alfonso Castelao, the prominent mid-twentieth-century Galician nationalist, could write blithely that Galicia was a pre-capitalist land without workers or bosses: all were property-owners.[66] The labour of the most subordinate groups, the sharecroppers and cottagers, was regulated by unwritten contracts; therefore, much of the prominent public debate of the *foros* ignored their existence. The warped political structures created by *caciquismo* did not represent them, and the declining rural clergy was unlikely to speak for them. Worse still, even nature seemed against them. In 1850 an infection hit Galicia's vineyards. In 1852, excessive rains ruined its harvests. In 1853, a cholera epidemic started, while parts of rural Galicia remained in conditions of near-famine. Riots forced the rural authorities to begin a public works programme to provide some minimum employment, but this, inevitably, was insufficient. Waves of social protest swept through the countryside in 1854 and 1855, calling for the fixing of bread prices and the banning of grain exports.[67]

Given these conditions, one might have expected that rural rebellion would have spread. This could never have happened in mid-nineteenth-century rural Galicia – although something akin to a rebellion would start a few decades later (a point which will be discussed in the next chapter). One explanation for the lack of rebellion has already been explored: the power of hidalgos and their *caciques*, who were able to contain any challenge to their hegemony. A second explanation lies in the 'closed' nature of Galician society: where could these rebels go? The towns were almost static; they rarely functioned as centres for critical debate. Instead, as Castelao perceptively noted, 'a Galician never rebels: he migrates'.

J. A. Duran presents a colourful list of the type of travelling trades with which Galicians were associated in the nineteenth century. They became Spain's acrobats, water-carriers, knife-grinders, buskers and harvesters, they were the beggars in ports, pilgrimages and processions, and they presented the puppet-shows.[68] To this list could be added the seasonal labourers who left each summer to travel to Andalucía and to Portugal to work on the harvest. When the poor were unable to change conditions in their home communities, they left. As Jose C. Moya sadly records, 'movement for many of them had become more an acceptance of defeat than a symbol of progress'.[69]

The other Galicia: Argentina

It is often suggested that trans-Atlantic migration was a direct result of Galicia's poverty. A moment's thought should be sufficient to correct this misconception: the journey across the Atlantic was expensive, and the one resource that the poor lacked was money. The desperate sharecroppers and cottagers of Galicia's villages left to join the list of itinerants identified by Duran; they would tramp round Spain, and maybe even reach Portugal, France or Italy, but they would never be able to cross the ocean. Subsidies for such journeys were rare: Moya estimates that only about two per cent of travellers benefited from them.[70] Instead, the bulk of the trans-Atlantic migrants were frustrated peasant farmers, unable to prosper within Galicia's closed agrarian economy, and looking to 'mejorar fortuna', to improve themselves and to make their fortune. Galicia's emigrants were, predominantly, young men with some education or skill, not poor, desperate rural labourers.[71]

The process of migration began slowly. When A Coruña was given the franchise for the trans-Atlantic post service in 1764, the Spanish Empire in Latin America and the Caribbean was already two and a half centuries old. Trading and shipbuilding quickly developed: the ports of Ferrol and Vigo followed A Coruña in developing trans-Atlantic links.

In 1778, the Crown made a specific appeal to Galicians to settle in Argentina. The new British presence on the Malvinas (probably better known to readers as the Falklands) was a threat to the Spanish colony of Argentina. It was proposed to populate Argentina's southern region of Patagonia as quickly as possible, to forestall any British initiatives. The Crown launched a substantial propaganda campaign to appeal for two hundred Galician families to migrate; it was expected that many would want to leave from this poor region.[72] In particular, the government wanted people with some skill, such as farming, cattle-rearing or a craft. It was judged that those who were *not* impoverished would be more likely to form stable communities. They were offered free passage to Argentina. Between 1778 and 1784 the migrants were ferried over the Atlantic in twelve crossings. A total of 2,028 people travelled; 1,956 of them left from A Coruña. However, Galicians proved relatively reluctant to travel: only about a quarter of the 'Two Hundred Families' came from Galicia (and most of these were from A Coruña itself). Another third were from Asturias, while the rest were from central Spain. The reason for this relative failure is now obvious: while migration was becoming a common part of Galicians' lives, as yet this tended to be a temporary, seasonal experience, usually involving single, young males. A permanent, family-based migration was something new and generally unwelcome.

Nonetheless, the episode of the 'Two Hundred Families' is an indication of Galicia's potential as a land of emigration. The development of this dynamic was, however, delayed by external factors. In 1779 Spain declared war on Britain, allying itself with the cause of the American Revolution. This conflict prevented easy travel across the Atlantic. In the 1790s, sea travel was disrupted by the French Revolutionary wars, and then in 1810 Argentina proclaimed its independence from Spain. The new nation welcomed migrants, but inevitably retained a certain hostility against the old colonial power. Spanish ships were refused entry into Argentine ports until the 1830s. It was not until 1850 that a new, liberal Argentine government declared a pro-immigration policy that welcomed Spaniards, and not until 1857 that Spain responded by withdrawing its bans on direct travel to Argentina. The Spanish government finally recognized the Argentine Republic in 1859.[73] The last element needed was the growth of a commercial trans-Atlantic ferry network which, significantly, was largely supplied by British, German and French firms. By the 1870s, crossing the ocean normally took less than four weeks.[74]

The exact number who travelled will never be known, and calculations are further complicated by the frequency with which migrants would return – sometimes to travel out once again. Villares suggests that about two million Galicians migrated across the Atlantic between 1836 and 1960. (It should be remembered that the *total* population of Galicia in 1900 was about two million: the number who left the region was extraordinarily high.) The peak of this wave was in the 1910s, when approximately twenty thousand left each year. Of this flood, about half went to Argentina, about a third to Cuba, and others to Uruguay, Brazil and Venezuela.[75] Migration of this type became part of ordinary life in Galicia. For example, in 1992 Carmen Cornes came to prepare her autobiography. She thought back to her early years, in the first decades of the twentieth century, and realized that she could not recall much about her father. This is not really surprising. He left for Buenos Aires before she was born, to return when she was five. Then, five years later, he travelled out to Cuba. Each time he came back with little money, barely enough to cover the costs of his journeys. Cuba, by reputation, was an unhealthy place. Certainly, it harmed Cornes's father: he returned ill and in debt, and died a few years later.[76]

Until 1898, Cuba was still a Spanish colony, and the policed nature of its society enclosed and limited the activities of the Galicians who migrated there. The Galician experience in Argentina was, instead, of the greatest importance, to the point where it seems justifiable to argue that without studying Argentina, one cannot understand Galicia. A popular quip in the early twentieth century asked 'What is the biggest city in Galicia?' The answer was 'Buenos Aires'. The Argentine authorities had wanted to encourage a modern, commercial form of export-oriented agriculture: they were looking for cattle-ranchers and shepherds to migrate. However, the final destination of the majority of the Spanish (and Galician) migrants to Argentina was the rapidly growing city of Buenos Aires (Table 2.4).

Table 2.4. The population of Buenos Aires, 1855–1936[77]

Year	Total population	Spanish population
1855	91,395	5,792
1895	663,854	80,352
1936	2,415,142	324,650

Approximately half the Spaniards in the city were Galicians; while the joke cited above may not be very funny, it is demographically accurate. The concentration of Galicians in the city was such that the term *Gallego* became a popular derogatory term for all Spaniards.[78] This wave of migration had three dimensions. Not only did Galicians leave Spain, they also left a rural society to live in a city, and they left agriculture to work in service industries. In a sense, this was a journey into modernity. Carmen Cornes was sixteen when she arrived in Buenos Aires in 1928. For her the biggest shock was the telephone. 'I had never seen a telephone in Galicia,' she recalls, 'nor a radio'.[79]

Young males were the most likely to leave. Often they were prompted by a wish to evade Spanish military conscription, but there were other factors in play. Moya argues that the growth of this dramatic flood of migrants may be explained, in part, by Galician ideals of masculinity. Men were supposed to be able to provide for their families, and the idea of travelling to do so was seen as positive.[80] This pattern of migration had a long-term effect on the gender balance of Galicia's population. Examining the district of Ortegal, on the region's north coast, Anxel M. Rosende found the proportions of men and women shown in Table 2.5.

Such imbalances were not unusual. They had serious effects on Galicia's population growth: fewer young men meant fewer marriages; fewer marriages meant fewer children. Because of migration, the proportion of old people in the Galician population was

Table 2.5. Relative proportions of men and women in the district of Ortegal, 1900–36[81]

Date	Women (percentage)	Men (percentage)
1900	59.2	40.8
1920	60	40
1936	55	45

growing. Furthermore, migration disrupted existing families. The great Galician poet of this period, Rosalía de Castro, wrote of the 'migration-widows': women whose husbands had migrated and either had never written back to their families, or had died while abroad. She described a desolate countryside, populated by mothers without sons and children without fathers, suffering from a 'deadly absence.'[82]

The situation changed somewhat in the last decades of the nineteenth century, when female migration grew more common. Galician maids became almost standard features of middle-class homes in Buenos Aires, and stereotypical characters in its theatre plays. Women's experience of the journey was quite distinct from men's: they were usually poorer, they were exploited by the ships' crews, and – worse still – there was a thriving trans-Atlantic sex industry, in which women were shipped from Spain to Argentina to become prostitutes.[83]

Something distinctive happened as Galicians set up home in Buenos Aires. In a state almost without any form of social service, Galicians had to create their own structures of mutual aid and security. 'Two cats form a society' was one popular Argentine saying about the proclivity of Galician migrants to establish new institutions. Another observer claimed that when a Basque arrived, he looked for a church, while when a Galician arrived, he looked for another Galician, and then formed a trade union.[84] In the mid-nineteenth century the new institutions tended to group together all Spanish migrants, but in the last decades of the nineteenth century there was an increasing trend for regional groups – Asturians, Aragonese, Catalans, Basques and Galicians – to form their own organizations.[85] The most prominent of these was the Centro Gallego, established in 1907, which was later to found the largest mutual aid society in Buenos Aires.[86]

The Galicians in Argentina usually tried to keep in contact with their region. In part, this can be seen by their efforts to create their own organizations, but it was also present in the letters that they sent back home. Indeed, Moya argues that it was these communications, rather than any initiative by either the Spanish or the Argentine governments, that was the most effective instrument for encouraging migration.[87] In a sense, Galicia was experiencing an early form of globalization: its people were learning to think of a bigger world, stretching out beyond their region, which was shaped by international forces.

One poignant reaction to this experience was the spread of *saudade*, an untranslatable Galego (and Portuguese) term for nostalgia. Cornes's autobiography illustrates this: having sailed to Argentina, she now missed Galicia.

> It is hard to explain. But I will always, always remember the rivers. The mountains, the valleys – always. I will always remember the sun setting at Cambados. I've got them under my skin. On one side, the sea, and then – look – the mountains, all of them worked, ploughed, and then up to another mountain . . . I can't find the words. But I think that it is only when you leave that you really get to appreciate them . . . I will never, never forget them.[88]

On the one hand, this might seem a very banal piece of writing. Who has not felt a bit homesick after a long journey? On the other hand, there is more to this passage than first meets the eye. As Cornes stresses, she is not simply remembering sunsets and mountains: she is recalling a peopled landscape, and this type of symbolism circulated among Galician writers. This leads us to our second qualification: Cornes's *saudade* was not an individual peculiarity but a collective experience, shared by several generations.

Rosalía de Castro (1837–85) was the poet of these new nomads. Her deceptively simple verses charted their journeys and their feelings, transforming *saudade* into an art form. One of her translators asks, rhetorically, 'Was this woman never happy?'[89] She wrote poems in both Galego and Castilian, and – as will be seen in the next chapter – was extremely important in the revival of Galego as a literary language. Her works do not suggest any specific political perspective, but they do acknowledge the poverty of some in the region, and they suggest that Galicians were suffering a specific hardship.

In the last chapter it was suggested that the development of the pilgrimage route to Santiago de Compostela set up a series of cultural exchanges, through which a particular identity for Galicia was created. In this chapter, we can see a second, similar process. Trans-Atlantic emigration created another series of experiences, images and counter-images, through which distinct identities were created. As Villares notes, these people were Galicians in the Americas, but were then 'Americans' when they returned to Galicia.[90] The really interesting point, of course, is what happened when these migrants returned to their home parishes, an issue which will be discussed in the next chapter.

A tourist's Galicia

In the second section of this chapter I referred to Pérez's popular novel, *La Casa de la Troya*, in which a father decides to send his student son to the Spanish university that is the most distant from Madrid.[91] He chooses Santiago de Compostela, but one can question his decision. In terms of simple distance, both Barcelona and Cádiz were further from Madrid than Santiago. Reading the comment in these literal terms is, however, absurd. The 'distance' referred to here cannot be measured in kilometres: Pérez is thinking of the cultural gap between 'the calm and peace of the city of stone' and Madrid. Conservative Santiago is posited as an attractive remedy to the modernity of Madrid, and in this fashion Pérez is validating the Galician capital. The conditions which might appear to an economic modernizer as shameful backwardness and to a social reformer as naked exploitation could appear, to an outsider, as the signs of a refreshingly peaceful region.

By the mid-nineteenth century commercial tourism was beginning. Inevitably, the clichéd presentation of Spain as the land of bullfights and flamenco rapidly began to dominate tourist literature, but it is interesting to see that there was some interest in Galicia. George Borrow, the indefatigable British bible-seller, visited Galicia while he was travelling in Spain. He recorded his surprise at the green, lush quality of the Galician countryside, and noted that Santiago de Compostela was 'a beautiful old town'.[92] Another pioneering mid-nineteenth-century text, part travel-writing, part tourist brochure, recommends that travellers should head out to the Galician mountains, where they could still find 'the simple and pure customs of those peaceful and hospitable people'.[93] Galicia's crosses, calvaries and statues were marvellous sights, its valleys and its 240 miles of coastline had to be seen. Of course, there was still a danger from highwaymen, but – the author assured his readers – this had been greatly exaggerated.

Conclusion

The key theme throughout this chapter has been the increasingly distinct nature of Galician society. This was often registered in negative terms: Galicia was a region which did not experience the commercialization of agriculture, the development of mass industry, the rise of an industrial bourgeoisie or the decline of the aristocracy. Despite its many ports, this was a region which did not benefit from the growth of the Spanish Empire. In many ways, during this period Galicia reflects some of the most conservative themes in Spanish history: *caciquismo* works in this region with near-textbook perfection, and there is no significant political challenge to the rule of the hidalgos. Lastly, mass emigration to Argentina and to other Latin American destinations created some specific social and cultural problems for the region.

Was there nothing positive? One can point to the development of the more vibrant, more go-ahead port communities, and – perhaps – to a handful of isolated writers and commentators who swam against the tide. But the dominant themes from this period are negative ones: Galicia's exclusion and decline.

Notes

[1] Stanley G. Payne, *Spanish Catholicism: An Historical Overview* (Madison, Wis.: University of Wisconsin Press 1984), p. 35.

[2] Henry Kamen, *Spain, 1469–1714: A Society of Conflict* (London: Longman, 1991), p. 33.

[3] Ibid., p. 44.

[4] Payne, *Spanish Catholicism*, p. 37.

[5] Ibid., p. 39; Sara T. Neale, 'Literacy and culture in early modern Castile', *Past and Present*, 125 (1989), 65–96 (69).

[6] Payne, *Spanish Catholicism*, p.45.

[7] Rey Castelao, 'Los Gallegos en el Río de la Plata durante la época colonial', in X. Nuñez Seixas (ed.), *La Galicia Austral* (Buenes Aires: Biblios, 2001), pp. 23–52 (p. 24).

[8] Henry Kamen, *Spain's Road to Empire: The Making of a World Power, 1492–1763* (London: Penguin, 2003), p. 307.

[9] Anthony Pagden, *Peoples and Empires* (London: Weidenfeld and Nicolson, 2001), p.64

[10] Kamen, *Spain's Road*, p. 454.

[11] Fernand Braudel, *Civilization and Capitalism, 15th–18th Century, Vol III: The Perspective of the World*, translated by Siân Reynolds (London: Fontana, 1984), p. 415.

[12] Idem, *The Mediterranean and the Mediterranean World in the Age of Philip II*, trans Siân Reynolds (London: Collins, 1973), p. 715.

[13] Jean-Michel Sallmann, *Géopolitique du XVIe siècle, 1490–1618* (Paris: Seuil, 2003), pp. 187–91.

[14] On the sociology of the aristocracy, see William J. Callahan, 'Crown, nobility and industry in eighteenth-century Spain', *International Review of Social History*, 11 (1966), 444–64.

[15] Villares, *Historia*, p.216.

[16] Pegerto Saavedra, *La vida cotidiana en la Galicia del Antiguo Régimen* (Barcelona: Crítica, 1994), p.79

[17] On the relationship between the Crown and the Galician aristocracy, see the stunningly lucid article by Manuel María de Artaza, 'Regional political representation in the Spanish monarchy during the *Ancien Régime*: the *Junta General* of the kingdom of Galicia', *Parliaments, Estates and Representations*, 18 (1998), 15–26.

[18] Saavedra, *La vida cotidiana*, p. 54.

[19] The material in the following paragraph is drawn largely from José Maria Cardesin Díaz, 'Paysannerie, Marché et Etat: la structure sociale de la Galice rurale au 19e siècle', *Annales HSS*, 6 (1996), 1325–46, and J. A. Duran, *Agrarismo y Movilización Campesina en el país gallego (1875–1912)* (Madrid: Siglo Veintiuno, 1977).

[20] Ramón Villares, *Historia de Galicia* (Vigo: Galaxia, 2004), p. 178.

[21] Ibid., p. 178.

[22] Saavedra, *La vida cotidiana*, p. 11.

[23] Villares, *Historia*, p. 287.

[24] Manuel Tuñón de Lara, *Poder y Sociedad en España, 1900–1931* (Madrid: Colección Austral, 1992), p. 123.

[25] Villares, *Historia*, p. 278.

[26] Carlos F. Velasco Souto, 'Repensado o caciquismo: algunhas reflexións e preguntas . . .' in L. Fernández Prieto, X. M. Núñez Seixas, A. Artiga Rego and Xesús Balbao (eds), *Poder local, elites e cambio social na Galicia* (Santiago de Compostela: Universidade de Santiago de Compostela, 1997), pp. 275–86; José Luis de la Granja, Justo Beramendi and Pere Anguera, *La España de los nacionalismos y las autonomías* (Madrid: Síntesis, 2001) p.43.

[27] Francisco Márquez Villanueva, *Santiago: tragectoria de un mito* (Barcelona: Bellaterra, 2004), p. 279.

[28] Villares, *Historia*, p. 215.

[29] Material in this section is drawn principally from Saavedra, *La vida contidiana*, pp. 275–302.

[30] Ibid., p. 280.

[31] Villares, *Historia*, p. 173.

[32] Saavedra, *La vida cotidiana*, p. 372.

[33] Ibid., p. 326.

[34] Payne, *Spanish Catholicism*, p.107.

[35] José Ramón Rodríguez Lago, 'Sociología y Comportamientos politicos del clero parroquial en la Galicia rural (1898–1936)', in L. Fernández Prieto et al. (eds), *Poder local, elites e cambio social na Galicia*, pp. 287–325 (p. 295).

[36] On Charles III and the Enlightenment, see Allan J. Kuethe and G. Douglas Inglis, 'Absolutism and enlightened reform: Charles III, the establishment of the *Alcabala* and commercial reorganization in Cuba', *Past and Present*, 109 (1985), 118–43.

[37] Villares, *Historia*, p. 234.

[38] Granja et al., *España de nacionalismos*, pp. 41–2.

[39] Pedro Antonio Sánchez, *La economía gallego*, ed. Xosé M. Beiras (Vigo: Galaxia, 1973), p. 59.

[40] Villares, *Historia*, pp. 254–6.

[41] Payne, *Spanish Catholicism*, pp. 83–5.

[42] See Cardesin, 'Paysannerie', pp. 1330–2.

[43] Villares, *Historia*, pp. 261–3.

[44] Ibid., p. 461.

[45] Ibid., pp. 185–98.

[46] *Memorias de un estudiante liberal (1903–1931)* (A Coruña: O Castro, 1987), pp. 41–3.

[47] Isidro Dubert, *Del Campo a la ciudad: migraciones, familia y espacio urbano en la*

historia de Galicia, 1708–1924 (Vigo: Nigrea Imaxe/Consorcio de Santiago, 2001), p.64.

[48] Enrique Martínez Barreiro, *La Coruña y el Comercio colonial gallego en el siglo XVIII* (A Coruña: O Castro, 1981), p. 34.

[49] Villares, *Historia*, p. 295; Dubert, *Del Campo a la ciudad*, p. 86.

[50] Martínez, *La Coruña*, pp. 41–5.

[51] Rey, 'Los Gallegos', pp. 30–1.

[52] Dubert, *Del Campo a la ciudad*, p. 59.

[53] Ibid., p. 155.

[54] Isidro Dubert, 'Domestic service and social modernization in urban Galicia, 1752–1920', *Continuity and Change*, 14:2 (1999), 207–26 (214).

[55] Dubert, *Del Campo a la ciudad*, p. 163.

[56] Jaime García-Lombardero, 'Economic transformations in Galicia in the nineteenth and twentieth centuries', in N. Sánchez-Albornoz (ed.), *The Economic Modernization of Spain, 1830–1930*, trans. K. Powers and M. Sañudo (New York: New York University Press, 1987), pp. 223–40 (p. 237); Villares, *Historia*, p.349.

[57] Ibid., pp. 273–4.

[58] *Poder y Sociedad*, p.33.

[59] Dubert, *Del Campo a la ciudad*, p.64.

[60] Xosé Rodríguez Galdo and Fausto Dopico, *Crisis Agrarias y Crecimiento Economico en Galicia en el siglo XIX* (A Coruña: O Castro, 1981), pp. 40–51.

[61] J. A. Duran, *Agrarismo y Movilización Campesina en el país gallego (1875–1912)* (Madrid: Siglo Veintiuno, 1977), p. 3.

[62] García-Lombardero, 'Economic transformations in Galicia', p. 226.

[63] Anna Champeney, 'Ethnography in north-west Spain: peasant crafts in Galicia: present and future', *Folklife*, 34 (1998), 83–99.

[64] Julio Cabrera Varela, 'Las precondiciones sociales de la identidad colectiva en Galicia', *Historia y Crítica*, 4 (1994), 209–38 (217).

[65] See his 'Paysannerie, marché et État', from which the analysis in this paragraph is drawn.

[66] Castelao, Alfonso R., *Sempre en Galiza* (Buenos Aires: Galicia, 1976), pp. 14, 47.

[67] Rodríguez and Dopico, *Crisis Agrarias*, pp. 15–30.

[68] *Agrarismo*, p. 5.

[69] Moya, José C., *Cousins and Strangers: Spanish Migrants in Buenos Aires, 1850–1930* (Berkeley, Calif.: University of California Press, 1998), p.93.

[70] Ibid., p. 52.

[71] Ibid., p. 30, and Alejandro Vásquez González, 'Factores de empuje y condiciones de transporte de Galicia hacia el Ríon de la Plata (1850–1930)', in Núñez Seixas (ed.), *La Galicia Austral* (Buenos Aires : Biblios, 2001), pp. 53–68.

[72] My analysis of this episode is taken from Rey, 'Los gallegos'.

[73] Moya, *Cousins and Strangers*, pp. 49–50, 62–3.

[74] Ibid., p. 37.

[75] Villares, *Historia*, pp. 267, 328.

[76] Beatriz López, *Hasta la Victoria siempre . . . testimonio de Carmen Cornes* (Sada: O Castro, 1992), p. 14.

[77] Moya, *Cousins and Strangers*, p. 148.

[78] Ibid., p. 15.

[79] López, *Testimonio de Carmen Cornes*, p. 59.

[80] Moya, *Cousins and Strangers*, p. 95.

[81] Anxel M. Rosende, *O Agrarismo na Comerca do Ortegal (1893–1936): a loita pola modernización da agricultura* (A Coruña: Ediciós do Castro, 1988), p.30.

[82] 'As viudas dos vivos, as viudas dos mortos: ¡Pra a Habana!', *Follas Novas*, in *Antología poética*, ed. Ernesto Sábado (Buenos Aires: Losada, 1998) p. 146; see also

Pilar Cagiao Vila, 'Género y emigración: las mujeres inmigrantes gallegas en la Argentina', in Núñez Seixas (ed.), *La Galicia Austral*, pp. 107–36.

[83] Cagiao Vila, 'Género y emigración'.

[84] Moya, *Cousins and Strangers*, p.277; Dolores Vieites Torreiro, 'La participación de los Gallegos en el movimiento obrero argentino (1880–1930)', in Núñez Seixas (ed.), *La Galicia Austral*, pp. 161–80 (p. 161).

[85] Alejandro E. Fernández, 'Los Gallegos dentro de la colectividad y las asociaciones españolas en el primer tercio del siglo XX', in Núñez Seixas (ed.), *La Galicia Austral*, pp. 139–60.

[86] Moya, *Cousins and Strangers*, p. 291.

[87] Ibid., p. 74.

[88] López, *testimonio de Carmen Cornes*, p. 35.

[89] S. Griswold Morley, 'Preface' to his translated edition of Rosalia de Castro's *En las orillas del Sar* (Beside the River Sar) (Berkelely, Calif.: University of California Press, 1937) p. x.

[90] Villares, *Historia*, p. 332.

[91] Alejandro Pérez Lugín, *La Casa de la Troya* (Santiago de Compostela: Galí, 1985), p. 14.

[92] George Borrow, *The Bible in Spain* (London: Dent, 1961), p. 245.

[93] Francisco Paulo Mellado, *Recuerdos de un viaje por Galicia en 1850* (A Coruña: Arenas, 1999 [1850]), pp. 4–5.

3

Politics and protests: Galicia, c.1850–1931

When did the Galician people first get involved in political action? Throughout the nineteenth century there were many popular political movements. One could cite the resistance to Napoleon after 1808, the military coup in Lugo in 1846 (discussed below), or the agitation associated with the First Republic (1873–4). All these examples, however, were little more than fleeting moments, which gripped a passionate minority, but passed over the majority of the population with little effect. A more convincing answer to the question posed above might be to cite the general election of 1891, in which all men had the vote. However, as will be seen, this election certainly did not allow all voters to express their opinions freely.

In this chapter I will turn from the long-term social and cultural themes debated in the previous chapters to consider the *quality* of the region's political activities. In particular, I will examine how Galician regionalism and nationalism developed.

People and politics: 1891

The first Spanish general election in which all men could vote was held in 1891. The population of Spain was then approximately 17.5 million: on average, each of the 399 deputies represented some 44,000 people.[1] There were 45 deputies to represent Galicia, distributed among the four provinces. Eight were chosen by urban areas, and the other 37 represented rural constituencies.

Galicia was slightly overrepresented in parliamentary terms: on average, each of its deputies would represent some 42,100 people. Secondly, looking at Table 3.1, one notes how the slow demographic drift westwards had continued: the easterly provinces of Lugo and Ourense now contained only 44 per cent of the region's population.

The Conservative Party was the favourite to win the 1891 election. Nationally, it won 253 of the 399 seats (63.4 per cent), while its principal rival, the Liberal party, won only 74 (18.5 per cent). The

Table 3.1. Provincial populations and parliamentary
representation in Galicia, 1891

Province	Population (1885)	Deputies
A Coruña	613,881	14
Lugo	432,165	11
Ourense	405,127	9
Pontevedra	443,385	11
Total	1,894,558	45

Republicans were still demoralized by the fall of the First Republic
(1873–4), and divided into ferociously antagonistic factions. They
did less badly than might have been expected, winning 31 seats (7.7
per cent).

The results in Galicia reflected these national trends: of the 45
deputies elected in 1891, 26 were Conservatives (57.7 per cent) and
14 were Liberals (31.1 per cent) (see Table 3.2).

The Liberal party performed better in Galicia than it did in Spain.
By the late nineteenth century the region was a secure base for liberal
notables, who could rely on *caciquismo* to guarantee a certain
minimum number of votes, even in bad years. Relatively speaking,
Lugo was the most Liberal of the four provinces, though this result is
somewhat confused by the existence of two 'non-party' (but not anti-
caciquismo) deputies in the province. On the other hand, Ourense
was clearly the most Conservative province.

There were few surprises in this election. In Pontevedra province,
two groups representing splits from, respectively, the Liberal and
Conservative parties each won one seat. The only real contest
occurred in A Coruña, where the region's one Republican deputy
was elected. This was the only area in Galicia in which the First
Republic had permanently changed political structures. The city's

Table 3.2. Deputies elected in Galicia, 1891[2]

Province	Republicans	Liberals	Conservatives	Others
A Coruña	1	5	8	0
Lugo	0	4	5	2
Ourense	0	2	7	0
Pontevedra	0	3	6	2
Totals	1	14	26	4

workers regularly voted for Republican candidates in both national and municipal elections.[3] In general, however, the *caciques* worked well, and voters followed their instructions. The forty-five deputies of 1891 may have represented the rich and powerful in the region, and they could even be seen as reflecting a regional balance of power, but they did not represent the region's people.

How was this situation to be changed? How was Galicia to become a region that played an active role, rather than one which was constantly shaped by outside events? In the early twentieth century, there were some important developments which indicated a shift in the region's status.

Caciquismo, *1898 and Regeneration*

One problem encountered by countries with unrepresentative political systems is that it is often extremely difficult to gauge what the public thinks. The Liberal and Conservative parties worked well as instruments to maintain stability, to repress dissident voices and to distribute jobs and favours. These two parties, however, failed to represent public opinion. This led to a type of 'cultural vacuum', within which many activists began to look, almost automatically, outside the political system for forms of real political representation.

In 1898 these structural defects within Spanish politics caused a wide-ranging crisis, which reached its tragic climax in 1936. This process worked at many different levels. In a sense, 1898 was Spain's last imperial crisis.[4] Of course, since the seventeenth century, Spain's empire had suffered many setbacks. The revolts by the colonies in Central and Latin America in the first years of the nineteenth century constituted one important reversal, demonstrating that Spain had lost its place as a leading world power. However, during the nineteenth century, new relations had evolved between the ex-colonies and the old imperial power; as was shown in the previous chapter, many Spanish people emigrated to Argentina. There was still a sense that a common culture united Hispanics on both sides of the Atlantic, which lessened the impact of the loss of the American colonies.

By the late nineteenth century Spain's last significant colony was Cuba. This was vital to Spain: arguably, the best-developed part of its economy was the Catalan textile trade, which depended on Cuba both for raw materials and as a captive market. Such structures demonstrate the nature of Spanish industrialization. Rather than creating new economic forms, the most go-ahead industrialists in Spain made use of antiquated imperial structures to protect their trade from international competition. Catalan textile magnates even campaigned against the abolition of slavery in Cuba, arguing that this would damage Spain's economic interests. They were joined by many in their campaign, including some merchants from Vigo. Cuba also allowed Spanish leaders to continue to represent their nation as an imperial power. For these reasons, when the colonists demanded greater autonomy or rebelled against central government (as happened in 1868–78, 1879–80 and 1895–8), their protests were ruthlessly crushed.

Many Galicians were resident in Cuba. Some began to draw comparisons between the situation of their region and that of the Cubans. Often they were sympathetic to the Cubans' demands for autonomy, a cause which was defended by Galician writers such as Manuel Curros Enríquez (1851–1908), who lived in Cuba in the 1890s.[5]

The crisis of 1898 began in April, when the USA issued a public declaration of support for Cuban independence from Spain.[6] In Spain, this was seen as tantamount to a declaration of war. Many experts judged that Spanish forces would be no match for the American navy, but Spanish politicians were misled by the appearance of widespread public support for war, an illusion created by a few fiery headlines in newspapers. Ships left from Galicia's ports, with Galician crews, carrying soldiers to Cuba. In July 1898 the Spanish navy suffered a crushing defeat. In August 1898 the government acknowledged that it had lost the war, and that Cuba had won its independence. Spain's beaten, exhausted troops sailed back from its last colony, to land on the quays at Vigo and A Coruña.

This military defeat had serious consequences. It was read as a sign of 'the depths to which Spain had been sinking behind the chauvinistic rhetoric of her leaders'.[7] A flood of critical works were published in the following months, as if all the political debate that had been repressed by *caciquismo* was now erupting into the open. New names began to attract public attention: Joaquín Costa, Miguel Unamuno, Ramiro de Maeztu and Ortega y Gasset all emerged in these months, and would remain prominent figures in the twentieth century. New concepts also emerged: 'Regeneration' was the most important of them. Historians now identify such writers as the 'Generation of 98', as if the defeat divided the old Spain from the new. The debate that these writers initiated was far-reaching and highly original: they debated Spain's identity, its reality and even its meaning. However, despite the wide-ranging protests which developed over the succeeding months, these writers and thinkers did not create a new political force.

In part, this was because the new generation of writers were uncertain about the best remedy for Spain's problems. Certainly, the defeat had demonstrated Spain's serious military weakness. Arguably, the overconfidence shown by many in power pointed to a second, equally serious, political problem: political opinion in Spain was shaped by irrational, venal forces, and was incapable of producing coherent and progressive policies. But how could this sickness be solved? What form would Spanish 'Regeneration' take? Regenerationists debated a near-endless series of questions. Should Spain become more like the rest of Europe? If so, was this to be done by imitating European industry, its learning or its political structures? Or, on the contrary, was there a unique Spanish path to modernity? Were Spain's problems to be solved by a stronger, more centralized form of government? Or was the solution to be found in decentralization, possibly in an appeal to the regions which had been so ignored by the centralizing and modernizing programmes of nineteenth-century governments? All these new writers tended to see *caciquismo* as a central problem that Spain faced, but how was it to be ended? By the ethical leadership of a rejuvenated monarchy? By a dictator, an 'iron surgeon', in the ugly expression that began to circulate? Or by a democratic republic?

The year 1898 should have been the great opportunity for the republicans. Instead, it took them off guard. Many of them were patriotic and, given their disgust with corrupt parliaments, still tended to see the army as a potential alternative power.[8] While they spoke of 'the people', few of them had any contact with or knowledge of popular concerns. Their organizations were little more than groups of notables, linked by a club or a circle, fired by their enthusiastic admiration for a single prestigious writer or leading activist. In the weeks before elections they would spring into life, only to fall back, after the predictable defeat of most of their candidates, into a self-serving contempt for a corrupt political system and the beguiled masses. In some cities – such as Valencia or A Coruña – they managed to seize control of the town halls.[9] But, on the whole, such small, stuffy groups were bewildered by the critical, anti-militarist attitudes which circulated in 1898.[10] When a snap general election was held in April 1899, the Republicans won only eighteen seats (including one in Pontevedra province) – five more than in 1898, but hardly a breakthrough.[11]

Instead, the long-term significance of 1898 was to encourage groups from outside the established political structures. The most immediate demonstration of this new attitude developed in Catalonia, in the north-east of Spain, the most modern and most industrialized region in Spain. Here, a new, politicized sense of Catalan identity grew, based on the fusion of at least two existing currents. During the nineteenth century, some militants had popularized Catalan cultural and linguistic activities, establishing Catalan as a literary language in its own right. But, equally important, there was a hard-edged, commercial aspect to the new Catalanism, epitomized by the famous Lliga Regionalista, which was created in 1901, described by Joseph Harrison as 'the first modern political party' in Spain.[12] The most prominent members of this group were Barcelona's textile magnates. They wanted an organization that would lobby the Madrid parliament on their behalf, obtaining commercial benefits.

In the 1907 general elections a new political coalition, Solidaritat Catalana, put up candidates. It drew support from Catholics and republicans, from monarchists and liberals, from conservative regionalists who saw Catalonia as an oasis of Catholic values in an immoral nation, and from progressive federalists who dreamt of a reborn Catalonia leading Spain to a new world of education and modernity. Solidaritat Catalana won 41 seats out of the region's 44 seats, and 68.4 per cent of the votes cast.[13] This was, first and foremost, a victory against *caciquismo*. It proved that modern, forward-looking political forces could develop in Spain. Could something similar happen in Galicia?

The Rexurdimiento *and regionalism*

In fact, there were similar moves across Spain. While governments and military leaders tended to stress the values of centralization and uniformity, in some regions different voices were emerging. Many factors were involved in the development of these alternative cultures. Often the values of European Romanticism, that great reaction to the political cultures of the French Revolution, were central to the new regionalisms of the nineteenth century. Romantics stressed the individual and distinct features of particular nations, and often admired medieval forms of religion, art and architecture. Through their inspiration, some writers began to study folk lyrics and peasants' tales. But other factors also encouraged the growth of regionalist movements. Regionalism could serve businessmen lobbying for a better deal, or clerical conservatives trying to hang on to their parishes. Provocatively, Isidro Dubert suggests that the first stimulus to Galician regionalism was the presence of new migrants in the region's tiny towns, provoking local oligarchs to adopt defensive and hostile forms of politics.[14]

The key point to grasp here is that there was no single cause or event which can convincingly be presented as *the* beginning of Galician regionalism. Instead, we need to think in broader terms: which factors were most likely to stimulate Galicians to consider their region as different from the rest of Spain? A qualification must be added here: for many, Galicia's apparent backwardness was proof of governmental neglect. To such observers, however, the most obvious solution was not to demand the separation of the region from Spain, but – on the contrary – to demand its greater integration. Above all, we should draw back from seeing an awareness of Galician distinctiveness as automatically producing a certain type of regionalist or Galician-nationalist political culture. Instead, this issue resembled an empty space, which could be filled with different political values.

The first programmes to integrate Catalonia and the Basque country into Castile's political structures started in the fifteenth century, and – arguably – the process was not completed until 1876. Both Catalans and Basques could draw on memories of older autonomous political institutions and traditions. As was seen in chapter 1, Galicians could not claim a similar historical experience. For these reasons, the first expressions of a specific, politicized assertion of Galicia were, understandably, confused, faltering, and – often – contradictory.

The earliest of these Galician movements was liberal and even left-leaning. As was seen in the last chapters, Galician participants in the eighteenth-century Enlightenment tended to look to the Spanish state to modernize and liberate their region. By the nineteenth century, it was becoming increasingly difficult to hold such beliefs. The legislation of 1833 had integrated the region into Spain's administration; by 1876 no regionally specific legislation remained within the Spanish constitution. Galicia was now an integral part of the Spanish state. One can identify the first flickers of Galician regional politics in this period, as a group of liberal students at the University of Santiago de Compostela, linked to the 'Progressive' faction within the Liberal party, began to debate regional questions in the 1840s. They attracted an audience among those who had bought up church lands following the *desamortización* legislation; such men were almost invariably liberal and anti-clerical. They staged public debates on literary and historical topics, and published an irregular series of journals and magazines between 1842 and 1845.[15] Their talks and papers allowed them to address topics which were not addressed by the university's courses. Some of them were probably also involved in the minor military rebellions which were staged in the region in 1840 and 1843, and in the rather more serious military coup in Lugo, in April 1846, which set off a series of protests throughout the region. Such rebellions were the inevitable by-product of Spain's ossifying political system, within which anti-establishment voices were unable to gain entry into parliament, and for these reasons they occurred frequently across the peninsula in the mid-nineteenth century: one historian has calculated that during Isabella II's thirty-four-year reign, from 1835 to 1868, there were no fewer than eighteen major military coups, and countless smaller rebellions.[16]

In April 1846 the coup's leaders were executed in Lugo. Although these men had little commitment to the cause of Galician separatism, they would later be seen as Galicia's first nationalist martyrs. This episode is distinctive, for several reasons. There are many examples of regional reactions against nineteenth-century forms of centralization. In most cases, however, a backward-looking aristocracy, using regionalism as a way to preserve its privileges against a modernizing state, is important as one of the first groups to make reasonably coherent demands. Galicia is unusual in that its first regionalists were clearly neither aristocrats nor conservatives.

Like other Spanish liberals, these students were trying to dress new political ideas in old clothes. They were inspired by the ambiguous new ideas of social Catholicism, which could be a genuinely assertive, original project to remake a Catholicism of the people, or which might merely be a Catholicism with a social conscience, a better form of charity. They proposed liberal, even democratic, reforms, they argued that Galicia was urgently in need of economic development, but they justified these proposals by referring to half-legendary regionalist precedents from the ancient past. Moreover, their blending of the central and the regional is difficult to grasp, for it translates only awkwardly into the political idioms of the twenty-first century. They never referred to Galicia as a nation, for this would imply that the land had a separate existence from the Spanish nation: instead, they used words such as 'province' and *patria*, or fatherland.[17] They attacked overcentralization and proposed a degree of decentralization in order to form political institutions which would manage this process of integration, not in order to leave the state. In later decades, these types of ideas would form the 'federalist' strand within Spanish republican thinking. Federalists wanted to remake Spain through a process of decentralization, which would recreate the nation as a federation of regions. Such ideas were neatly summed up by a phrase from a federalist-republican in 1869: Galicia would be independent, but an integral part of the nation.[18]

Federalist ideas acquired a larger audience in Galicia during the First Republic (1873–4). The prestigious Galician novelist Emilia Pardo Bazán was both impressed and alarmed by the revolts and social agitation of these years. Her well-known novel, *La Tribuna* (1882), describes the new popular audience for republican politics that developed. Pardo Bazán depicts the women of the cigar factories of A Coruña listening intently as republican papers are read out. The novel's heroine 'learns to think in the style of a newspaper article, and to talk in the same manner'.[19] Pardo Bazán herself, while a republican, was actually rather sceptical of these developments. Her disgust with *caciquismo* led her to despair of popular or democratic movements.[20] However, as will be seen later, A Coruña became a major centre of republican activism in the early twentieth century.

After 1846 regionalist ideas seemed to spread from Santiago de Compostela, with A Coruña becoming a centre of debate. Certainly, of thirty-one publications which can be identified as sympathetic to the regionalist cause from 1846 to 1881, fourteen were based in A Coruña.[21] This was no political movement, however, merely a loose network of ideas and debate.

The second wave of Galician regionalists were less likely to be political activists. Unable to change their world, these were often amateur scholars who took refuge in a half-imagined world of ancient mystery. The Celts were now rediscovered as the holders of a glorious past. There was an interesting cultural specificity here: while across Europe, the discovery of Celtic traditions usually meant the reassertion of Celtic languages, in Galicia the Celts were nearly always understood as a 'a complex cultural concept', not as a linguistic group.[22] Of course, as in other regions, there were political issues raised by language use in Galicia, but in this region such debates centred on the status of the Romance language Galego, not on the promotion of Celtic languages. In 1853, the first book was published in Galego.[23] From 1875 to 1891 thirty-six books of poetry, seven plays and six works of prose were published in Galego.[24] This new use of Galego as a literary, poetic and theatrical language was the most obvious sign of the Galician *Rexurdimiento*, or Renaissance. However, Castilian clearly remained the dominant language in the press and in political and social writing.

A passage from the autobiography of Emilio González López, a republican activist from A Coruña, illustrates the awkward relationship between the two languages. Here, he describes how his father, a trade union activist, and his mother made use of them.

> My father was gripped by an unquenchable love for the written word – something he had gained from his years as a print worker. But while he was a carpenter, he learnt the value of the spoken word: not that of normal, everyday conversation, but that of speeches and conferences. In both modes, he only used Castilian. It was in this language that he could express himself with greatest spontaneity, although he always spoke Galego with my mother and his workmates . . . Galego was my mother's language; she spoke it naturally and spontaneously, and she always used it with my father and her children.[25]

Of course, González's family cannot be cited as some scientifically chosen representative sample. But we can draw from this example an illustration of how the use of the two languages was evolving: many people in Galicia were effectively bilingual, and could choose which language to use in which context. They tended to reserve Castilian for formal, public speech (or writing), and Galego for more private conversations. To some extent, this difference followed lines of gender: men were more likely to be literate, more likely to have attended school, more likely to participate in public events, and therefore more likely to use Castilian than were women.

While Rosalía de Castro wrote her simple folk lyrics in Galego, published as the *Cantares gallegas* in 1863, her husband, Manuel Murguía (1833–1923), published a five-volume history of Galicia in Castilian. His intention was to provide a scientific basis for Galician identity; to this end he based his research on original documents, and made reference to the sciences of linguistics, archaeology and palaeography. The first volume was published in 1865, the fifth in 1913. His work proposed a world-view based on a Darwinian competition between superior and inferior races.[26] Murguía was one of the first to argue that the Celts had left a distinct ethnic legacy to the modern Galicians, which made them different from the rest of Spain. Galicia's Celtic roots had then been reinforced by the Suebes, and this 'racial purity' had been preserved into the nineteenth century.[27]

This second wave of Galician regionalism was less obviously politicized than the first; it had fewer links to Spanish national politics. It was dominated by conservative themes, principally the need to protect an idealized rural community from the threat represented by, variously, the modern state, rationalism or industrialization. Like the first wave, this was not a well-organized political movement with a clearly edited manifesto. Murguía's political values are difficult to interpret; alongside his avowed connections to Spanish and European liberals, the quasi-racist determinism of his writing suggests some deeply conservative themes. The failure of the First Republic (1873–4) would push many regionalists to the right. Yet, at the same time, these late nineteenth-century regionalists detested *caciquismo*, and retained something of the social conscience of the first wave.

Alfredo Brañas's *El regionalismo*, published in 1889, could be cited as the most representative text from this second wave. Clearly inspired by reactionary Carlist ideas, *El regionalismo* called for a revival of Spain's ancient regions, and for the creation of corporate structures to reunite rich and poor in moral communities. Brañas criticized the evils of industrialization, capitalism and liberalism, but his solution was a revival of medieval guilds.[28] In his work, he argued that Galicia formed a region within the larger structure of the Spanish nation.

An 'Asociación Regionalista Gallega' was finally created in 1890 in Santiago de Compostela, with Murguía as president. Local committees were also formed in Lugo, A Coruña, Ourense, Pontevedra

and Tui.[29] A few notables and scholars joined; mainly liberal professional people. A handful of meetings were held. In 1891 they
sponsored the revival of a medieval poetry competition, the Xogos
Frorais, or Floral Games, in which poets competed to win prizes
bearing flower motifs, a distant cousin of the Welsh Eisteddfod. The
Galician regionalists were not the first to promote such events:
Catalan regionalists had revived their 'Jocs Floral' in 1859. The
Asociación Regionalista Gallega collapsed in 1893.[30] These scholars
stressed the need to distance the region from the nation. However,
this was not a call for Galicia's independence from Spain, but more a
project 'to rebuild the state from below' – in other words, to renego-
tiate the integration of Galicia into Spain.[31]

The most significant assertions of Galician culture and language
often took place outside the region. Clubs, networks and associations spread across Spain, and even over the Atlantic. For example,
the foundation of a literary society, Galicia Literaria, in Madrid in
1875 played a vital role in the formation of some future Galician
militants.[32] Emilio González López, a teenager from A Coruña, first
exhibited his paintings in the Galician Centre at Gijón, a port to the
west of Galicia.[33] Cuban exiles subsidized the publication of
Murguía's five-volume history.[34] In Argentina, new elites among the
Galician migrants were demanding to be treated with respect by the
rest of the population. They were swift to echo some of the key
themes of the new Galician regionalism, reflected by the publication
of two journals in 1879. *El Gallego* was republican, left-leaning and
federalist in its politics, while *La Revista Galaica* was conservative
and regionalist.[35] There were also some similar moves in Cuba,
beginning with the publication of the *La Tierra Gallega* journal in
April 1894.[36]

Another vital extra-Galician factor in the development of
Galician political life was the return of the 'Americans'. Those who
had emigrated to Argentina and Cuba, it should be remembered,
were not the poorest of the poor. Instead, they are better understood
as frustrated sub-elites, often desperate to raise money to buy themselves freedom from the *foros* and to modernize their farms. In
Argentina they learnt – the hard way – about how to organize institutions and develop social movements. When they returned to
Galicia, they were often quick to reject the apathy and fatalism of
the countryside. In particular, the peasants who lived near the ports
of A Coruña and Pontevedra were able to observe the new militancy

of among some urban workers, as socialist and anarchist ideas began to spread.

Agrarismo: *the revolt of the countryside*

Caciquismo initially appears as a simple example of corruption and manipulation. In practice, it could work in quite subtle ways. Hidalgos and *caciques* presented themselves as the natural protectors of rural communities.[37] They gave advice to the ignorant, they warned the unwary. Above all, they represented themselves as the leaders of an imaginary community of rural property-owners, united in their rejection of the unjust exactions of the state and, in particular, in their constant efforts to evade taxation. Such ideas were endemic across Spain: they had, for example, frustrated the drawing up of an accurate land survey, for this would have been the first step to a fairer tax system.[38]

In the last years of the nineteenth century, the first signs of the decay of this enforced consensus in Galicia emerged. It was marked by the growth of *agrarismo*, or 'agrarianism'. As was the case with the emergence of Galician regionalism, this was 'a movement of quite extraordinary complexity . . . rich in contradictions', which cannot be reduced to a simple cause-and-effect analysis.[39] The process unfolded at different paces in different localities. Certainly, the influence of individual 'Americans' was vital, alongside the activities of public-spirited professional people and merchants, some inspired by the Regenerationist ideals of 1898. In some places, the parish clergy were at the centre of the movement, leading to the later creation of Catholic agrarian trade unions. By 1907, the movement had reached into all four provinces.

The information in Table 3.3 allows us to understand this movement more clearly. Firstly, it was unequally distributed across the region: the conservative eastern provinces were far less affected than the more dynamic west. In Pontevedra province there was one society for every 2,000 rural workers; in Lugo one for every 27,000.[40] The most important expression of the movement was the formation of agrarian societies of peasant-farmers, but it also appealed to cattle-ranchers. Lastly, the list of 'others' demonstrates the variety of forms that the movement took: it also led to the creation of rural banks, mutual aid societies and cooperatives. Often, their immediate

Table 3.3. Agrarian societies in Galicia, 1898–1907[41]

Provinces	Total	Farmers' groups	Ranchers' groups	Trade unions	Others
A Coruña	114	55	36	6	17
Lugo	12	6	3	–	3
Ourense	27	22	–	2	3
Pontevedra	120	104	12	2	2
Galicia	273	187	51	10	25

aims seem quite modest: to create forms of association, to alleviate rural misery. Why did they arouse such excitement? The answer lies in their forms. The agrarians were independent of the *caciques'* political parties and usually explicitly neutral in religious matters. These two points meant that they constituted an immediate challenge to the social and religious rulers of the countryside.[42]

Often these societies had political connections, even if these were not immediately obvious. Observers would need to be sensitive to minute differences in names. Groups with titles such as 'Sociedad Agrícola' (Agricultural Society) or 'Sociedad de Labradores' (Farmers' Society) would probably be open to the big property-owners, and therefore be integrated into the structures of *caciquismo*. On the other hand, the title 'Sociedad de Obreros Agriculturas' (Agricultural Workers' Society) was a sure indication of an anarchist or socialist influence.[43] In practice, diverse political groups helped start this movement. Socialists were active in agrarian societies near Pontevedra, Vigo, Ourense and Betanzos (in A Coruña province). Anarchists worked with *agraristas* near A Coruña; they even formed their own much-feared Unión Campesina (Peasants' Union). Following their defeat in the Third Carlist War (1872–6), the remaining Carlist activists were rethinking their methods. This change of strategy was marked by a new name: 'Traditionalists'. Together with some dissident Catholics, Traditionalists helped agrarians in Arzúa and Betanzos (both in A Coruña province). Galician regionalists were also associated with the agrarians around Pontevedra.[44] In Ortegal (Lugo province), the movement took a relatively benign form, loosely linked with the Liberal party, and concentrating on developing self-help institutions.[45]

These agrarian radicals usually met with a ferocious and entrenched opposition. According to one priest, the agrarians were demons, Freemasons and Protestants.[46] Priests, even bishops, would preach sermons against them; the *caciques* would use their contacts with the administration to have them banned.[47] Following instructions from the archbishop of Santiago de Compostela, Cardinal Herrera issued the following circular in 1903.

> We have been deeply saddened to see that, in so many parishes . . . there are men immersed in the most pernicious doctrines of socialism who labour to realize its ends. They are opposed to Religion, to authority and to private property. They organize themselves, not for the honest ends of a Christian life, but to put into practice their ideas, opposed to social order . . . They have formed a league of resistance to legitimate authority. While they invoke terms such as the freedom of thought, of speech, of meeting and association, they fight to turn the existing order upside down.[48]

Because of the ferocity of opposition, many were reluctant to join the agrarians openly. In some small parishes, an agrarian society might look more like the organization of a single family rather than a whole class, with only a few dozen members joining. Most societies had over a hundred members, but none had more than a thousand. Duran calculates that in 1907 there may have been about thirty thousand agrarians in Galicia, perhaps representing about a tenth of the total rural labour force.[49] Because of the fear of persecution, often the local head of a society might be a doctor, an artisan, even someone who held a *foro* – all people with some independence from the *caciques*.[50] Joining an agrarian society was a courageous act. When the *caciques* felt threatened, they would turn to violence, and the agrarians had to fight back with the weapons that they had to hand: bitter strikes, which divided communities, and the burning of farm property.

Step by step, these methods gained some success; peasant-farmers slowly were able to buy themselves out of the obligations which the *foros* had imposed. Agrarianism was the most visible sign of a new sense of confidence, which allowed peasants to stand up to hidalgos. However, the movement had its limits: after 1907, its political focus grew more blurred. The agrarians almost became respectable. They were the organizers of cooperatives and popularizers of agricultural improvement, tending always to be oriented towards the landowning small farmers. In later decades, groups from across the political spectrum would lobby for their support.[51]

While peasants were eventually able to gain full ownership of their land, this reform did not change the pattern of scattered, minute land-holdings. Edward Malefakis estimated that by the 1960s there were some fifteen million separate plots of land in Galicia, six for every inhabitant.[52] This pattern was an obstacle to any substantial agricultural modernization.

Regionalists and agrarians had very different origins: while the first group idealized the Galician countryside, the second actually worked on the soil. But the two did share some common goals, principally the aim to cleanse the region of *caciquismo*. Could they work together?

Solidaridad Gallega

Galician regionalists and nationalists admired the success of Solidaritat Catalana in 1907. Their praise for the movement runs through their speeches and writing. Barcelona was the only place in Spain where conscious, clear thinking flourished, wrote the Galicia nationalist Roberto Blanco Torres in 1919; this was due to 'its citizens' unique spiritual force', which made their city 'the unique organ of European efficiency' in Spain.[53] For Victor Casas, another nationalist, Catalonia was 'the vanguard of movement' in Spain, while Barcelona represented 'the best of Spain'.[54] The Catalan deputies recognized the potential similarity of their two movements, and attempted to assist their Galician cousins. In 1907 a group from Solidaritat Catalana travelled round Galicia, giving lectures explaining the success of their movement.

Could this movement be imitated in Galicia? In July 1907 a new weekly appeared in A Coruña: *Galicia Solidaria*. This followed the Catalan model in being open to all tendencies who would work for the region, and attracted interest from some of Galicia's republicans (principally based in A Coruña), its regionalists (also based in A Coruña) and its Traditionalists (often based in Lugo province). *Galicia Solidaria* was then followed by a second weekly, *A Nosa Terra* (Our Land), which was designed deliberately as a voice for regionalist politics. A manifesto was issued, announcing the creation of Solidaridad Gallega. Its words demonstrated the political ambiguity of the new movement.

> Solidaridad Gallega aims to affirm and validate Galicia's personality through more substantial decentralization, to win and to affirm its rightful representation in all spheres of law and [to improve] the welfare of those concerned, within the structures of the Spanish state.

> Solidarists are united by this positive concern, and affirm their fullest
> toleration for all the various opinions of each particular member.[55]

Once again, we can note that this was not a movement which aimed
to separate Galicia from the rest of Spain; rather, its aim was to rene-
gotiate the integration of the region in the nation. Another point
which the manifesto quite deliberately sidestepped was that of the
movement's political values. Were they republicans? Regionalists?
Constitutional monarchists? Or Traditionalists? In fact, the
Traditionalists were growing increasingly interested in both the
Catalan and Galician movements.

A second manifesto, written by Rodrigo Sanz and issued in
September 1907, did nothing to clear up these political ambiguities.
It was 'a strange balancing act, with indeterminate and elusive
language'.[56] However, there was some clearer sense of focus. The
solidarists' enemy was obvious: the *cacique*. Their methods were
clarified: Solidaridad Gallega's key struggle was to be the electoral
one. Sanz's rhetoric balanced between the conservative and the
republican-federalist interpretations of regionalism. On the one
hand, he called for a 'New Reconquest' of Spain, suggesting the
region's Catholic legacy, but on the other hand he scrupulously
avoided all explicit mention of Church and king, suggesting a
modern, secular, nationalism. His references to Galicia's economic
problems were equally vague: while *caciquismo* was condemned, no
solution was suggested to the *foros*, beyond a demand for a more
dignified relationship between *señor* and labourer. The plight of the
cottagers, the sharecroppers and the urban workers was ignored.
Lastly, Sanz attempted to spell out the organization's attitude to the
questions of regionalism and separatism. Solidaridad Gallega was
not a regionalist organization, but 'a regional nucleus of a force of
national regeneration'.[57]

In October 1907 Solidaridad Gallega organized a series of meetings to publicize its cause. Very quickly, there was a setback. On 7
October the meeting in A Coruña was disrupted by crowds of republicans, who shouted slogans hostile to the 'Carlists'.[58] This was close
to a disaster: A Coruña was arguably the most politically advanced
town in the region, with the most experienced, active and intelligent
electorate. If these people showed such implacable antagonism to
Solidaridad Gallega, what chance had it got in the rest of the region?
The reaction of A Coruña's papers was also revealing. The liberal
Voz de Galicia was extremely hostile. *El Noreste*, a conservative daily,

supported decentralization and showed some interest in the region-
alist cause. The republican *Tierra Gallega* clearly opposed
Solidaridad Gallega. Its one defender was, curiously, *El Eco de
Galicia*, a paper funded by the archbishop of Santiago de
Compostela, which moved from suspicion of the new movement to
consistent support.[59]

To their surprise, the solidarists found that there was some support
for their cause in the countryside. The Agrarians and some priests
worked to provide them with halls and audiences.[60] This was significant: it suggested that regionalism could acquire a social base. But
the movement was not sustained. The hostile reception in the towns
and the increasingly right-wing drift of the movement's backers
disoriented many of Solidaridad Gallega's supporters. At the next
general election, in May 1910, there was only one regionalist candidate (who was unsuccessful), and by 1912 the movement had
collapsed. In fact, something similar happened in Catalonia: the
Solidaritat Catalana coalition rapidly split into rival factions after its
1907 victory, although Catalan regionalism (and nationalism) did
survive in other forms.

There are some important lessons to be learnt from Solidaridad
Gallega. The first is perhaps an obvious one, a point which should
have been clear to the solidarists themselves: the process which had
been pioneered in Catalonia could not be mechanically imitated in
Galicia. In fact, Solidaridad Gallega's connections with the Catalan
movement may well have alienated some of its potential supporters,
who associated Catalonia with the rich merchants who invested in
Galicia. Above all, there was no Galician equivalent to the textile
magnates who supported Catalonia's Lliga Regionalista. Of course,
the solidarists could have chosen to work more closely with the
agrarians, but their clerical and conservative supporters would have
been reluctant to accept any demand for peasant rights. Despite both
opposing the rule of the *caciques*, the two movements did not share
any positive principles.

Secondly, like its Catalan mentor, Solidaridad Gallega was based
on an unstable coalition of different forces. While each, in their own
way, was inspired by the ideal of Regeneration, and therefore all
opposed *caciquismo* and were committed to the cleansing of
Galicia's politics, they were not agreed on how this should be done.
In particular, these coalitions, in Galicia and Catalonia, were unable
to develop firm political structures of their own.

The Brotherhood of Friends of the Language

Following Solidaridad Gallega's failure, regionalist debate declined. The next development was quite different, representing a type of recasting of the regionalist project. In March 1916 Antón Villar Ponte, a well-known regionalist activist, published a pamphlet of Galician culture, proclaiming the need for the defence of the Galician language as a priority. This was a controversial point: up to this date, even Galician regionalists had been reluctant to make use of Galego for formal, public occasions. Orators speaking in Galego at public meetings would be insulted as 'illiterates' by hecklers.[61] In May 1916 Villar organized a meeting in Santiago de Compostela, which attracted some forty people, including prominent Traditionalists and republicans.[62] They formed the first 'Hirmandade dos Amigos da Fala', or Brotherhood of Friends of the Language. ('Irmandade' is an alternative Galego spelling of 'Hirmandade'; it later became the more commonly used.) In the weeks that followed, new sections were formed in Monforte, Ourense and Vilalba; another was created in Pontevedra, but soon collapsed. Unlike Solidaridad Gallega, this organization's aims were clear: to encourage the use of Galego in speech and writing, to defend Galician culture and to develop research into the region's past. Local groups undertook a wide range of activities: choirs, drama groups, meetings, evening classes and exhibitions.[63]

There was one noticeable absence, however: the Irmandade did not develop a political discourse. Was this a weakness? Not necessarily. Their apparently innocent activities did not attract the immediate opposition of the *caciques*. Their apolitical nature allowed regionalists, Traditionalists and republican-federalists to attend the same events without conflict. More importantly, within their activities some political values were developing: a love of their region, and a sense of shared struggle to preserve and develop an identity. One point which quickly developed was a sensitivity to the manner in which Galicians were portrayed elsewhere in Spain (and even in Argentina). Anti-Galician jokes infuriated this new generation of militants, who demanded that Galicians stay silent no more.[64]

Rather than seeing the absence of an explicit political discourse as a weakness, it might better be analysed as a clever tactical move, sidestepping awkward and divisive debates, and avoiding a head-on clash with the forces of *caciquismo*. Correspondingly, the Irmandade chose not to contest the municipal elections of November 1917, although a few individual members stood, usually on other lists. One sympathetic councillor was elected in A Coruña, two in Santiago de Compostela.[65] In the February 1918 elections, the Irmandade worked with the Mauristas, a radically reformist, anti-*caciquismo* strand within the Conservative party.

Numbers grew steadily in this period (Table 3.4). The biggest group was that in A Coruña, which attracted about half of the Irmandade's membership.

Table 3.4. Estimates of membership of the Irmandade, 1916–18[66]

Date	Members	Groups
December 1916	200	6
November 1918	700	13

By November 1918 it was impossible for the Irmandade to avoid debating the movement's political values. Some clear tendencies were emerging. Priests were growing suspicious of the movement, and tending to leave. In A Coruña, the Irmandade tended to be liberal and democratic, sometimes even socialist. On the other hand, the Irmandade's second biggest group in Ourense was markedly more conservative, perhaps more in the line of Murguía's politics, but also inspired by Traditionalist arguments. The two tendencies were expressed through two different Galego-language journals: the A Coruña group revived the older title *A Nosa Terra*, while after 1920 the Ourense group published *Nós* (Ourselves). The second group proved to be more forceful and original in its political arguments, a point I will explore in the next section.

The Irmandade met in Lugo in November 1918 to formalize their organization. This date was not a coincidence: the First World War was ending, and western European politicians were considering the implications of the Fourteen Points drawn up by the American president, Woodrow Wilson. These proclaimed the right of all nationalities to be recognized. While Spain had stayed neutral in the First World War, it was nonetheless affected by the conflict.

The Irmandade's meeting was entitled the 'First Nationalist Assembly' – a title which was a political statement in itself. After two years of relatively anodyne cultural activities, this grouping was now making the claim that it represented Galicia: a claim which none of the earlier regionalist groupings had made. The Irmandade's *Manifesto* of November 1918 made clear the significance of this move. It began with the following declaration:

> Considering that Galicia possesses all the essential features of nationhood, henceforth we will call ourselves Galician nationalists, as the term 'regionalist' does not articulate all our aspirations nor does it express the intensity of our problems.[67]

This was not quite the same as calling for Galician independence. The Irmandade's preferred solution was a new Iberian federation, including Galicia, Catalonia, the Basque country and Castile, and possibly extending to Portugal. Within this federation, all the constituent parts would be treated as equal partners, and each would benefit from a substantial degree of autonomy, allowing each nation to legislate on matters such as justice, education, agriculture, industry and commerce. Within Galicia, Galego would have equal status with Castilian.

How were the Irmandade, with their seven hundred members, to achieve this goal?

Strategies and politics

It should be remembered that the Irmandade were the inheritors of almost eight decades of debates and discussion. In 1918, the idea that Galicia was a distinctive area, different from the rest of Spain, was not new. The Irmandade of 1918 were somewhat more experienced than their predecessors, but their dramatic declaration of November 1918 did not introduce any radical change to the tactics and ideas inherited from the previous movements.

Both the republican group at A Coruña and the more conservative group in Ourense were faced with the same fundamental problem: if Galicia was a nation, then why did the majority of its population show such little interest in the theses of the new nationalist groups? How could seven hundred unelected people claim to represent two million people of Galicia?

Both groups tended to answer such questions with awkward forms of sidestepping. Galicia's status as a nation was not to be demonstrated with reference to the expressed will of two million inhabitants, but through a consideration of its history. Murguía's influence here was vital; his work provided the model for such arguments. Galicia was formed as a nation through the very processes of history. Its Celtic inheritance, its distinctive language, its customs, all demonstrated the reality of this nationhood. In the words of Blanco Torres, 'geographically, linguistically and ethically we are a people, a nationality'.[68]

Within the ranks of the Irmandade, the key thinker on such matters was Vicente Risco (1884–1963). A new recruit to the cause, Risco had previously been a dabbler in strange and exotic thought, studying works as diverse as Nietzsche's philosophy, French decadent poetry and Hindu religious texts. His first essays, dating from the beginning of the twentieth century, evoked the decadence of the West and praised the aesthetic sense of the Orient.[69] He worked as a civil servant in Ourense, and contributed to the local press. Like many of the post-98 generation, he saw Spanish political life simply as an example of corruption, and seemed willing to consider any alternative, no matter how romantic or exotic. It was not until 1917 that he began to show an interest in Galician culture: in this year he wrote an essay in praise of its folklore.[70] Early in 1918 he joined an Irmandade and also converted to Catholicism.

In 1920 Risco wrote his masterwork, the *Teoría do nazonalismo galego*. This work reflected his strengths and his weaknesses. Risco argued that nationality was an objective fact, 'a spiritual reality', which existed independently of state forms – or even of popular opinion.[71] While he admired the heroic struggles of the Poles and Irish – 'our brothers in sad, green Ireland'[72] – his conception of nationalism, with its emphasis on the construction of nationalism through age-old historical forces, was quite distinct from their voluntarism. A nation, for Risco, was 'a community of spiritual and economic interests determined by nature'.[73] The task facing nationalists was not to *construct* the nation, but to rebuild it by the 'spiritual, political and economic reconstitution of Galicia'.[74]

Risco proclaimed the value of Galicia's Atlantic, Celtic specificity, and rejected the Mediterranean values of decadent Castile. He divided Spain into the Euro-Iberia of the north and the Afro-Iberia of the south.[75] The north had been betrayed by, in turn, the Catholic kings, the French Revolution and the anti-Napoleonic Cortes of Cádiz (1812). Galicia was different from the rest of Spain: it was the oldest and the most European land in the peninsula, rooted in Celtic and Germanic values.[76] Even its economic structures were distinct, argued Risco. Its small rural properties demonstrated that the Galicians were instinctively democratic, while big capitalism was an alien form, imported into the region.[77] These distinctive traits had to be preserved: this was the duty of all nationalists.

Risco opposed the entire culture of the modern world; he condemned the nineteenth century as 'the stupid century'.[78] Nineteenth-century liberal and democratic ideas were deeply alien to him. His long-term strategy was precisely to attempt to avoid mass politics by effecting a type of spiritual change in Galicia, implemented through its writing and culture. 'It is better to be Galician than to be free', he wrote.[79] Instead of mobilizing the people, the small band of Galician nationalists were to constitute 'the nationalist elite, the intellectual minority . . . an intellectual aristocracy' who would interpret 'the voice of blood' from the 'soul of the people'.[80] Even his attitude to popular Galego forms of writing and speech was more complex than it seemed. Risco understood 'popular literature as the outward and visible sign of an informing and sacramental collective spirit'.[81] In other words, despite having an apparent admiration for the literature and language of the people, Risco did not consider these as products of the people. On the contrary, it was the people who were being produced by this nebulous and mysterious Galician spirit, rooted in the earth and the language. His long-term aim, accepted by most of the Irmandade at this point, was to construct a new type of Iberian confederation, of which Galicia would be an equal part.[82]

One can question, therefore, the usefulness of Risco's political guidance to the new nationalists. His first instinct was to advise them to avoid politics, to abstain from standing as candidates and – even – not to vote. But when, within the Irmandades themselves, he was faced with an unavoidable political dilemma, his attitudes grew more disquieting.

In February 1922 the Fourth Nationalist Assembly, held in Monforte, debated the issue of participating in elections. The A Coruña group was leading a type of internal rebellion against Risco's advice, and the meeting was to vote on a proposal from them. By this point, the Irmandade's numbers had dropped somewhat: there were maybe five hundred members, of whom three hundred were in A Coruña. In a straight vote, it seemed likely that the A Coruña group would win. However, Risco argued that *on principle* such simple counting of individual members was wrong. Instead, each Irmandade group should be counted separately: he argued that this reflected the corporative spirit of the nationalist movement better than the 'individualism' of voting. Risco enlarged on this point. The Irmandade were 'a movement of the elite'. For these reasons, 'quality must count as much or more than quantity'.[83] Of course, following his criteria, the dozen or so small groups scattered across Galicia were able to outvote the big A Coruña group.

One might have expected that the republican-linked A Coruña group would have countered with a defence of democratic values against Risco. Nothing of the sort occurred. This point is revealing: it suggests that we are examining not so much a nationalist left and right as two different attitudes to political action. Risco was essentially a pessimist. He feared that contact with other political forms and political groups would damage the new nationalist movement. The A Coruña group were more confident: they considered that they could participate in politics, even in coalition with other non-nationalist groups, without compromising on principles. More importantly, they were looking for practical political gains, rather than Risco's rather nebulous spirituality.

This republican-leaning wing of the Irmandade never produced a theorist of Risco's stature. Their leading members were, above all, activists, good speakers who know how to sway a hostile crowd, and men who were brave enough to fight the entrenched powers of *caciquismo*. They were not, however, men of great intellectual powers. They were represented by men like Víctor Casas and Ramón Suárez Picallo. Casas (1900–36) had been a travelling salesman, and was largely self-taught. What he learnt of political theory came from the polemical exchanges he entered into as a journalist.[84] Suárez (?–1964) had learnt his political theory in a still rougher school: the labour movement of Buenos Aires. He was proud of his working-class origins. 'I am not a lecturer,' he proclaimed, 'it's only on the street that I'm active.'[85]

Such self-taught men, with their improvised sense of political tactics, were unable to counter Risco's eloquence. True, one can find some differences of emphasis; where Risco stressed race and earth as the roots of identity, the A Coruña group tended to concentrate on the more voluntaristic qualities of culture and language. While some of Risco's followers argued that there was a specific Galician Catholic spirituality which had to be protected, the A Coruña group were more likely to be anti-clerical. But they were not socialists: they argued that there was no class struggle in Galicia, and they tended to reduce all political dilemmas to Galicia's opposition to Castile, its eternal enemy. Insofar as they had a social programme, it was directed towards the independent, property-owning peasant-farmers of the agrarian movement, not to the cities, the landless rural labourers or the industrial workers.[86] Lastly, they tended to replicate Risco's empty and rhetorical assertions about the movement's ability to represent the region. 'We are the true Galicia', wrote Casas.[87]

The one point of open disagreement between the two strands concerned the status of culture in the Galician nationalist movement. The A Coruña group argued that while the defence of Galician language and culture was vital, it was also essential that the nationalists create a political organization. But this did not necessarily lead the A Coruña group into an assertion of democratic values. When talking of taking nationalism to the urban masses, Casas argued that 'we are the doctors and Galicia is the patient'.[88] This is a revealing comment, for it suggests a highly unequal, paternalistic relationship: Casas's nationalists would tell the Galicians what they required.

The tension between the two groups grew in the early 1920s, resulting in a formal split in February 1922, with Risco and the smaller groups leaving to form the Irmandade Nazonalista Galega.

This first generation of nationalists was fired by a passionate rejection of all things that they identified as coming from Castile. Often, this worked to blur important social and political distinctions. For example, *caciquismo* was frequently presented as an omnipresent explanation for all that was wrong in the Galicia countryside. But, by scapegoating the *caciques* in this manner, nationalists avoided discussing other important questions concerning rural social hierarchies: they ignored the sharecroppers and cottagers.

There was also a curious paradox in the Galician nationalists' attitudes to the countryside. The bulk of the Irmandade's support came from middle-class people in Galicia's towns, and they were bitterly (and usually effectively) opposed by the *caciques* who ruled in the countryside. Yet these new nationalists idealized Galician rural society, praising it as a healthy, moral alternative to the world of modern industry.[89] 'The fields hold the soul', commented the Galician nationalist writer Ramón Otero Pedrayo, a close colleague of Vicente

Risco. He produced novels which idealized the old, feudal social relations of the countryside, including some fervent praise for the reign of
the *señores*. He did not criticize the Galician landowners for being
exploitative, or for organizing *caciquismo*, but for following Madrid's
fashions and for forgetting how to speak Galego.[90] Even Casas
considered that the towns were the least Galician parts of Galicia, and
called on the Irmandade to make a special effort to enter them.[91]
Perhaps this paradox is simply unresolvable, but one can speculate
that its answer must lie in the social position of these first Galician
nationalists. They were not hidalgos. A survey of their members,
drawing data from the period 1916 to 1931, reveals that almost half
their members were urban professionals (principally lawyers, but also
writers or doctors), and almost a quarter were urban petitbourgeois
(shopkeepers or traders).[92] (In some cases, however, they were distant
descendants of hidalgos.)[93] Perhaps these early nationalists were
people who felt that they *ought* to have been hidalgos, and who
blamed the Spanish state for their apparent decline in status.

Anti-Castilianism was a politically expedient stance for these
Galician nationalists. Blanco wrote an essay entitled 'Collective
Degeneration', full of rage against not just central government, but
the other peoples of Spain. They were degenerate, psychopathic,
marked by a history of political disasters:

> A people formed of masses, with no resources other than their instincts,
> with no higher ideal than the banal praise for each new day, with no sense
> of ethics: an ignorant scum, uneducated and servile – never will such a
> people be able to act as true patriots, an act which only a free and conscious
> people can do.[94]

Obviously, such ideas are closer to racism than a reasoned argument
for political autonomy.

Politics under the Dictatorship (1923–30)

Such early political debates swiftly came to a halt after September
1923. Political tensions in Spain had erupted into open conflict,
which was seen most dramatically on the streets of Barcelona, where
company hit-men exchanged pistol shots with the armed anarcho-
syndicalists of the CNT. Catalan regionalists were confused by this
issue, uncertain whether to back the police, and – ultimately – the
army, against the CNT. Other issues added to the sense of crisis: the

Spanish Cortes was investigating the military defeat at Anual in Morocco in August 1921. The army felt beleaguered, and so supported the *coup d'état* organized by General Primo de Rivera in September 1923, which suspended parliament and political parties.

At first, many felt some optimism about Primo de Rivera. Regeneration had been debated since 1898, but there was no evidence of reform. Political parties seemed as corrupt as ever. Perhaps Primo de Rivera would be the 'iron surgeon' that some had dreamed of in 1898: the dictator who would act decisively to end *caciquismo* and to modernize the nation. The A Coruña group of the Irmandade even felt some initial confidence in Primo de Rivera's commitment to reform, and Risco was at first willing to cooperate with a rather shallow scheme to introduce a type of federation of municipalities in Galicia.[95] Mauristas – conservative reformists – in Galicia could also be persuaded to join the regime's equivalent to a political party, its Unión Patriótica.[96]

These hopes soon faded. In the absence of opinion polls or elections, it is difficult to be certain about political tendencies, but there is every indication of a growing sense of opposition and – more importantly – a new, important growth in republican sympathies. Galician nationalists realized that Primo de Rivera's commitment to decentralization was hollow. One prominent sign of this new opposition was the growth of the Federación Universitaria Escolar (FUE), a student federation which started in Madrid in 1926, and spread to university campuses across Spain in the following years. The FUE opposed the censorship enacted by Primo de Rivera's regime. It first campaigned on behalf of prominent dissident lecturers who were victimized by the regime, but it rapidly began to act as a propagator of new republican values, critical of the old, inward-looking Republican parties.[97] By 1928 there was an active group in Santiago de Compostela.

While republicans organized, Risco's Irmandade turned to cultural work. A study centre, the Seminario de Estudos Galegos, was created in October 1923. *Nós* developed into a serious and prestigious review, which demonstrated that Galego was more than a literary language; it could also be used to discuss political philosophy, history and sociology. But the number of Irmandade supporters fell. Between 1919 and 1923, the Irmandade could count on between five and six hundred members; after Primo de Rivera's coup, their support shrank to a hard core of some two hundred.[98]

FUE militants were also instrumental in drawing A Coruña's semi-clandestine Republican groups into greater public activity. An established Republican figure, Santiago Casares Quiroga, re-emerged to lead them in 1929. The city's Irmandade were actively involved in this Republican revival. New groups were created with surprising rapidity. Following the foundation of an A Coruña group, a meeting in Santiago de Compostela in 1929 established ORGA (the Autonomous Galician Republican Organization), which worked to set up centres across Galicia. It included representatives from the FUE and from Lerroux's Spanish-patriotic Radical party – the latter soon left. ORGA was part of a Republican revival across Spain, and the FRG (Galician Republican Federation) was created as a platform for Republican candidates in Galicia. These new Republicans were committed – or, perhaps more accurately, seemed committed – to the cause of Galician autonomy, and so attracted support from many of the Irmandade.

Primo de Rivera stepped down from power in January 1930. There then followed an awkward fifteen-month hiatus, in which Berenguer, a conservative general, attempted to steer Spain towards another authoritarian regime. As part of this process, municipal elections were held in April 1931. There was only limited freedom of the press and freedom of meeting. The old monarchist parties, the Liberals and the Conservatives, were confident that they could use the established structures of *caciquismo* to win this contest. The final results were something of a surprise (Table 3.5).

Table 3.5. Councillors elected in the April 1931 municipal elections (Spain)[99]

Political group	Councillors	Percentage
Communists	67	0.8%
Socialists	4,813	5.9%
Republicans	34,688	42.8%
Total anti-monarchists	40,168	49.4%
Monarchists	40,324	49.8%

While, technically speaking, the results suggested a paper-thin majority for the monarchist parties, it was widely recognized that the anti-monarchist forces had won a moral victory. General Berenguer stepped down, and the Second Republic was declared on 14 April 1931.

Table 3.6. Councillors elected in the April 1931 municipal elections in Galicia[100]

	A Coruña	Lugo	Ourense	Pontevedra	Totals
Abstention	45%	38%	38%	58%	
Communists	2	–	–	2	4
Socialists	40	19	14	48	121 (2.3%)
Republicans	439	349	200	170	1,158 (22.4%)
Monarchists	383	540	88	292	1,303 (25.3%)
Others	166	74	648	141	1,029 (19.9%)
Unknown	413	–	800	322	1,535 (29.8%)

The results in Galicia looked a little different (Table 3.6).

In nearly all cases, those classified as 'others' or 'unknown' were monarchist candidates backed by the *caciques*. Among the Republicans were a handful of Galician nationalists and regionalists.

A number of surprises emerge from these results. Firstly, with the exception of Lugo, the towns had voted republican. These results also demonstrate the establishment of a socialist left, mainly in the suburbs of A Coruña, Vigo and Pontevedra. Secondly, they show that while A Coruña remained the most progressive province in the region, there was also a surprising degree of republican support in Lugo. Lastly, however, Galicia was clearly a more conservative area than the rest of Spain, and *caciques* were still in control of over half of its voters in 1931.

Conclusion

This chapter began with a question: when did the Galician people first get involved in political action? During the late nineteenth and early twentieth centuries, Galicia's political environment was slowly starting to change. The old coalition of the hidalgos and *caciques* was being challenged in a number of different ways.

On the far right, the Traditionalists attempted to modernize the old certainties of Carlism. They were clearly a minority in the region, and never commanded the loyalty of either the hidalgos or their tenants. However, even these stubborn conservatives were showing signs of adaptation. They participated in the creation of agrarian societies and they attempted to influence the regionalist groups.

On the left, the republicans were establishing bases in the urban areas, principally around A Coruña, Vigo and Pontevedra. Significantly, the opposition to Primo de Rivera was expressed through support for republican parties, leading to the dramatic jump in their votes in April 1931. However, as yet, the republicans had found it difficult to create structures of mass organization. Until 1929 they still resembled the small, closed circles of notables that had run Republican municipalities in the 1890s. Would their new organizations be able to establish more open and more substantial structures in the Second Republic?

Lastly, the most ambitious innovation of this period was that represented by the Galician regionalists and nationalists. They faced many obstacles: the opposition of the *caciques*, their inexperience in organization, and their fumbling, awkward attempts to create political structures. In the late nineteenth century and early twentieth century they had some real success in promoting Galician culture. However, it was clear that a love of Galicia did not translate easily into a political programme. Galician patriots could be regionalists or nationalists, republicans or monarchists, Catholics or anti-clericals, conservatives or democrats. Their one model was that provided by Catalonia – and, on a number of occasions, it had been proved that this was of limited use to them. Galicia was different from the other regions of Spain, and Galician nationalists could not simply copy other groups.

In 1931, this was still a population whose political thinking was largely controlled and limited from outside. While often there was all the appearance of political life – such as parties and elections – the reality was absent. The *caciques* had stunted the region's thought; the First Republic and Regeneration had had little effect. Would the Second Republic be different?

Notes

[1] Data from Miguel M. Cuadrado, *Elecciones y Partidos Políticos de España (1868–1931), Vol. II* (Madrid: Taurus, 1969), pp. 882–9.

[2] Ibid.

[3] Ramón Villares, *Historia de Galicia* (Vigo: Galaxia, 2004), p. 303.

[4] My analysis of this process is drawn principally from two excellent studies: Martin Blinkhorn, 'Spain, the "Spanish problem" and the imperial myth', *Journal of Contemporary History* 15 (1980), 5–25, and Christopher Schmidt-Nowara, '"La España Ultramarina": colonialism and nation-building in nineteenth-century Spain', *European History Quarterly*, 34:2 (2004), 191–214.

[5] Carlos Casares, *Conciencia de Galicia: Risco, Otero, Curros; Tres Biografías* (Vigo: Galaxia, 2004), pp. 55–6.

[6] See José Varela Ortega, 'Aftermath of splendid disaster: Spanish politics before and after the Spanish–American War of 1898', *Journal of Contemporary History*, 15 (1980), 317–44.

[7] Blinkhorn, 'Spanish problem', p. 11.

[8] On this point see, for example, José Alvarez-Junco, *The Emergence of Mass Politics in Spain: Populist Demagoguery and Republican Culture, 1890–1910* (Brighton: Sussex Academic Press, 2002), pp. 67–87.

[9] On the nature of Spanish Republicanism, see the perceptive studies in Nigel Townson (ed.), *El Republicanismo en España (1830–1977)* (Madrid: Alianza Editorial, 1994).

[10] See José Luis de la Granja, Justo Beramendi and Pere Anguera, *La España de los nacionalismos y las autonomías* (Madrid: Editorial Síntesis, 2001), p. 50.

[11] Martínez Cuadrado, *Elecciones y Partidos*, p.914.

[12] See his excellent study, 'Big business and the failure of right-wing Catalan nationalism, 1901–1923', *Historical Journal*, 19:4 (1976), 910–18. More generally, see the introductory textbook by Albert Balcells, *Catalan Nationalism, Past and Present*, trans. Jacqueline Hall (Houndsmill: Macmillan, 1996).

[13] Cuadrado, *Elecciones y Partidos*, p. 745.

[14] Isidro Dubert, *Del Campo a la ciudad: migraciones, familia y espacio urbano en la historia de Galicia, 1708–1924* (Vigo: Nigra Imaxe/Consorcio de Santiago, 2001), pp. 226–9.

[15] Granja, Beramendi and Anguera, *La España*, pp. 43–4.

[16] On Spain's peculiar and distinctive military culture, see Gabriel Cardona, *El Problema militar en España* (Madrid: Historia 16, 1990); for calculations of the number of coups, see Gerald Brenan, *The Spanish Labyrinth* (Cambridge, CUP: 1978), p. 58.

[17] Justo G. Beramendi and Xosé M. Núñez Seixas, *O Nacionalismo Galego* (Vigo: A Nosa Terra, 1996), pp. 22–3.

[18] Cited in Ibid., p. 39.

[19] Emilia Pardo Bazán, *La Tribuna* (Madrid: Alianza Editorial, 2002), p.101.

[20] David Henn, 'Looking for scapegoats: Pardo Bazán and the war of 1898', in A. H. Clarke (ed.), *A Further Range* (Exeter: University of Exeter Press, 1999), pp. 44–60.

[21] Granja, Beramendi and Anguera, *La España*, p.45; Beramendi and Núñez, *O Nacionalismo Galego*, pp. 19–21.

[22] See Beatriz Díaz Santana, *Os Celtos en Galicia: arqueología e política na creación da identidade galega*, trans. Rosa María Peña Guerrero (A Coruña: Toxosoutos, 2002), pp. 53–9.

[23] Casares, *Conciencia*, p. 35.

[24] Granja, Beramendi and Anguera, *La España*, p. 100.

[25] Emilio González López, *Memorias de un estudiante liberal (1903–1931)* (Sada: Do Castro, 1987), pp. 18–20.

[26] Manuel Murguía, *Historia de Galicia*, edited selections in Justo G. Beramendi, 'Pensamiento Político Galleguista (c.1840–c.1950)', in J. Antón and M. Caminal (eds), *Pensamiento Político en la España Contemporánea, 1800–1950* (Barcelona: Teide, 1992), pp. 751–85 (pp. 762–3).

[27] See Francisco Bobillo, *Nacionalismo Gallego: La Ideologia de Vicente Risco* (Madrid: Akal, 1981) pp. 41–3, and Díaz, *Os Celtas*, p. 65.

[28] Granja, Beramendi and Anguera, *La España*, p. 101; Beramendi and Núñez, *O Nacionalismo*, pp. 47–8.

[29] Ibid., p. 60.

[30] Granja, Beramendi and Anguera, *La España*, pp. 101–2.

[31] Xosé Manuel Núñez Seixas, 'The region as essence of the Fatherland: regionalist variants of Spanish nationalism (1840–1936)', *European History Quarterly*, 31:4 (2001), 483–518 (491).

[32] Casares, *Conciencia*, p. 36.

[33] González, *Memorias*, p. 78.

[34] Beramendi and Núñez, *O Nacionalismo*, p. 76.

[35] Xosé Manuel Núñez Seixas, 'Emigración y nacionalismo Gallego en Argentina, 1879–1936', *Estudios Migratorios Latinoamericanas*, 5:15/16 (1990), 379–406.

[36] Casares, *Conciencia*, p. 53.

[37] J. A. Duran, *Agrarismo y Movilización Campesina en el país gallego (1875–1912)* (Madrid: Siglo Veintiuno, 1977), pp. 21–4.

[38] See Juan Pro Ruiz, 'Fraude, statistique et pouvoir dans l'Espagne libérale (1840–1868)', *Revue d'histoire moderne et contemporaine*, 41:2 (1994), 253–68.

[39] Duran, *Agrarismo*, pp. 141–3.

[40] Ibid., p. 145.

[41] Ibid., p. 144.

[42] Ibid., pp. 150–1.

[43] Ibid., p. 150.

[44] Ibid., pp. 145–6.

[45] Anxel M. Rosende, *O Agrarismo na Comarca do Ortegal (1893–1936)* (A Coruña: Edicións do Castro, 1988).

[46] Duran, *Agrarismo*, p. 153.

[47] Ibid., p. 147.

[48] Circular issued on 10 March 1903 in the archbishop's *Boletín Oficial*, cited in Duran, *Agrarismo*, p. 155.

[49] Ibid., pp. 149–50.

[50] Ibid., p. 159.

[51] See, for example, José Manuel Poase Antelo and Herminia Pernas Orozo, 'O desenvolvemento da política local no marco dun concello rural: A Baña, 1900–1936', in L. Fernández Prieto, X. M. Núñez Seixas, A. Artiga Rego and Xesús Balboa (eds), *Poder local, elites e cambio social en Galicia* (Santiago de Compostela: Universidade de Santiago de Compostela, 1997), pp. 373–92.

[52] Edward E. Malefakis, *Agrarian Reform and Peasant Revolution in Spain* (New Haven and London: Yale University Press, 1970), pp. 17–18.

[53] Roberto Blanco Torres, *Xornalismo Irmandiño* (Vigo: A Nosa Terra, 1999), p. 39.

[54] Victor Casas, *Escritos Políticos* (Vigo: A Nosa Terra, 1996), pp. 78–9.

[55] Cited in Duran, *Agrarismo*, p. 179.

[56] Bobillo, *Risco*, p. 49.

[57] Cited in Duran, *Agrarismo*, p. 181.

[58] Ibid., p. 192.

[59] Ibid., p. 197.

[60] Ibid., p. 177.

[61] Casares, *Conciencia*, p. 112.

[62] Beramendi and Núñez, *O Nacionalismo*, p. 95.

[63] Ibid., p. 96.

[64] See, for examples, Blanco Torres, *Xornalismo Irmandiño*, p. 25, and Xosé M. Núñez Seixas, 'Colón y Farabutti'.

[65] Beramendi and Núñez, *O Nacionalismo*, p. 97.

[66] Information from Ibid., p. 98.

[67] 'Manifiesto de la I Asamblea Nacionalista. Noviembre de 1918', in Granja, Beramendi and Anguera, *La España*, pp. 388–90.

[68] Blanco, *Xornalismo*, p. 32.

[69] See Bobillo, *Risco*, pp. 26–8.

[70] Casares, *Conciencia*, p. 106.

[71] Vicente Risco, *Obra completa, I: Teoría nacionalista* (Madrid: Akal, 1981), p. 43.

[72] Ibid., p. 47.

[73] Ibid., 57.

[74] Ibid., p. 44.

[75] Ibid., p. 51.

[76] Ibid., p. 58.

[77] Ibid., p. 61

[78] Ibid., p. 34.

[79] Ibid., p. 260.

[80] Ibid., pp. 69–70, 258.

[81] Derek Flitter, 'Icons and imperatives in the construction of Galician identity: the "Xeración *Nós*"', *Forum for Modern Language Studies* 36:3 (2002), 296–309.

[82] Risco, *Teoría Nacionalista*, p. 38.

[83] Casares, *Conciencia*, p. 124.

[84] See Alberto Romasanta, 'Víctor Casas: O compromiso galeguista', in Casas, *Escritos*, pp. 7–60.

[85] Baldomero Cores Trasmonte, *Ramón Suárez Picallo: Socialismo, Galleguismo y Acción des masas en Galicia* (Sada: O Castro, 1983), p. 11.

[86] Beramendi and Núñez, *O Nacionalismo*, pp. 113–17.

[87] Victor Casas, *Escritos*, p. 65.

[88] Casas, *Escritos*, p. 68.

[89] Beramendi and Núñez, *O Nacionalismo*, pp. 107–8.

[90] Ibid., pp. 104–8; Casares, *Conciencia*, pp. 277–8; Ramón Otero Pedrayo, *Prosa Miúda: Artigos non coleccionadas (1927–1934)* (Sada: Ediciós do Castro, 1988), pp. 53–4, 130.

[91] Casas, *Escritos*, p. 68.

[92] Beramendi and Núñez, *O Nacionalismo*, p. 130. I have adjusted the statistics given by Beramendi and Núñez by factoring out those whose profession was unknown.

[93] Xavier Castro Pérez, 'Las bases sociales del nacionalismo gallego' in Justo G. Beramendi and Ramón Maíz (eds), *Los nacionalismos en la España de la II Republica* (Madrid: Siglo XXI, 1991), pp. 255–73 (p. 259).

[94] Blanco, *Xornalismo*, p. 76.

[95] Beramendi and Núñez, *O Nacionalismo*, pp. 136–8.

[96] González, *Memorias*, p. 148.

[97] Ibid., p. 168.

[98] Beramendi and Núñez, *O Nacionalismo*, p. 129.

[99] Cuadrado, *Elecciones*, p. 855.

[100] Ibid., pp. 1000–1.

4

Republic, civil war and repression: Galicia 1931–1976

Franco came from Galicia. He was born in the naval port of Ferrol, some twenty kilometres east of A Coruña, in December 1892. The two ports were very different. In the seventeenth century Ferrol was just a small fishing village but, following the establishment of the Arsenal in 1750, it expanded quickly in the late eighteenth century to become a major centre of naval shipbuilding.[1] In the nineteenth century, a social elite of naval officers dominated the town.[2] While dissident voices, republican and Galician, developed in A Coruña, Ferrol was a Spanish-patriotic port. Few people there spoke Galego, and the Irmandade never attracted much support.[3]

Franco's father, an administrator for the Spanish navy, wanted his son to become a naval officer. Franco failed the entrance exam and – one could argue – he spent the rest of his life attempting to compensate for this failure. In 1906 he left Ferrol for the Military Academy in Toledo, in central Spain. He showed little affection for his native region in his later life.

Franco's family is a reminder of another Galician culture. The region's ports could act as crucibles for innovative, challenging voices, open to influences from the seven seas; but they could also be outposts for a conservative, conformist Spanish patriotism. In the crisis years which followed the creation of the Second Republic in 1931, Galician political cultures grew increasingly polarized. People like Franco's family would, eventually, act brutally and decisively to stifle the critical voices emerging from cities like A Coruña.

The Second Republic

The surprise creation of the Republic in April 1931 led to an explosion of 'euphoria and hope' throughout Galicia.[4] In part, this can be measured by the number of small reviews and journals which sprang up in Galicia's towns and cities, debating literary theories and presenting local artists.[5] The articles by Victor Casas, a Galician nationalist journalist, neatly capture some key aspects of this excitement. He looked forward to a single, united, progressive political movement developing in the region, based on two key concepts: 'a free Galicia and a federal Republic'. *Caciquismo* and the corruption of the monarchy just seemed to fade away. After all, 'monarchy and *caciquismo* are synonyms',[6] and the old rulers were uncertain how to act. Censorship of the press, restrictions on public meetings and political organizations were ignored, and a new society seemed to emerge, 'with prudence, serenity and calm'.[7]

A general election was quickly arranged: it took place in May 1931. This election was to choose the deputies who would agree a new constitution for Spain. Under the circumstances, it was almost certain that the republicans were going to win a stunning victory. However, there were still some important questions concerning these elections. Firstly, their structure was different from previous contests: voters chose lists for big, multi-member constituencies, which were designed to prevent the old structures of *caciquismo* working. This system benefited big parties, and encouraged small groups to join coalitions.

More importantly, the *newness* of these elections has to be stressed. These were the fairest elections which had ever been fought in Spain: all men over twenty-three could vote, and the republicans passed a law enfranchising all women later in 1931. But this same point also means that these elections brought together inexperienced parties with inexperienced voters. While republicanism had been a political force in Spain for almost a hundred and forty years, the only experience that republicans possessed of forming governments came through the short-lived First Republic (1873–4) – during which the rivalry between the various republican factions had developed to a near-suicidal level. The long decades of opposition during the Restoration (1875–1923) and Primo de Rivera's dictatorship (1923–30) had done little to modernize or to improve these little groups.

One immediate consequence of this legacy was that there was no big, well-organized republican party which could provide a clear focus for programmes and policies. In Stanley Payne's assessment of the 1931 elections, he lists no fewer than eleven republican groups present in the new Cortes (the Spanish parliament) – and there is no doubt that his list simplifies a more complex political reality. Between them, the republicans won 407 seats. On the other side were 6 separate non-republican groups, plus an ill-defined collection of 19 'miscellaneous rightists', with some 51 seats.[8] A weakness of the republicans is revealed as one glances down the figures. By far the biggest group in the ranks of the republicans were the socialists of the PSOE, with 113 seats. Yet the socialists were quite different from many middle-of-the-road republican parties: they wanted something more than the abolition of *caciquismo* and monarchy; they wanted radical social reform, to benefit industrial workers and rural labourers. In practice, it would prove almost impossible to hold together these two forces, the socialists and the republicans.

These considerations also mean that comments about the precise meaning of the Second Republic's three elections have to be made with great care. A basic pattern is clear: in May 1931 there was a great republican advance; in the November 1933 election, a right-wing backlash followed; then, finally, in January 1936, a new left-wing coalition was forged, the Popular Front, resulting in a second left-wing victory. But beyond these basic points, it is often extremely difficult to track the evolution of particular groups, let alone specific individuals.

In Galicia, the political situation was made still more complicated by the existence of Galician autonomy as a separate issue, which could push together unlikely allies and also divide groups who agreed on almost every other point on the political agenda.

Having made these qualifications, let us turn to examine the results of what could be seen as the first elections in Galician history which were not directed by the *caciques* (Table 4.1).

Many people voted in these elections, but not in as large a proportion as in Spain as a whole. In particular, the voters of Pontevedra

Table 4.1. Participation rates in the general election in Galicia, May 1931[9]

Province	1931
A Coruña	64.58%
Lugo	68.16%
Ourense	67.69%
Pontevedra	52.19%
Spain	70.13%

province seemed relatively apathetic, a trend which would continue throughout the Second Republic. One alarming possibility, however, is that rather than measuring the political liberation of Galicia's citizens, these voting figures may actually quantify the continuing effectiveness of *caciquismo*. It is noticeable that the province with the highest participation rates – Lugo – was also the province in which the old notables, campaigning with new labels, did best. In fact, the electoral commission judged that Lugo's elections had been distorted by corrupt practices, and Lugo was the only one of the fifty Spanish provinces in which by-elections were held later in 1931.

The figures in Table 4.2 must be treated with caution: except for the Socialists, there were no well-organized parties fighting these elections, and any classification of a grouping as 'rightist' or 'republican' involves an element of judgement. Certainly, many deputies for Lerroux's Radical Republican party (which won eight seats) were to drift to the right in the next two years. Lastly, the Galician nationalists did not contest these elections as a separate group, but as members of the republican coalition.

Having made these qualifications, however, a general pattern is clear. These elections amounted to a surprising breakthrough for the republicans, a major setback for the older monarchist parties, and – most remarkable of all – also saw the election of the first socialist deputies in Galicia's history. Socialist support was principally from the urban areas. As for the Galician nationalists, the results were ambiguous. Were voters choosing the nationalists because they supported Galician patriotism, or because they were republicans? I will return to this point in the next section.

As we examine the records from the years that followed, it becomes clearer that the election results from 1931 are a political turning-point in the region's history. Republican groups soon developed and

Table 4.2. Election results in Galicia, May 1931[10]

Province	Socialists	Republicans (Nationalists)	Rightists
A Coruña	3	9 (1)	4
Lugo	2	8 (1)	1
Ourense	1	9 (1)	–
Pontevedra	4	5 (1)	3
Totals	12	31 (4)	8

Table 4.3. PSOE (Socialist Party) and UGT (General
Union of Labour) presence in Galicia, 1928–32[11]

	1928	1932
PSOE groups	7	78
PSOE members	499	3,500
UGT members	10,746	24,862

expanded, particularly in the towns. To the left of the republicans, a
sizeable and well-organized socialist movement was developing (see
Table 4.3). In these years, the UGT, the trade union federation linked
to the Socialist Party, gained support from construction workers,
metal workers, miners and – most surprisingly of all – among some
agricultural workers.

There were other groups on the left, apart from the socialists. The
beleaguered Spanish Communist Party (PCE) was also finding
supporters, principally among the workers in Galicia's small mines.
In the municipal elections of April 1931, two Communist councillors
were elected in A Coruña, and two in Pontevedra.[12]

While the figures in Table 4.4 show some inconsistencies, the

Table 4.4. Estimates of Communist Party
members in Galicia, 1931–6[13]

Year	Estimated membership
1932	282
1933	792
1934	527
1935	1,093
1936	3,212

overall trend is clear: the number of Communists in the region was
growing, particularly after 1934.

Lastly, the anarcho-syndicalist CNT grew quickly. A regional
federation had been created in August 1922. Its main support came
from workers in Vigo and A Coruña.[14] While it managed to survive
during Primo de Rivera's dictatorship (1923–30), its membership
plummeted, from 25,536 in 1922 to 13,218 in 1931. During these
years its activists were in contact with the republican underground.
After 1931, many of its members were attracted to the more

moderate strand of anarcho-syndicalism, symbolized by the 'Manifesto of the Thirty', published in Barcelona in 1931, which proposed the development of a large, well-organized and responsible movement, willing to negotiate with bosses and even to consider the creation of a Syndicalist party. It grew rapidly in Galicia: 32,517 workers had joined its unions by 1932, eight thousand more than in the rival UGT. Like the UGT, it won support among miners and metalworkers, but there were some significant differences between the two federations. While the UGT was successful in building an agrarian wing, the CNT gained less support in the countryside. On the other hand, more than eleven thousand fishermen were CNT members in 1932.[15] Bitter strikes in Ferrol and Santiago de Compostela, involving armed clashes between CNT militants and police forces, led to an increasingly revolutionary stance by the organization.

Research by Emilio Grandío Seoane allows us to track the development of political life in some more detail. Grandío has studied political groups in A Coruña province, which remained the most lively of Galicia's four provinces during the Second Republic. A list from 1935 records all the political groups which were officially registered in the province (see Table 4.5). Inevitably, we need to approach this list with some caution. The right-wing government which came to power in November 1933 began to dismantle the social reforms of

Table 4.5. Registered political organizations in A Coruña province, 1935[16]

Organization	Number of local groups
Radical Party	29
CEDA	29
Republican Unity	18
Republican Left	6
Radical Democrats	3
Socialist Party	15
UGT	24
CNT	18
Communists	2
Agrarians	5
Traditionalists	1
Falange	3
Spanish Renovation	2
Partido Galeguista	1

the previous left-republican government. The old *caciques* had recovered some of their confidence, and were using extra-legal means to restrict left-wing groups. Therefore, in 1935, one might expect that left-leaning groups might have been reluctant to become officially registered. Lastly, while this list allows us to make some estimate of the geographic extent of a particular organization, it is obviously a less reliable indication of the numbers who may have supported the group.

Perhaps predictably, the two most extensive organizations in the province were both right-wing. The first of these was the Radical Party, led by Alejandro Lerroux. This was a familiar sight: a republican party which functioned as a fan club for its leader, and as an instrument to distribute jobs and favours. After 1933 the Radicals were in terminal decline, leaving behind the virulent anti-clericalism of their youth to expire in a corrupt conservatism. Worst of all, they could no longer even be considered as an anti-*caciquismo* party: instead, they had instituted a counter-*caciquismo* of their own. Their actions in Pontevedra province during the 1936 elections would become notorious. In the December 1933 elections this group became the biggest single party in the region, winning no fewer than fifteen seats.[17] It is no surprise that this group had built up an extensive network of contacts, supporters and clients in A Coruña province in 1935.

CEDA (the Confederation of Autonomous Right-Wing Organizations) was an innovation on the political scene: a modern, mass, right-wing organization which did not stress the issue of the monarchy, but instead presented itself as principally a coalition of Catholic groups. It was this group that had spearheaded the right-wing victory of 1933, and which pushed for the dismantling of the republicans' social legislation. It was particularly well organized in the provinces of Pontevedra and A Coruña.[18] It was the second biggest party in the region, winning ten seats in 1933.

Next on Grandío's list are the republican groups, predictably split into three different strands, with minute differences in policies. While not as extensive as CEDA and the Radicals, they clearly had developed out from their pre-1931 enclaves, into the small towns of the countryside.

Following the Republicans are four left-wing groups. The UGT (General Union of Workers) and the CNT (National Confederation of Workers) were both highly politicized and active trade union organizations, the first socialist, the second anarcho-syndicalist. Their presence on this list suggests that even in the difficult conditions of 1935 they still played an active public role, maybe in the form of opening a meeting-hall or a library, or running evening classes. They represent quite a shift in popular political culture, breaking the old illusion that Galicia was a region of small property-owners, and suggesting that new ideas of class consciousness were spreading. Both groups were concerned by the rise of the far right, and – unusually – were considering forms of united action.[19] Alongside the UGT and CNT, the Socialist Party had a reasonably extensive presence, while the Communists were still clearly a minority group.

By 1935 the agrarians were no longer the radical mass movement that they had been at the turn of the century. They were now more likely to function as an apolitical movement that supported co-operatives and agricultural improvement.

Then there are the three groups of the far right, each representing different forms of radicalization, like distinct archaeological strata. The Traditionalists were the direct descendants of the old Carlists, still obsessed with their sixteenth-century theocratic utopia. They attracted little support in the region. Spanish Renovation was, potentially, a more serious group, begun by José Calvo Sotelo, a native of the region. Calvo had been part of the generation of 1898, but rather than moving towards an advocacy of democracy or decentralization, he was loyal to that other strand of Regenerationist thought: the 'iron surgeon'. He had worked with Primo de Rivera's Unión Patriótica, and, following the fall of the monarchy, had created Spanish Renovation as a project to remodel monarchism in the light of mid-twentieth-century far-right thinking. Lastly, there were the three Falangist groups. The Falange is often seen as the true representative of fascism in Spain. Led by José Antonio Primo de Rivera, the son of the dictator, the Falange blended an intense, lyrical passion for modernization and even – in a sense – for social reform, with a proclamation of nationalist-authoritarian values.

None of these three strands of far-right thinking had attracted substantial support in Galicia. Their principal base was among students at Santiago de Compostela. But, as in other cities in Spain, increasingly violent conflicts between the far right and the far left were fought out on Santiago's streets. Militants shifted from using their fists to firing pistols at each other.[20] The older notables were still sceptical of these new organizations' value, and while the conservative Republic of the Radicals and CEDA was working to short-circuit social reform, they were generally willing to accept the Republic's structures. However, it is significant that there were far-right militants active before 1936 in the region.

Lastly, at the end of our list is the one Partido Galeguista group, the new organization of the Galician nationalists. This clearly marginalized position is worth considering. While Galician nationalists might claim that they were the true representatives of Galicia, in the province of A Coruña they clearly had failed to convince the mass of the population. In part, however, their marginalized position was a result of renewed activity by *caciques*. In October 1934 *A Nosa Terra*, the Galician nationalist journal published in A Coruña, was suspended for several months by the civil governor (the main representative of central government in the region). In these years, it was difficult for Galician nationalists to organize.[21]

The Partido Galeguista, 1931–6

The Second Republic was a difficult period for the Galician nationalists. As we have seen, they had some great hopes in April 1931. Victor Casas looked forward to a Galician–Republican coalition winning the support of the region, and leading it to political autonomy. What went wrong?

In 1929 and 1930, the Republicans acted faster than the Galician nationalists. Their federations – ORGA and the FRG – were both formed before the proclamation of the Republic in 1931. The A Coruña group of Galician nationalists were willing to cooperate with this rising tide of republican activism, while Risco and the Ourense group were bewildered by the speed of events. In 1930 Risco found it impossible to oppose the principle of cooperation with Republicans, but did succeed in preventing the Irmandade as a body from committing themselves to either republic or monarchy.

The relative success of the Galician nationalists in the May 1931 elections – in which they won four seats – seemed to prove that the A Coruña group had been right. But events later that year proved an unpleasant shock. The constitution which was approved by the Cortes in December 1931 was not that of a decentralized, federal republic, but of a centralized, 'integral' republic, on the French model. It did contain some unusual aspects: for example, it made no reference to the Spanish nation, instead using the phrase 'Spanish people'. It also allowed for the formation of politically autonomous regions within its borders, although the rigorous procedure for the establishment of such areas suggested more hostility than welcome for such projects. Spanish remained the official language of the Republic.[22]

Galician nationalists were bitterly disappointed by this measure. Initially, ORGA had appeared to back the idea of Galician autonomy, but its members did not criticize the new constitution. The Galician nationalists reacted swiftly. A congress was called in Pontevedra in December 1931, and a new party was created: the Partido Galeguista. ('Galeguista' is the Galego term for a Galician patriot.) This amounted to a reunification of the two strands of Galician nationalism: the A Coruña group was now more sceptical about the usefulness of an alliance with the republicans, while Risco was prepared to concede the viability of political action. The Partido Galeguista's founding manifesto declared Galicia to be a 'cultural unity ... an autonomous people ... a cooperative community ... [and] a cell of universalism'.[23] It proposed political autonomy, the defence and development of Galician culture and language, coupled with a mildly social-reformist programme that included, for example, women's rights, labour legislation and the abolition of child labour.

Like the republican and left-wing groups, the new party grew swiftly under the conditions of relative political liberty of the Second Republic. Possibly Grandío's list of groups in A Coruña province seriously underestimates the extent of Partido Galeguista support, or – more probably – 1935 represented a low point for the new party, during which members were less willing to attract attention to themselves. In particular, the party grew extremely quickly following the left-wing victory in February 1936, a point which explains the

Table 4.6. Estimates of Partido Galeguista organizations in Galicia, 1931–6[24]

Date	Groups	Members
December 1931	32	700
December 1932	38	2,300
October 1933	60	3,000
February 1936	89 / 120	3,337

confusion about the number of Partido Galeguista groups in February 1936. While the number of groups and members should not be exaggerated – they were very far from representing the whole region – there can be no doubt that the Partido Galeguista established Galician nationalism as a significant current within Galician political life during the early 1930s.

Table 4.7 lets us see some of the strengths and weaknesses of the organization. The centres of Galician nationalism remained what they had been in 1917, with the creation of the Irmandade: the republicans of A Coruña and the cultural conservatives of Ourense. Of the four provinces, Pontevedra appears to be the most resistant to Partido Galeguista's message; possibly the explanation for this relative weakness lies in the strength of the Republicans in Vigo and Pontevedra.

Table 4.7. Estimates of the distribution of Partido Galeguista organizations in Galicia, 1936[25]

Province	Groups	Other bodies
A Coruña	30	3
Lugo	21	2
Ourense	23	10
Pontevedra	15	15

In many ways, however, the Partido Galeguista was different from the older Irmandade. Firstly, it was a proper political party, with a permanent structure and clear programme. It put up candidates at elections, and actually won some contests. Secondly, its social support was far broader. True, an analysis of some three thousand Partido Galeguista members shows that about eight per cent were students, five per cent were teachers or lecturers, and four per cent were from the urban liberal professions. But alongside such typical supporters of romantic nationalism there was evidence of a far broader social appeal. More than a quarter of the party's members were farmers, and about an eighth were artisans and other independent manual workers.[26] Despite this record of moderate, but real, successes, the party grew divided. At first, frustration with the republican record could unite the two wings. For example, one can read in Casas's journalism from as early as November 1931 the warning that 'a Republican *caciquismo*' could develop which would be 'as terrible as that which we endured under the monarchy'.[27] The linking of those two words – 'republican' and '*caciquismo*' – in his writing is a clear indication of the great disillusion that he already felt with the republicans. By 1932, Casas was still more forthright: the struggles of 1931 had ended in a 'clear failure'. ORGA was an adulterated, muddled grouping, with one foot in Galicia and one foot in Madrid. Worse still, it was the section in Madrid that gave the orders.[28] The new republican governments treated Galicia 'worse than the monarchy'.[29]

Risco's scepticism about the new Republic grew deeper after 1931. Like many conservatives, he was particularly alarmed by its anti-clerical legislation, which threatened the Church's leading role in schools. He did not oppose the standing of Partido Galeguista candidates in December 1933, but after their defeat – not one PG candidate was elected – he felt vindicated. The party should be independent of the republicans. One important factor in his political evolution was his stay in Berlin for six months in 1932. Risco was horrified by what he saw. Casares, one of Risco's biographers, notes: 'Risco was an intellectual who was born and bred in a little rural town, tied into an agricultural land. He was shocked by this encounter with a modern, cosmopolitan, industrial city like Berlin, which caused him a permanent agony.'[30] While in Berlin, Risco was able to observe the Nazi movement. He was never a supporter of such ideas; Risco identified with an older form of conservatism, based on a weak state and the preservation of a village culture. But, following his stay in Berlin, some anti-Semitic phrases entered his writing. The final lesson for him, however, was the necessity of a strong religious culture. The Catholic faith could save Galicia from the danger of both the Jews and the Nazis; the Church was 'the only effective force against chaos'.[31]

Risco was therefore more annoyed than ever when leftist tendencies began to emerge within the Partido Galeguista. These were best represented by Suárez Picallo, based in Pontevedra. Suárez was one of the four Galician nationalists elected in 1931. He found he could work with the socialists on some projects: for example, a programme to protect and develop the Galician fishing industry. Moreover, he was delighted when, late in 1933, the socialists began to campaign for the cause of Galician autonomy.[32] While Suárez considered that it would be inappropriate to follow a Marxist political strategy in Galicia, a region with an extremely small industrial proletariat, he felt some sympathy for Marxism. He certainly prevented Risco from forcing the Partido Galeguista into an explicitly anti-Marxist position.[33]

The Partido Galeguista's congresses in January 1934 and April 1935 were therefore tense, awkward meetings. At the latter, Ramón Otero Pedrayo, a close colleague of Risco, proposed that the party should officially support the Church: a stance which would imply an anti-republican position. The majority of the Party rejected this, with the result that the Partido Galeguista split. A Dereita Galeguista (Galician Nationalist Right) was formed in Pontevedra; in February 1936, Risco led most of the Ourense group into it.[34] A manifesto by this group proclaimed, 'we consider that the Catholic religion is fundamental to the indigenous Galician tradition, that the two are consubstantial and inseparable'.[35]

Meanwhile, the newly republicanized Partido Galeguista joined the Popular Front coalition in January 1936. Three of its candidates, standing as part of the Popular Front, were elected: one in Pontevedra and two in A Coruña. The Popular Front triumphed in the provinces of Pontevedra and A Coruña; the right held Ourense; while a curious mixture of right-leaning republicans and centrists won in Lugo. For a few months, the coalition of republicans, socialists and Galician nationalists seemed to work well: all campaigned vigorously in favour of a statute of autonomy, and the Cortes finally accepted a proposal. It was put to a regional referendum on 28 June 1936.

Table 4.8. Results of the June 1936 referendum on Galician autonomy[36]

Registered voters	1,343,135
Voters participating in the referendum	1,000,963
Number voting 'yes'	993,351

The results of the referendum were unmistakeable: it demonstrated massive popular support for the cause of Galician autonomy – a breadth of support which reached far wider than did the support for the Partido Galeguista.

The military rebellion, July 1936

In July 1936 many of Galicia's leading politicians were in Madrid to celebrate the results of the autonomy referendum. In some cases, this saved their lives.[37]

On 18 July 1936 Santiago de Compostela's local paper carried a short announcement of difficulties of communication with Madrid. This was the first sign of the military rebellion against the Republic. Four of the Republic's twenty generals led their soldiers to revolt against the democratically elected government. Franco joined a few days later. His participation was vital: he commanded the battle-hardened Spanish Foreign Legion, which had been fighting against Arab Moroccan nationalists. The rebel generals thought they would win as quickly as Primo de Rivera had won in September 1923. It was widely assumed that the divided Republic would not last two weeks.

Instead, an unusual coalition of forces rallied to the defence of the Republic. A new republican police force, the Assault Guard, was generally loyal. They were joined by workers organized in the UGT and CNT. Many soldiers disobeyed the instructions from their officers, and deserted to defend the Republic. By 20 July 1936, a pattern was clear: the rising had revealed a new political geography. Vast stretches of northern, rural Spain, the bedrock of Spanish Catholicism, supported the rebels, while southern Spain and urban Spain defended the Republic. The rebels held less than half of Spain's land and less than a third of its population. Catalonia remained staunchly republican, but the Basque country was split between monarchists, who backed the rebellion, and Basque nationalists, who – with great misgivings – often supported the Republic.

These were terrible days in Galicia. Left-republicans, socialists, Communists, anarchists and members of the Partido Galeguista had some idea of what was happening. In Santiago de Compostela the Partido Galeguista mayor attempted to get reassurances from the local army commander that he would not rebel. The replies were equivocal, but seemed to indicate that there would be no fighting. A municipal commission formed to monitor the city. All these efforts proved useless. Late in the evening on 20 July, troops left their barracks and occupied the city. Santiago's small group of Falangists rapidly joined them. They made an important contribution to the rebellion, for they brought a sense of political direction to it.

There was some sporadic fighting in Galicia, principally in A Coruña and in the small town of Tui, close to the Portuguese border. Many Communists and anarchists from the region rushed to get to A Coruña but – in most cases – they arrived too late. Nowhere in Galicia was there the type of mass urban movement that saved Barcelona and Madrid in 1936, principally because the region had not produced the deep-rooted, experienced, militant mass organizations that these cities contained. Significantly, the best Galician novel concerning the rebellion – Manuel Rivas's *O lapis do carpinteiro* (The Carpenter's Pencil) – is set among republicans held in Santiago de Compostela prison, waiting to know their fate.

The killing started almost immediately. Opponents of the uprising could lose their lives in many ways. A few were killed in the sporadic, hopeless clashes with the army. Others were identified by Falangists as friends of the Republic: they might be beaten, they might be thrown into the army's improvised prisons, they might be killed. Sometimes radicals and dissidents were brought before military courts, and accused of republican loyalties. They had little opportunity to defend themselves. As Alvaro Jaspe stresses, we should not see the rebellion as a meticulously planned conspiracy. It was a messy, haphazard affair, involving personal vendettas as much as political principles. It was run by confused, frightened men who rarely understood the consequences of their actions. While the rebellion had gone to plan in Galicia, it had failed in Madrid, Barcelona and Valencia. Where was their quick victory? Jaspe cites the reports in the local press, asking for witnesses to come forward to identify the corpses found at dawn along the roads. The police authorities often seemed genuinely bewildered by such events.[38]

How many died in the region? Later Galician nationalist and republican refugees spoke of fifty thousand, even one hundred thousand deaths. These are undoubtedly massive exaggerations, although they say something about the shock and terror that the exiles felt. Jaspe cites some more moderate estimates (Table 9.4).

There is some good reason to think that these figures significantly underrepresent the true horror of the repression. The recent careful studies coordinated by Santos Juliá – which, unfortunately, do not extend to Galicia – suggest that, on average, about three thousand people were killed in each province. The figures cited above, if accurate, would suggest that there was less blood spilt in Galicia than anywhere else in Spain.[40]

Table 4.9. Estimates of victims of Francoist repression, 1936–9[39]

Province	Assassinations	Other killings	Death sentences	Total
A Coruña	8	303	607	918 (51.1%)
Lugo	10	165	59	234 (13.0%)
Ourense	4	155	17	176 (9.8%)
Pontevedra	11	346	109	466 (25.9%)
Total	33	805	792	1794

The one point which emerges clearly from Table 4.9 is the geographic pattern of the repression: the western provinces of A Coruña and Pontevedra suffered far more than the eastern provinces of Lugo and Ourense. One could even argue that the repression was the revenge of the conservative east against the innovative west, in particular against the radical city of A Coruña.

Francoism in Galicia

One simple point needs to be borne in mind as we consider the succeeding years: in 1939, no one could have predicted that Franco would remain ruler of Spain for another thirty-six years. After all, Primo de Rivera had survived for only six years, from 1923 to 1929. This obvious point, however, explains much of the confusion shown by opposition groups. They were unprepared for the military coup in July 1936, and they needed many years to understand the gravity of the situation they faced.

'Francoism' is an awkward term, and is probably misleading if it suggests a coherent political philosophy. Franco's reign was sustained by a balance of forces, 'a collection of heterogeneous clans', as Raymond Carr and Juan Pablo Fusi remark.[41] The first favourites appeared to be the Falange – or the Falange Española Tradicionalista y de la Juntas de Ofensiva Nacional Sindicalista (Spanish Traditionalist Phalanx and the Committees of the National Syndicalist Offensive), to use its full name. By 1939, this was no longer the small band of fanatical social visionaries who had gathered behind José Antonio Primo de Rivera. The republicans had killed José Antonio the Falangist leader in 1936, and Franco then followed them by annihilating the core of his organization. The

Falange was forcibly united with the reactionary Carlists in April 1937, and civil servants were required to join it. By 1939 the organization had become bloated and almost directionless. For example, early in 1936 there were four hundred members in its women's section; by 1939 there were six hundred thousand.[42]

During the early years of the Second World War this lack of direction was partly hidden by the Falangists' fervent optimism that they were on the winning side. While Franco ensured that Spain remained neutral during the Second World War, it did offer some support for the German war effort. For example, German submarines were permitted to reprovision at Vigo.[43] The Falangists' optimism declined as it became obvious that the forces of the Third Reich were in retreat. In 1945, Franco enforced a type of ideological makeover. His regime was no longer pro-Fascist, it was anti-Communist. The Falange were pushed down, a little, and Catholic and monarchist politicians were allowed to rise into the government. In 1947 Franco declared that Spain would revert to a monarchy after his death, but it remained unclear what type of monarchy this would be.

One cause uniting the Falangists, Traditionalists, monarchists and Catholics who supported Franco was the ideal of Spanish unity. The Second Republic was condemned for its moves towards regional autonomy, its legislation withdrawn, and regional languages banned from all public spheres. In schools, churches, offices and on the radio, only Castilian was spoken.[44] One of the regime's posters proclaimed: 'If you are Spanish, then speak Spanish.'[45] This point should not be exaggerated: it was never actually *illegal* to speak in a non-Castilian language, but the opportunities to do so were severely limited, often as much by strong informal pressures as by formal legislation. For example, Carballo Calero was a Partido Galeguista member who was held in prison from 1939 to 1941. When his friends wrote to him, they always used Castilian, for they knew that a postcard written in Galego would probably never get to him.[46]

After July 1936, Galicia lost its political leaders. González gives a brief survey of Galicia's Popular Front deputies in 1939: it is a useful indication of the disarray and confusion caused by the Civil War. Two deputies from A Coruña province had been shot. Two more were in prison. One was in hiding; he eventually got out to Uruguay. A sixth from A Coruña province remained in hiding within Spain. Two socialist deputies from A Coruña worked for the Socialist Party in Madrid, and effectively gave up their status as representatives. Two deputies from Pontevedra province stayed in republican Spain until 1939; a third had left for France in 1936.[47]

After 1939, it was as if time had stopped in Galicia. The advances of the previous decades: the mobilization of the farmers, the opening-up of political debates, the rooting of left-wing organizations in the towns and even in the villages, the assertions of the dignity and honour of traditional Galician culture – all ended or, at best, were restricted to an underground formed by tiny circles of trusted friends. No matter exactly how many were killed in the months following July 1936, the survivors had learnt the lesson that the Francoists wanted to teach: don't ask questions, don't criticize. The words of a character in a short story from 1967 by Carlos Casares eloquently sum up the situation. 'You can't speak out, you can't, you just can't and you've got to hold out and forget about your rights and your heroics.'[48]

This was also a time of poverty, when living standards were in decline. In A Coruña province, a nine-year-old girl started farm work in 1947, after only one year at school. Her parents were relatively rich: they could afford to buy her shoes to wear in winter. The poor were hardly ever sick, she later recalled, because 'then, the sick simply died'.[49] Living on the other side of the Atlantic, in Buenos Aires, Carmen Cornes gave up thoughts of returning to Galicia. She could see that 'there was no future' in Galicia. Franco's rule had imposed three years of compulsory military service for young men. Many deserted and crossed the ocean, knowing that they could never return. The region's women were left to run their family's farms.[50]

Fugitives and guerrillas

From the start, there were a few fugitives: a handful of people who had come out on the wrong side in July 1936, who had seen how the Francoists dealt with opponents, and who then took to the hills. They had nowhere to go; the ports and the towns along the coasts had become bases for the Francoists, and the roads were watched. They were desperate people, simply looking to survive. But in order to do this, each fugitive needed support. Luis Lamela García makes a neat point about the soon-to-be famous (or infamous) outlaw 'Foucellas', late in 1936. In hiding, he depended on the efforts of three women: his wife, his mother and his sister. They played a dangerous game of cat-and-mouse with the authorities, attempting to guess the movements of the Civil Guard, and passing 'Foucellas' from one hiding-place to another.[51]

The Second World War was the first good news for such people for many months. They could not conceive of any internal, Spanish movement that could destroy Francoism; the only way that the regime could be ended would be from outside. The fugitives hoped that the allies would launch an attack on Franco's Spain. By the early 1940s the methods for hiding fugitives grew more sophisticated. Attempting to stay close to the towns was dangerous. Their best chances for survival were out in the countryside, up in the hills, away from the populated and policed western areas and towards the more desolate east.

Curiously, the regime often seemed to be creating its own enemies. Many fugitives guessed that there was a death sentence on their heads for their actions in 1936. Even those who might have been willing to compromise then found that they were caught in a second trap. By hiding out during the civil war, they had escaped conscription into the Francoists' forces: the penalty for this was execution. They therefore felt that they had no choice but to continue to hide out in the countryside. Some patterns of cooperation with the villagers developed. Whether they were motivated 'by fear, friendship, money, idealism or ignorance', Galician villagers provided vital support for these early fugitives.[52]

Their situation changed as the Second World War progressed. Even under conditions of Francoist censorship, it was possible to realize that Hitler's forces were losing. A slow, spasmodic transformation took place among the groups of fugitives. In fact, north-west Spain led the way: early in 1942, a Federation of Guerrillas in Galicia and León (the province immediately to the east of Ourense) was created. By 1944 there were two more guerrilla groups operating in A Coruña province, one of which was controlled by the Communist Party.[53]

The status of these groups changed after 1945. The Allies had defeated Nazi Germany and Fascist Italy. Many assumed that next they would turn to Falangist Spain. The refugees in France, Mexico and Argentina began to plan their return, and there were several awkward attempts to unite the exiled political groups under one banner.[54] There was also a brief upsurge of confidence among the victims of Francoism in Spain itself. On 1 May 1945, republican and Communist flags were flown in many Galician towns.[55]

Francisco Martinez-Lopez's autobiography gives us one example of this change in attitudes. He was born in 1925 near Bierzo, in León province, just to the east of Ourense province. He was too young to participate in the brief anti-Falangist struggles in July 1936, but he saw the results. The Falangists imposed order by terror: by 'punishments and pillaging, by intimidation and killings'.[56] He started work in 1943 as an assistant in a laboratory attached to a mine. In 1944, he felt certain that Franco's reign was soon to end, and joined an underground Communist organization. In 1947 he helped distribute Communist leaflets, calling for a strike and for the sabotage of the mine. Fifteen suspects were arrested and badly tortured, but Martinez escaped. On 22 September 1947 he took for the hills. There he joined a group of seven guerrillas, who took him westwards into the hills of Galicia. He was amazed at what he saw there: his words are worth recording at length.

> The next day we reached La Goldra. Our meeting-point was the village bar. All the locals supported the guerrillas. They came over to see us, to hear the news, to talk and to play cards, because many of us enjoyed a game. All of this was very far from my idea of 'the underground'. It was a revelation which made me grow more enthusiastic. I got the idea that I was staying in a half-liberated zone, run by two parallel powers: the unofficial power, and the official power five kilometres away. I felt that in La Goldra I was living in a different world. This collective effort, which was so enthusiastic, encouraged me to commit myself more firmly to armed struggle. The support that we attracted meant a lot, although we still had to be careful not to underestimate the enemy's resources. In our eyes, this support showed how well-founded was the cause that we shared with the majority of people, and how right we were to defend it. The pleasure of such moments in the heart of those villages – and there were many – compensated for other times, more deadly and hostile . . .
>
> From 1948 to 1950 we continued to think that guerrilla actions would stimulate a wider anti-Francoist struggle. In the provinces of León and Ourense this involved thousands of democrats and hundreds of households. Many teachers and priests supported us. Our network was linked to other Spanish regions . . .
>
> First of all, we were active in the villages. We developed propaganda activities, we organized the young people. Above all, we helped the peasants to escape the traps that the tax office set them, to resist the tax officials who turned up, and to develop the most basic forms of disobedience to the regime's representatives. As the peasants developed solidarity with us, they also developed solidarity among themselves, and this feeling contributed to a real anti-Francoist culture.[57]

Martinez was not alone in feeling this sudden surge of confidence. Other young men, alienated from their work and tired of the deprivations of the Franco regime, felt that this was the right moment to commit themselves to the opposition. Networks formed around A Coruña, Pontevedra and Lugo. Many of them came with political ideas: they were socialists, Communists or anarchists. Initially, these differences did not matter. They were united by a sense of solidarity in their fight against a single enemy.[58]

While the exiled republicans placed their hopes in Allied action against Franco, Communists and anarchists organized these guerrilla groups in Spain. The Socialist Party was more cautious, and less active in its contacts with the guerrilla groups. The Partido Galeguista explicitly refused to be involved in guerrilla activity.[59]

For a few years, a highly original structure of political activity developed in parts of Galicia. In the past, the villagers of the eastern half of the region had been the most resistant to radical ideas: few republicans had been elected here, and even the agrarians found more support in the west. Men like Foucellas and Martinez were drawing a new map of the region, bringing a new sense of hope and political idealism to parts of the east, overturning the old conservative certainties. In a sense, there was one continuity: the suspicion of the state. The old *caciques* had exploited this sentiment to create their myth of a united community of property-owners, resisting the tax demands of the liberal, modernizing state. Here, in 1947, the villagers were resisting a Francoist state, and their age-old suspicions now drew them closer to Communists and anarchists. The villagers' sense that their communities had been ignored, mistreated and exploited was now taking on a critical, radical edge.

The movement traced out by Martinez and Foucellas did not last long. Firstly, despite Martinez's enthusiasm, it should be stressed that his group reached only a minority of villages. Secondly, the Allies failed to act: with the onset of the Cold War, Francoist Spain became too valuable an ally.[60] The same shift in international politics isolated the international Communist movement from other leftwing political groups, and caused divisions among the exiles. In 1948, Stalin advised Communists to cease guerrilla activities.[61] Within Spain, the Francoists proved adept and persistent enemies, ruthlessly cutting away at the guerrillas' support, particularly through the creation of the semi-legal 'contras', who would launch terrorist-style attacks on villagers who were suspected of aiding the guerrilla groups. In the late 1940s, it was clear that the guerrillas were losing their campaign.

The Politics of survival

After the brief moment of hope of 1945 had faded, Galicians had to accept that Franco was going to be in power for a long time. There was a slow, awkward, coming to terms with this situation. An example of the difficulties they faced can be drawn from the work of Alfonso Daniel Rodríguez Castelao (1886–1950). Exiled in Mexico and then in Argentina, Castelao was one of the few surviving leaders of the Partido Galeguista outside Spain. He worked on the text that was to become a masterpiece of Galician nationalist political culture, *Sempre en Galiza*, or 'Forever in Galicia'. There were five sections to this work, each written in a different place.

A prologue, written in Badajoz, in southern Spain, in 1935.
The first part, written in Barcelona and Valencia in 1937.
The second part, written in New York and in transit, 1940.
The third part, written in Buenos Aires in 1943.
The fourth part, written while travelling to France in 1947.

The difference in political values between the first and second parts is astonishing. In the first, written during the Civil War, Castelao is attempting to fuse the cause of Galician nationalism with that of Spanish republicanism. Remarkably, this section takes the form of a commentary on Stalin's well-known essay *Marxism and the National Question*. For all its faults, Stalin's text has the advantage of setting up some clear criteria concerning which polities truly constitute nations.[62] Castelao spends a hundred pages or so arguing that, according to Stalin's criteria, Galicia is clearly a nation, and therefore it deserves to be recognized as such by the republicans.

In part two of his work, everything has changed. There is no longer any likelihood that the republicans can win; the civil war has been definitively lost, and Castelao is correspondingly more bitter and more critical. He notes that a second civil war has now begun, among the exiles, as they argue about who to blame for their defeat.[63] Castelao refuses to participate in these rivalries; instead, he notes the 'incapacity, incompetence and intransigence' of the republicans.[64] Such sectarian politicians can offer only centralized systems. Castelao advises Galician nationalists to turn their back on such disputes, and to organize themselves. In particular, Castelao recommended a more democratic form of Galician nationalism, a point to which I will return shortly.

There is one revealing moment of doubt in this section. At one point Castelao asks: 'is it possible that Galicia could be fascist?' In context, this is clearly supposed to be a rhetorical question which could elicit only the response, given a few sentences later, 'no, Galicia will never be fascist'.[65] But was this so obvious? On the same page, Castelao cites the name of Calvo Sotelo, the Galican who created the far-right grouping Spanish Renovation. Looking more widely, one thinks of the Francoist historians who were willing to praise the loyalty and the strengths of the Celto-Iberians, and to value Spain's northerners more highly than its southerners – all themes which Galician nationalist historians had previously rehearsed.[66] Risco, the most prominent leader of the Partido Galeguista, survived in Galicia. He still published works, but stressed his commitment to Catholic values and said little to annoy the Francoist authorities. Alvaro Cunqueiro (1911–81) had also been a member of the Partido Galeguista, in 1931. In 1936, he worked as a journalist for the Francoists, and in the 1940s and 1950s produced interesting – but innocuous – travel-writing, journalism and some mildly comic retellings of Arthurian legends. Lastly, many members of the youth wing of the Partido Galeguista had been conscripted to fight for Franco. Perhaps Galicia was not fascist, but in the 1940s there were certainly plenty of signs that its inhabitants could cooperate with the new Francoist authorities.

After the failure of the guerrilla movements in the late 1940s, there were few signs of open dissent in Galicia. This was not a region in which the trade union confederations, either the socialist UGT or the anarcho-syndicalist CNT, survived underground in any significant number.

The fate of Calero, the Galician nationalist playwright, is revealing. After two years in prison, he was released in 1941, and saw his young daughter for the first time in five years. He looked for work in private colleges, for he knew that he would never be accepted in a state school. In 1946 he began to contribute to a Carlist paper, *El Noche*, that – unusually – maintained an interest in Galician regional culture. He used a pseudonym for his articles. In 1950 he finally found a permanent job in a private college in Lugo, where he stayed until 1965. He remembered this period as a time of marginality, isolation and humiliation. 'I stayed in the same building, and never went out, except at the weekends. I spent all my time working.'[67]

The gap between those who remained in Galicia and the republican exiles outside, in France, Mexico and Argentina, grew wider. The exiles wanted to see signs of militant opposition in their region: this alone would confirm their status as the legitimate representatives of a people struggling to be free of Franco. Instead, they saw apathy and compromise.

It was not until 1950 that a Galeguista movement re-emerged. This was led by Ramón Piñeiro, another member of the old Partido Galeguista. Piñeiro devised a remarkable cultural strategy, drawing on some elements of Risco's ideas, and transforming them to take account of the radically changed circumstances. Francoism did allow a small grey area of toleration for regional cultures, if they were safely restricted to the private sphere. Piñeiro correctly estimated that any attempt to create a mass rebel movement would be crushed by the Francoist police. He therefore called on the remaining Galician nationalists to throw their energies into the cultural sphere (a strategy which had been previously adopted during Primo de Rivera's dictatorship). More specifically, he proposed the creation of a publishing house, to specialize in Galician matters, publishing – where possible – in Galego. By 1950, Piñeiro had found 125 shareholders who would support his project, and the Galaxia publishing house was created in Vigo.[68] (It survives to this day.) Twelve books were produced in 1951. One of Piñeiro's constant aims was to demonstrate the subtlety and richness of Galego by using it as a medium for the most complex and modern prose, and so Galaxia published, in Galego, the first editions of works by Heidegger and Sartre to be issued in Spain. While the Francoist regime tolerated the use of Galego in the countryside and in traditional ceremonies, the use of Galego in publishing was viewed with far greater hostility. The regime's police watched closely the activities of the network of people around Galaxia: on occasion, informal intimidation prevented initiatives.[69]

The fascinating point about Piñeiro is that this was clearly something more than simply making the best of bad circumstances.[70] He argued that Galaxia would provide a type of Galician nationalist education for the young, thus guaranteeing the future of the movement and establishing a kind of leadership-in-waiting. In Piñeiro's terms, this would produce the 'galeguización' of Galician society, without any head-on confrontation with the authorities, without even the formation of a political party. On the contrary, Piñeiro argued that there was no need for Galician nationalist politics:

instead, militants should aim to infuse *all* Galician parties with a consciousness of the region. It was time to transcend nationalism, and instead to embrace the cause of European federalism – an ideal which, in the post-war context, was attracting many sincere and inspired followers among the Catholic left across Europe.

Many elements of Piñeiro's thinking were already present in Risco's earlier works. Risco, too, had been sceptical of party politics, and had stressed the value of 'cultural' work. Piñeiro's radical innovation was his explicit rejection of nationalism itself.

Many reacted angrily against Piñeiro. One important centre of criticism was in Argentina. After the end of the Second World War, migration to Argentina increased massively: this was the last great trans-Atlantic exodus. A total of 286,437 Galicians left for Argentina between 1946 and 1960.[71] The relations between Spain and Argentina were governed by a new international treaty, agreed in 1948. Should these people be seen as political exiles? There can be no doubt that the first reason that pushed them to leave was the dire economic condition of the region. Resentment of poverty then often stimulated wider and deeper anti-Francoist thinking. Buenos Aires became 'the cultural and political capital of that ideal Galicia that Castelao had proclaimed'.[72] From 1939 to 1944, twelve books were published in Argentina in Galego, while none were produced in Galicia itself.[73]

Galician institutions in Argentina went through a phase of politicization. Most of them were, at least initially, firmly committed to the republican cause. The national day of Galicia, 25 July, was celebrated with great fervour, and a lively exile press was produced. Moreover, there were important political debates: Galician nationalists talked to republicans and socialists. Castelao's presence in Buenos Aires was also important. He led Galician radicals into a strong, clear defence of their separate identity, and he criticized Risco's thinking. His *Sempre en Galiza* suggested a reformulation of Galician nationalist ideas, stressing the action of the people, and infusing the cause with progressive and democratic values.[74]

For these reasons, the Argentine exiles were highly critical of Piñeiro's ideas. *A Nosa Terra* – now edited in Buenos Aires – complained that Galaxia published some works in Castilian: a betrayal! More importantly, it noted how Piñeiro's ideas reduced Galician nationalism to the actions of an 'academic elite', unrepresentative of the masses.[75] This point is important: it was the first time within Galician nationalist circles that the issues of the *representative* quality of the militants had been raised; it suggested a radical break with the old, conservative, deterministic certainties of Murguía and Risco.

The new nationalism

During the 1950s, Francoism evolved once more. The simple clerical conservatives of the post-war years were gradually replaced by members of the mysterious Catholic Opus Dei organization, which often seemed like a counter-Freemasonry, with a similar stress on secrecy and behind-the-scenes activities. Opus Dei planned Spain's industrial modernization, involving a massive shift away from the agricultural domination of Spain's economy. In 1939, about half the labour force worked in agriculture; by 1977 only about a quarter.[76] While these moves certainly affected Galicia, the region was never Opus Dei's priority. Galician agriculture changed more slowly than elsewhere in Spain. Some have even seen the years from 1939 to 1970 as marking a 're-ruralization' of Galicia.[77] During the 1970s Galicia became a popular tourist destination for Spaniards who wanted to remember what the old Spain used to look like.[78] On the other hand, the Francoist regime did finally initiate a long, complex process of land concentration, which began the reform of rural Galicia's age-old pattern of miniscule land-holdings.

Opus Dei planned for a particular form of industrialization, concentrating on the development of centres of advanced activity. The opening of the SEAT car factory in Barcelona in 1952 was one of the first signs of this programme: by 1970 it employed twenty thousand workers.[79] Migrants flocked to Catalonia, crowding in so fast that they exceeded the region's housing capacity. Barcelona was surrounded by a vast shanty-town of tents and sheds, inhabited by migrant workers. Among their numbers were many Galicians, who briefly became famous for their near-monopoly of tramdrivers' positions.[80] Later, Galician industrial development began; the opening of a large oil refinery near A Coruña in 1962 and the Citroën car factory near Vigo in 1972 marked important stages in the region's economic history.

With this new wave of industrialization came new forms of labour discontent, no longer based on the old UGT and CNT structures, but led by a new generation of militants, who had grown up under Franco. There were some spectacular, violent labour confrontations in Barcelona and the Basque country in 1951, in Asturias in 1958, and then in all three regions in 1962.[81] In the early 1970s, this combativeness spread to new areas, including Galicia.

Other forms of protest also emerged in the 1960s. In part, the new radicals were inspired by world events: by the revolution in Cuba in 1959, by the long revolutionary process in Algeria from 1954 to 1962, and by the battle against American forces in Vietnam from 1965 to 1975. One lesson that was drawn from these events was very simple. The authorities were not impregnable. Through the right combination of will and strategy they could be beaten, a heady and inspiring thought to anyone who had grown up under Francoism. The growth of the Basque nationalist terrorist organization, ETA (Euzkadi Ta Askatasuna – Basque Land and Liberty), provided a closer example of the same lesson. In the same period, there was also a revival of Catalan culture, innovative and critical of the regime, and an increasing disengagement by the Church from the Francoist regime.

One Galician was extremely prominent in these years: Manuel Fraga Iribarne, who was born in Vilalba, in Lugo province, in 1922. Fraga had studied law in Santiago de Compostela, Madrid and Valencia. He occupied some minor administrative positions in the early 1950s, a typical representative of the well-educated, conservative Catholic generation who were replacing the old Falangist militants. In July 1962, however, Fraga was appointed Minister of Information and Tourism, and in this position pioneered the regime's new press law of 1966. This dismantled the formal procedures of censorship, whereby a paper had to submit its pages to a censor *prior* to publication. However, there remained strict limits on the issues that papers were allowed to discuss, and heavy penalties for those who overstepped the mark. In many cases, the 1966 law initiated a period of self-censorship, in which editors discouraged journalists from raising awkward questions.

By this point, even Francoist loyalists were considering how the regime might evolve. Fraga accepted that some political modernization had to accompany economic modernization, but rejected democracy. In the 1960s he considered that an opening-up of the structures of the Falange, allowing a degree of criticism to be heard, would be the best strategy for the survival of the regime.

During the 1960s, one could detect odd, isolated incidents of dissent in Galicia. For example, early in 1967 there was a strike in Bazan, in A Coruña province. Five hundred workers walked out of their factory: such moves were strictly illegal, and shocked conservative Francoist opinion. But, worse still, a priest marched at their head.[82] In 1967 Galaxia published a collection of short stories by Carlos Casares (1941–2002). The collection included one title, 'The Wolves', which was a coded criticism of the Francoist methods. In the first edition, this passed almost unnoticed. The collection sold well, but when Galaxia came to publish the second edition, the authorities protested, and demanded that the book be banned. The editors hid their copies, and eventually the book was distributed, to selected bookshops, for 'under the counter' sales.[83] Xosé Manuel Beiras, a leading intellectual in an underground Galician nationalist group, became the head of the Faculty of Economic Sciences at the University of Santiago de Compostela in 1968. The sense of crisis was even beginning to affect the regime's natural supporters. In 1959 there were 166 new priests ordained in Galicia, the highest number in the post-1945 period. Numbers then decreased steadily: by 1969 there were only 66 ordinations, by 1973, only 27.[84]

Such incidents, in themselves, proved nothing. However, there is much evidence to suggest that they were signs of greater, more substantial changes within Galicia. Two new political groups were created underground in the early 1960s, representing two different strands of radical Galician nationalism. The Unión do Povo Galego (UPG – Union of the Galician People) was initiated by a group of Galician students in Madrid in 1963, and established contacts in Santiago de Compostela and Vigo in 1964. This group attempted to fuse some of the classic themes of Galician nationalism with revolutionary Maoism. Initially, the two ideologies might appear very different, but there were some points of contact. Mao had debated how to plan a Marxist revolution in a land with almost no industrial proletariat. His answer was to consider a revolution in stages, and during the preliminary – or 'national-popular' – stage, the vast majority of the population would act against the tiny minority of exploiters. The UPG argued that this lesson could be applied to Galicia. It stressed the similarities between Galicia and colonies in an imperialist system: for this reason lessons could be learnt from Algeria, Cuba and Vietnam. In the late 1960s, the UPG gained a couple of hundred members, principally in Vigo and Madrid.[85] Joining an illegal group like the UPG was highly dangerous, and it seems likely that many others were intimidated from joining by the threat of police action.

The Partido Socialista Galego (PSG–Galician Socialist Party) was created in August 1963 in A Coruña. It represented a revolt against Piñeiro's passivity and cultural elitism, and marked an important step in the development of Galician nationalism. Although a small left-wing Galician nationalist party had been created in 1932, it had attracted little support, and soon collapsed. Instead, as has been shown, there was a substantial right-wing presence within the Partido Galeguista. The PSG was designed to develop left-wing ideas in Galicia. Initially, it defined its key principles as federalism, socialism and democracy: significantly, it did not mention Galician nationalism.[86] Moreover, it was critical of Marxist-Leninism and the model of the Soviet Union, and instead drew inspiration from European Social Democratic parties. However, in the early 1970s, the PSG began to evolve in a more radical direction. It debated and accepted the thesis that Galicia was a colony, suffering from under-development, and called for the right to self-determination.

One clear difference between the two groups was that, initially, the UPG was simply more active than the PSG. It held small, illegal and highly dangerous demonstrations in the late 1960s, it worked within apparently harmless and legal cultural associations, and in the early 1970s was involved in strikes in Ferrol and Vigo.[87]

The use of the image of the 'internal' colony, accepted by both these groups, is a striking example of the degree to which Galician nationalism had changed. It suggested a new type of political culture, no longer a backward-looking defence of some ethnic or cultural purity, but something closer to an economic and political assessment of Galicia's fate within the Spanish nation. It identified Galicia's struggle with the other great anti-colonial struggles of the epoch, and pushed Galician nationalists into using an increasingly radical, left-wing, vocabulary. Above all, it stressed the necessity of mass, popular activity in a manner that previous Galician national-ists had tended to ignore.

On the other hand, there are many signs of these groups' weak-nesses. They were both tiny. Their militants had little practical experience in politics: would their passion and optimism be enough?

Conclusion

Francoism was the revenge of the conservative Spanish nationalists against the new Spain which had emerged in the Second Republic. It cut short many of the most promising developments of that regime, and – in their place – demanded an unthinking loyalty to some increasingly outdated beliefs. But despite the Francoist regime's avowed conservatism, much changed during his reign. Large-scale industrialization evolved in Galicia, drawing labourers out from the eastern provinces. Franco's repression provoked a politicization of language use on a scale never seen before. Lastly, the new generation of revolutionary, Maoist nationalists was also, paradoxically, a result of his rule.

The political identity of the region remained more confused than ever. Franco had replaced the enabling, positive political cultures of the Second Republic with a spirit of silence and passivity. Politics belonged to the minorities: to the regime's supporters, growing more divided among themselves in the 1960s and early 1970s, and to the tiny marginalized groups of the cultural, political and labour undergrounds.

Notes

[1] Ramón Villares, *Historia de Galicia* (Vigo: Galaxia, 2004), pp. 242–3.

[2] Paul Preston, *Franco: A Biography* (London: HarperCollins, 1993), pp. 2–3.

[3] M. A. Fernán and F. Pillado Mayor, *Conversas en Compostela con Carballo Calero* (Barcelona: Sotelo Blanco, 1986), pp. 23–37.

[4] Ibid., p. 75.

[5] See Modesto Hermida García, *As revistas literarias en Galicia na Segunda Republica* (Sada: O Castro, 1997).

[6] Victor Casas, *Escritos Políticos* (Vigo: A Nosa Terra, 1996), p. 114.

[7] Ibid., p. 118.

[8] Stanley G. Payne, *Spain's First Democracy: The Second Republic, 1931–1936* (Madison, Wis., University of Wisconsin Press, 1993), p. 51.

[9] Carmen Ortega Villodres, 'Participación y abstención electoral: La Segunda República en perspectiva comparada', *www.ciere.org/CUADERNOS/Art%2049*, accessed on 23 July 2004.

[10] Emilio Grandío Seone, *Caciquismo e eleccións na Galiza da II Republica* (Vigo: A Nosa Terra, 1999), pp. 56–60.

[11] Paul Heywood, *Marxism and the Failure of Organised Socialism in Spain, 1879–1936* (Cambridge: CUP, 1990), p. 212; Dionisio Pereira, *A CNT na Galicia, 1922–1936* (Santiago de Compostela: Laiovento, 1994), p. 219.

[12] Baldomero Cores Trasmonte, *Ramón Suárez Picallo: Socialismo, Galleguismo y Acción des masas en Galicia* (Sada: O Castro, 1983), pp. 94–5.

[13] Roberto Cruz, *El Partido Comunista de España en la II Republica* (Madrid: Alianza Universidad, 1987), p. 304.

[14] Pereira, *CNT*, p. 29.

[15] Ibid., pp. 216–18.

[16] Emilio Grandío Seoane, 'O poder local na pronvincia da Coruña durante a II República', in L. Fernández Prieto, X. M. Núñez Seixas, A. Artiga Rego and Xesús Balbao (eds), *Poder local, elites e cambio social na Galicia* (Santiago de Compostela: Universidade de Santiago de Compostela, 1997), pp. 243–74 (p. 271).

[17] Grandio, *Caciquismo,* p. 75.

[18] Ibid., p. 64.

[19] Pereira, *CNT*, pp. 120–1.

[20] José Antonion Tojo Ramolla, *Testimonios de una represion: Santiago de Compostela, julio 1936–marzo 1937* (Sada: O Castro, 1990), pp. 103–11.

[21] Justo G. Beramendi and Xosé M. Núñez Seixas, *O Nacionalismo Galego* (Vigo: A Nosa Terra, 1996), p. 161.

[22] José Luis de la Granja, Justo Beramendi and Pere Anguera, *La España de los nationalismos y las autonomías* (Madrid: Editorial Síntesis, 2001), pp. 115–17.

[23] 'Programa fundacional del Partido Galeguista. Pontevedra, 6 y 7 de diciembre de 1931', in Ibid., pp. 393–6.

[24] Beramendi and Núñez, *O Nacionalismo*, pp. 147, 150–1.

[25] Ibid., p. 151.

[26] Ibid., p. 153.

[27] Casas, *Escritos*, p. 130.

[28] Ibid., pp. 133–4.

[29] Ibid., p. 145.

[30] Casares, *Conciencia de Galicia: Risco, Otero, Curros* (Vigo: Galaxia, 2004), p. 142.

[31] Ibid., p. 156.

[32] Cores, *Ramón Suárez Picallo,* pp. 79–83.

[33] Ibid., p. 96.

[34] Beramendi and Núñez, *O Nacionalismo*, p. 163.

[35] 'Bases programáticas de la Derecha Galleguista. Ourense, abril de 1936', in Granja, Beramendi and Anguera, *La España*, pp. 399–401.

[36] Alberto Romasanta, 'Víctor Casas: O compromiso galeguista', in his edition of Víctor Casas, *Escritos Políticos* (Vigo: A Nosa Terra, 1996), p. 47.

[37] The following paragraphs are largely drawn from Tojo, *Testimonios*, pp. 21–6.

[38] Alvaro Jaspe, 'The military uprising of 1936 and the repression in Galicia', *Galician Review*, 3–4 (1999–2000), 77–102.

[39] Ramón Salas Larraázabal, *Perdidas de la Guerra*, cited in ibid., p. 78.

[40] Santos Julía (ed.), *Víctimas de la Guerra civil* (Madrid: Historia, 1999), pp. 410–12.

[41] *Spain: Dictatorship to Democracy* (London: George Allen and Unwin, 1981), p. 6.

[42] Mercedes Carbayo-Abengózar, 'Shaping women: national identity through the use of language in Franco's Spain', *Nations and Nationalism*, 7:1 (2001), 75–92.

[43] Preston, *Franco*, p. 475.

[44] Manuel González González, 'La recuperación del gallego', *Revista de Filogía Románica* 3 (1985), 101–19.

[45] Miquel Siguan, *España plurilinguë* (Madrid: Alianza Universidad, 1992), p. 68.

[46] Fernán, *Conversas*, p. 103.

[47] Emilio González López, *Memorias de un diputado republicano en la Guerra civil española* (Sada: O Castro, 1990), p.179.

[48] Carlos Casares, *Wounded Wind*, trans. Rosa Rutherford (Aberystwyth: Planet, 2004), p.12.

[49] Hans C. Buechler and Judith-Maria Buechler, *Carmen: The Autobiography of a Spanish Galician Woman* (Cambridge, Mass.: Schenkman, 1981), pp. xxv, 1–3.

[50] Beatriz López, *Hasta la victoria siempre . . . testimonio de Carmen Cornes, emigrante gallega y militante de la vida* (Sada: O Castro, 1992), p.53.

[51] *'Foucellas': el riguroso relato de una lucha antifranquista (1936–52)* (Sada: O Castro, 1993), pp. 24–5.

[52] Ibid., p. 13.

[53] Francisco Moreno, 'La represión en la posguerra', in Santos Juliá (ed.), *Víctimas de la Guerra civil* (Madrid: Historia, 1999), pp. 275–406 (pp. 370–3).

[54] See Alicia Alted Vigil, 'La oposición republicana, 1939–1977', in Nigel Townson (ed.), *El Republicanismo en España (1830–1977)* (Madrid: Alianza Editorial, 1994), pp. 223–63.

[55] Lamela, *Foucellas*, p. 69.

[56] Francisco Martinez-Lopez, *Guerrillero contre Franco: la guérilla antifranquiste du León (1936–1951)* (Paris: Syllepse, 2000), p.37. NB: as Martinez-Lopez's work was published in France, his name has been spelt according to the rules of French orthography.

[57] Ibid., pp. 50–1, 68–9.

[58] Ibid., p. 57.

[59] Beramendi and Núñez, *O Nacionalismo*, p. 174.

[60] On the international context, see Enrique Moradiellos, 'The Potsdam Conference and the Spanish problem', *Contemporary European History*, 10:1 (2001), pp. 73–90.

[61] Morena, 'La represión', p. 374.

[62] Some excerpts of the essay can be found in John Hutchinson and Anthony D. Smith (eds), *Nationalism* (Oxford: OUP, 1994), pp. 18–21.

[63] Alfonso R. Castelao, *Sempre en Galiza* (Buenos Aires: Galicia, 1976), p. 141.

[64] Ibid., p. 158.

[65] Ibid., p. 189.

[66] Fernando Wulff, *Las esencias patrias: historiografía e historia antigua en la construcción de la identidad española* (Barcelona: Crítica, 2003), pp. 231–2.

[67] Fernán, *Conversas*, p. 134.

[68] Beramendi and Núñez, *O Nacionalismo*, p. 194.

[69] See Victor F. Freixanes, 'Conversa con Francisco Fernández e Xaime Isla Conto', *Grial*, 157 (2003), 50–7.

[70] I have drawn my analysis of Piñeiro from Beramendi and Núñez, *O Nacionalismo*, pp. 200–4.

[71] Marcelino X. Fernández Santiago, 'Asociacionismo Gallego en Buenos Aires (1936–60)', in X. Núñez Seixas (ed.), *La Galicia Austral* (Buenos Aires: Biblios, 2001), pp. 181–201 (p. 182).

[72] Fernández, 'Asociacionismo Gallego', p. 182.

[73] González, 'Recuperación', p. 105.

[74] Ramón Maíz, 'El galleguismo de Castelao: Nacionalismo Organicista y democracia política', in J. Antón and M. Caminal (eds), *Pensamiento Político en la España Contemporánea, 1880–1950* (Barcelona: Teide, 1992), pp. 787–809.

[75] Beramendi and Núñez, *O Nacionalismo*, p. 200.

[76] Carr and Fusi, *Spain*, p. 49.

[77] Julio Cabrera Varela, 'Las precondiciones sociales de la identidad colectiva en Galicia', *Historia y Crítica*, 4 (1994), pp. 209–38 (p. 223).

[78] Carr and Fusi, *Spain*, p. 64.

[79] Ibid., p. 12.

[80] Ibid., p. 68.

[81] Ibid., pp. 138–9.

[82] X. Antonio Martínez García, *A Igrexa antifranquista en Galicia (1965–1975)* (Sada: O Castro, 1995), pp. 17–18.

[83] Rosa Rutherford, 'Introduction', Carlos Casaves, *Wounded Wind* (Aberystwyth: Planet, 2004), pp. i–viii.

[84] Martínez, *A Igrexa antifranquista,* p. 241.

[85] Manuel Anxo Fernández Baz, *A formación do nacionalismo galego contemporáneo (1963–1984)* (Santiago de Compostela: Laiovento, 2003), p. 48.

[86] Beramendi and Núñez, *O Nacionalismo,* pp. 230–3.

[87] Ibid., pp. 217–19.

The Iberian peninsula, showing the relative positions of Galicia (shaded in grey), Portugal and Spain. Image produced by Catherine Evans (University of Glamorgan).

The four provinces of Galicia, and their most important towns. Image produced by Catherine Evans (University of Glamorgan).

The cathedral at Santiago de Compostela, dominating the Plaza do Obradoiro. Photograph by Mariola Mourela.

The statue of the poet, Rosalía de Castro, in Santiago de Compostela (see chapter 3), a figure central to the nineteenth century revival of Galego and the construction of a modern Galician identity. Photograph by Mariola Mourela.

The End of Franco (see chapter 5). The destruction of the last public statue of Franco in Galicia, in July 2003. Photograph courtesy of *La Voz de Galicia*.

The western coast of Galicia in December 2002, following the *Prestige* oil-slick. Photograph by Mariola Mourela.

Volunteers work to clean the coastline following the *Prestige* oil-slick, December 2002 (see chapter 6). Photograph by Mariola Mourela.

A Nunca Máis demonstration, spring 2003 (see chapter 6). Caricatures of Fraga (left) and the Spanish prime minister Aznar (right) are hoisted displaying the symbol of the Falange. The nationalist BNG flag is visible to the left. Photograph courtesy of *La Voz de Galicia*.

The small horreo stone-built barn used by Galician peasants has today become an emblematic symbol of Galicia.

5

The Autonomous Community: Fraga's Galicia, 1977–2005

On 9 July 2003 the *Voz de Galicia* announced that the last public statue of Franco in Galicia, located in Ponteareas (in Pontevedra province), had been dismantled. They published a splendid photo of the object: a giant, four-foot-high marble representation of Franco's head, raised high on a plinth, besmirched and splattered, with sticky black paint running down his cheeks and graffiti covering the stand. But the new municipal council, a coalition of Galician nationalists and socialists, was taking no chances. Having separated the statue from its plinth, it was transported off the site at 1 a.m., as silently as possible. After discussions, the council decided not to arrange a public ceremony to mark the moment.[1]

The man may have died, and his last statue finally been removed, but his influence can still be felt in the region in which he was born. In this chapter and the one that follows, I will survey the changes in Galicia since 1975. This chapter will first examine Galicia's social evolution, and then concentrate on the rise of a remarkable conservative grouping – the Partido Popular (Popular Party) – that governed the region from 1981 to 2005. The next chapter will discuss some challenges to their rule.

Galician society after Franco

In 1980 Carmen Cornes returned to Galicia from Argentina. She had been away from the region for over five decades, and eventually left Argentina only as a result of her protests after her son's 'disappearance' during the repression carried out by the Argentine military dictatorship. On her return, she found that little had changed in Sisán, the parish in Pontevedra province in which she was born. Of course, there were some differences: the roads looked straighter and cleaner, the houses were bigger, and most of them had baths, and the farmers ploughed with tractors instead of oxen. 'But in the hamlets the work was much the same, whether taking care of animals or working the land: all much the same.' Above all, Cornes identified the single most important continuity in her birthplace. 'The young people wanted to get out. The system had not changed.'[2]

She came back with very little money, and so had little choice but to accept her brother's offer of a room in his house. This made her uneasy: she was still more embarrassed when she realized that she would have to stay in her young niece's bedroom. When she opened the bedroom door, however, she saw a sight which immediately made her feel at home. Her niece had a large poster of Che Guevara on the wall. In this little incident, we suddenly get a glimpse of an informal radical political culture that crossed the Atlantic, uniting protestors in Argentina and Galicia.

Was Cornes right to say that nothing much had changed in the fifty years that she had been away? Certainly, there is plenty of evidence to the contrary. This was the period during which many left the land: by 1975, for the first time, the majority of Galicia's population lived in towns and cities. At the same time, this meant a renewed shift westwards, as people left the agricultural areas in Lugo and Ourense for the towns along the coast. A new, mixed, peasant culture developed among those who remained in the villages. Women became full-time farm managers, taking care of both the animals and the fields, and guaranteeing a basic minimum of food for their families. Men tended to travel more widely, looking for work, but they were now more likely to go to Switzerland for construction work than to Argentina or Cuba.[3] When they returned with their savings, they would often build new houses in the style of the Swiss buildings on which they had worked.[4]

The shift in population has changed the relative size of the four provinces.

As can be seen in Table 5.1, a century ago one could estimate very approximately that each of the four provinces contained about a quarter of the region's population. By 2003, only about a quarter of Galicia's population lived in the eastern provinces. Most remarkably of all, the population of the two eastern provinces – Lugo and Ourense – has actually shrunk since 1950.

Many of these people moved from villages in the east of the region to the cities in the west, resulting in a boom in the urban population, as can be seen in Table 5.2. Of the region's seven biggest cities, only two are in the eastern provinces, and the two biggest cities – A

Table 5.1. The population of Galicia's provinces in 1900 and 2003[5]

Province	1900	1950	2003
A Coruña	653,556 (32.9%)	971,641 (35.9%)	1,120,814 (40.7%)
Lugo	465,386 (23.5%)	521,213 (19.3%)	360,512 (13.1%)
Ourense	404,311 (20.4%)	494,283 (18.3%)	342,213 (12.4%)
Pontevedra	457,262 (23.1%)	714,666 (26.4%)	927,555 (33.7%)
Total	1,980,515	2,701,803	2,751,094

Table 5.2. Cities with over 50,000 inhabitants in 2000[6]

Province	City	Population
A Coruña	A Coruña	241,769
A Coruña	Ferrol	81,255
A Coruña	Santiago de Compostela	93,903
Lugo	Lugo	88,235
Ourense	Ourense	108,647
Pontevedra	Pontevedra	75,212
Pontevedra	Vigo	285,526

Coruña and Vigo – are both ports. Vigo represents something of an administrative peculiarity: it is the biggest city in Spain that is *not* a provincial capital. This shift in population has radically affected the profile of Galicia's cities. For example, in 2002, 43.3 per cent of those living in Santiago de Compostela were born outside the city.[7]

Galicia's economy still shows signs of late development. In 1975, approximately half of Galicia's population worked in agriculture. Today, less than a fifth work in this slowly modernizing sector: far less than a generation ago, but still more, relatively speaking, than in Spain as a whole (see Table 5.3). Galicia's principal agricultural exports are milk, wine and vegetables. In recent years,

Table 5.3. Numbers of employed people (in thousands) by economic sector in Galicia and Spain in 2000[8]

Sector	Galicia	Spain
Agriculture and fishing	177.0 (17.9%)	989.0 (6.8%)
Industry	175.5 (17.8%)	2,879.0 (19.9%)
Construction	116.6 (11.8%)	1,591.8 (11.0%)
Services	517.4 (52.4%)	9,014.0 (62.3%)
Total	986.6	14,473.7

Galician farmers have found it difficult to compete with other European producers. Following four separate land-consolidation laws (in 1952, 1955, 1962 and 1973), the process of pulling together Galicia's land-holdings has begun – but no more than that. Since 1954, consolidation measures have been applied to slightly more than a third of Galicia's agricultural land, involving 18.4 per cent of its landowners. But each of the region's farmers still owns – on average – 8.3 plots of land each, and this 'complex mosaic' is clearly inefficient and costly, a factor which still hinders all attempts to modernize Galicia agriculture.[9]

Fishing is more seasonal work: during 2001, between 28,800 and 35,700 people were employed as fishers.[10] While this represents a fairly small minority in Galicia's total workforce, and while even these numbers are in decline, there is still a case to be made that fishing represents a vital sector in the Galician economy. Fishers provide employment for shipbuilders, and the fish they catch are then processed within some of the most advanced factories in the region. Unfortunately, there is yet another reason for this sector's importance: some fishers also operate as smugglers, and in recent years have switched from smuggling tobacco to smuggling cocaine. The supply originates in Colombia, is shipped out from coastal islands off Venezuela, and then transferred on to Galician fishing boats in the mid-Atlantic. In 2003, some 60 per cent of all cocaine seized in Europe was taken off or near the coast of Galicia.[11]

The numbers working in industry and the services are still significantly lower than in the rest of Spain. These sectors are under some strain. For example, textile production in Galicia is closely integrated with firms over the border in Portugal. They employed about two hundred and thirty thousand people in 1999, but only about one hundred and sixty-seven thousand in 2003. Most jobs were lost in this sector as a result of firms that 'delocalized' production by moving their factories to countries such as Morocco and China, in which wage rates are significantly lower.[12] On the other hand, the Galician construction industry is growing faster than in most of the rest of Spain: the new migrants to the western cities need houses. In 1994, 1.17 million people were employed in construction; in 2003 there were 1.98 million.[13] Secondly, there is some expansion in the tourist industry, a point to which I will return at the end of this chapter. In August 2002, 7,666 people worked in hotels in Galicia, of whom about half were working in Pontevedra province (3,876).[14]

However, unemployment remained a serious problem. In 1999 and 2000 unemployment levels were, on average, higher in Galicia than in the rest of Spain. While the region's farmers and fishers benefited from relatively low rates of unemployment, industrial workers were not so fortunate: in 2000, while 6.8 per cent of industrial workers in Spain were unemployed, 9.0 per cent of Galicia's workers were jobless.[15] More recently, there have been signs of improvement: in 2004 there was a sustained seven-month period in which new jobs in services and industry more than compensated for the loss of work in the agricultural and fishing sectors. In fact, concluded one trade union survey in 2004, in recent years Galicia's economy has begun to resemble the Spanish economy.[16] Wages, however, remain low. In late 2004, the average Spanish worker earned 1,641 euros per month, while in Galicia the average monthly salary was 1,391 euros, the third lowest of the seventeen regions.[17]

There are many indications that Galicia remains relatively deprived. In 2003, house prices in Galicia were 60.5 per cent of the national average, the second lowest of the seventeen regions in Spain. Across Spain, 25.2 per cent of all households had access to the Internet: in Galicia only 16.9 per cent enjoyed this facility, the third lowest of the seventeen regions.[18] In the villages of old-fashioned eastern provinces, modern technology was often slow to arrive. In 1988 Susana de la Gala González, an anthropologist, stayed in the little village of Mourisca in Ourense. There were twenty-nine houses in the village: half of them were empty. Gala was amazed when she realized that in the entire village, there was only one telephone.[19]

The Galician economy still urgently needs investment to permit its modernization. Regional authorities have a vital role to play here, as they distribute EU funding.[20]

Perhaps most seriously, this is an ageing population. In typical years, such as 1998, 1999 and 2000, the number of deaths in Galicia exceeds the number of births by nine or ten thousand.[21] The populations of Lugo and Ourense provinces have been declining for over five decades, and the same point can be made for many of the rural areas of A Coruña and Pontevedra provinces. In fact, Galicia has the second-lowest birth rate and third highest death rate of the seventeen Spanish regions. This point has an effect on many social and cultural issues that might seem quite distant from demographic structures. For example, take the issue of the Galego language. One notes that Catalan is developing rapidly as a commercial language, and is

frequently used in advertising. Is business likely to take a similar attitude to Galego? No, for it is seen as a language of old people with
little purchasing power. In the last analysis, this process becomes
self-reinforcing. While old people rule Galicia – a point epitomized
until recently by Fraga's grasp on power – young people feel alienated, and so leave. Santos Solla presents a pessimistic view of
Galicia's future. Except for some dynamic sections between A
Coruña and Vigo, he fears that Galicia will become a land of
'exploitation of forests, insignificant but competitive farms and an
immense park for tourists'.[22]

One last peculiarity remains. Migrants still form a vital part of
Galician society. According to one estimate, some 1.2 million
Galicians live outside Spain, and another half-million live outside
the region, but within Spain. For example, there are approximately
one hundred and fifty thousand Galicians in Catalonia, and some six
thousand Galicians hold an informal monopoly over Barcelona's
taxi services.[23] 268,452 Galicians living abroad had registered to vote
in the elections to the Galician parliament in 2001: they formed more
than 10 per cent of the total regional electorate.[24] In some cases, this
led to odd results, typified by the village of Avión in Ourense
province. Here, no fewer than 2,307 citizens of Avión's total population of 4,498 – or 51.2 per cent – were registered as living abroad.
Large numbers of emigrants were registered to vote in all of
Galicia's major cities: 11.8 per cent of the electorate of Ourense, 10.3
per cent of Pontevedra and 6.5 per cent of Santiago de Compostela.
These figures have some political consequences, as these migrants
have in the past voted for the conservative Partido Popular (PP).
Observers have noted some suspicious aspects about them. For
example, in 2003 no fewer than 473 Galician voters who were registered as living in Buenos Aires were over a hundred years old, while
the whole of 'mainland' Galicia contains only 359 centenarians.[25]

This situation can also result in some anomalies. In 2003 there
were almost eleven thousand Spanish nationals living in Argentina
who benefited from some form of health care. Approximately six
hundred of them were from Andalucía: their health care was
provided free by the Andalucían regional authority. But the Galician
Xunta was faced with paying for 9,148 Galicians: it insisted that
these emigrants contribute eleven euros a month to a health-care
plan before it would provide them with aid.[26]

Lastly, like Cornes, these migrants can return. In fact, since 1983, more people have entered Galicia than have left: some of these are new immigrants, but the majority are 'returning'. The economic depression in Latin America encourages many to go back: some eleven thousand did so in 2003. Predictably, they usually settle in the larger cities, such as A Coruña or Vigo, rather than in the rural parishes in which they were born.[27] An increasing number of the migrants are relatively old, and therefore less likely to make an active contribution to Galicia's economy. In 1988, 23 per cent of the returning migrants were over fifty-four; in 2000 33 per cent had reached this age. An enquiry conducted in 2003 found that 2.0 per cent of these returning migrants came back to Galicia to start a business, 5.9 per cent to find work and 13.7 per cent to retire.[28] Few others come to Galicia. Some may not welcome immigrants, but it is clear that their presence is a sure sign of a country's economic dynamism. In January 2004 it was estimated that there were almost 2.4 million unauthorized immigrants in Spain: only 42,364, some 1.76 per cent of the total, were in Galicia.[29]

Returning to Carmen Cornes's comments, we can reply that she probably underestimated the socio-economic changes of the late twentieth century, but that her appreciation of the mood among the region's young people was more accurate. For many, this seems a closed society, from which they must escape *before* they start a family. Without their contribution, the Galician population is growing older: it is in danger of becoming a region to which people retire.

The new nationalism: Galician politics and autonomy, 1975–80

The UPG and the PSG both argued that Galicia's ills had been caused by the region's status as a colony, subordinate to the political dynamics of the Spanish state and exploited by outside investors. 'The primary instrument of colonial oppression in Galicia, which has lasted five centuries, is the centralized Spanish state', argued the PSG in 1974.[30] In the years that followed, such arguments were put to the Galician electorate.

Spanish historians now talk of a *tardofranquismo*, a late Francoism, to distinguish the last years of the declining regime. One distinguishing mark of this period was the growing realization, even among the most stubborn of conservative loyalists, that change was inevitable. For this reason, Franco's death on 20 November 1975 did not mark the beginning of a substantial reform process – debates, even in a confused and awkward form, had begun long before, and often remained unresolved long after. This was not an occasion like 14 April 1931, when the announcement of the creation of the Second Republic drew jubilant crowds on to the streets. In 1975, the Civil Guard still controlled public space strictly, and any radical demonstration faced their determined opposition. In fact, many in the police forces saw this as their last chance to prevent the country falling into anarchy, and were more vigorous than ever in beating back protesters. Demonstrations during this period were often ugly, violent confrontations. As a result, there were a number of deaths caused by police actions: for example, on 3 March 1976 three workers at a demonstration in Vitoria, in the Basque country, were killed by police, and in April 1978 a protester died of her injuries following an angry demonstration by striking workers in Vigo.[31]

The process of reform in the mid 1970s was more nebulous and opaque than it had been in 1931. Francoist bureaucrats and politicians publicly issued calls for modernization and *aperturismo* – literally 'opening-up', but the Russian word *glasnost* probably better captures the resonances of the term. Manuel Fraga played an important part in this process. From 1973 to 1975 he was Spain's ambassador to the United Kingdom. In October 1973 he issued a call from London for the creation of a vast reform coalition, stretching from the 'modern right' to Catholic-inspired social democrats.[32] Fraga was rapidly establishing himself as one of the most clear-thinking and forward-looking of the last Francoists, and his proposals now carried some weight. In March 1977, he led seven political organizations into the formation of a new party, the Alianza Popular. Fraga was elected general secretary of this organization; he became its president in December 1979.

On the other hand, many were sceptical. Could Francoism reform itself? Was there not a serious danger that the same people would remain in power, creating a Francoism without Franco? Against such proposals, radicals argued for a clear 'rupture' from the established authorities. The problem for such radicals was that they could not propose an alternative centre of authority. The republican exiles, out in Argentina, Mexico and France, had now lost all credibility; they could no longer claim to represent Spain. But within Spain, there was no single centre to the opposition, for the obvious reason that nearly forty years of repression and censorship had smashed the best organizations of the left, the regionalists and other dissident groups.

For these reasons, rhetoric played a vital role. In terms of concrete support, all the anti-Francoist groups were tiny: none of them had had the opportunity to enrol members in an open, public manner. None of them had secure sources of finance, none of them had any practical experience in organizing institutions or governments. Of course, there were some bases for the opposition. Universities and – more generally – increasingly critical publishing houses could provide homes for dissident thinkers. The Church had effectively broken with Franco, and the number of priests fired with a desire to reform their society was growing. More tentatively, one could also point to the shadowy re-emergence of a labour movement, already split between social Catholics, socialists, Communists and far leftists. But, having made these qualifications, it remains true that the anti-Francoist opposition's greatest resource was rhetoric or, more bluntly, talk. This point explains the ferocity with which Galician nationalists deployed their excessive Maoist polemics against the structures of colonialist centralist Spain.

The political evolutions of this period resemble the realignment of some vast galactic structure: the creation of a new group, the publication of a manifesto, even just the coining of a phrase – such as 'rupture' – were each, in themselves, small modifications which *potentially* could signify a gigantic shift in the public life of a whole society. Events moved fast. Disparate, inexperienced anti-Francoist militants were motivated in equal share by the passionate hope for a new society, by their profound scepticism concerning the reform projects of ex-Francoist bureaucrats, and by their pervasive fear of a police crackdown. They worked hard to construct reliable structures to represent the entirety of the opposition. By December 1976, after only a few months of legality, the socialist PSOE was claiming that it had seventy-five thousand members – an astonishing feat, if true.[33] In April 1977 the PCE, the Spanish Communist Party, was finally relegalized – a still more surprising accomplishment. During the course of 1977 the Galician nationalist PSG held four long congresses in Galicia – the first legal congresses that the organization had been able to hold since it began, in 1963.[34]

In June 1977 these new or revived parties were put to the test in Spain's first free general election for forty years. A second general election followed, in March 1979. The results of these contests were surprisingly bad for the Galician nationalist groups. There were some obvious reasons for this: the inexperience of their militants, the absence of funding, and even their legal status. The PSG became a legally recognized party only in 1977. The UPG's first congress, held in August 1977, was – technically speaking – illegal, for the UPG was not authorized as a legal party until July 1978.[35] For this reason, it founded the Bloque Nacionalista-Popular Galego (BN-PG) as a legal 'front' organization to fight the 1977 election.

The first point to note about the 1977 and 1979 elections is that they were marked by extremely high levels of abstention in Galicia. The development of political democracy was not greeted with enthusiasm by the electorate, but more by a sense of worry and confusion. While this point is valid for the whole of Spain, Table 5.4 demonstrates that the problem was particularly acute in Galicia.

Table 5.4. Abstention rates in the general elections of 1977 and 1979 in Galicia and Spain[36]

	1977	1979
Galicia	39.3%	50.3%
Spain	20.1%	31.7%

In 1977, abstention rates in Galicia were almost double those in the whole of Spain. The problem was more acute in the villages in the east than in the towns and along the coast. It seems to be the result of a number of factors.[37] Firstly, the new peasantry of the late twentieth century had reverted to an economic position of self-sufficiency: perhaps this economic status also encouraged a spirit of 'political self-sufficiency' according to which the peasants preferred to ignore political life. Secondly, one should remember the geographic pattern of the rural settlements, scattered in their networks of households, hamlets, villages and parishes. For many rural Galicians, the polling booth was far away from their homes. As a result, they may well have been reluctant to make the effort to participate in a process which seemed to have little relevance to their lives. Lastly, it is also possible that the recorded rate of abstentions may be a result of technical errors, by which those who had either moved to the towns of the west or who had emigrated were still registered in their old residences.

While the gap between Galician participation rates and the all-Spanish averages has narrowed in recent years, Galicia continues to show a relatively high rate of abstentions in elections to this day.

The election results from 1977 and 1979 show the domination of the region by national, Spanish parties (Table 5.5).

Table 5.5. Galician voting figures for the general elections of 1977 and 1979[38]

Party	1977	1979
UCD	606,726 (53.6%)	515,891 (48.3%)
PSOE	175,149 (15.5%)	183,958 (17.2%)
AP / CD	148,239 (13.1%)	148,139 (13.9%)
PCG	34,147 (3.0%)	43,691 (4.1%)
PSG / UG	27,366 (2.4%)	58,036 (5.4%)
BN-PG	23,109 (2.0%)	64,106 (6.0%)
PPG / PGSD	23,014 (2.0%)	–
Others	94,239 (8.3%)	53,551 (5.0%)
Total	1,131,989	1,067,372

In both elections, the UCD (Unión de Centro Democrático – Union of the Democratic Centre) did extremely well. This was a short-lived party of Francoist officials, whose apparent commitment to reform made it briefly the largest party in Spain. The socialist PSOE was Galicia's second party, although their support was far smaller than that of the UCD. Their greatest strength was in A Coruña province, although in the 1979 election they gained some votes in Lugo province.

The AP (Alianza Popular) and CD (Coalición Democrático) were both organizations created by Fraga. While the UCD talked about reforms, Fraga's parties were more reticent. The AP's 1977 programme spoke of the 'unity of the nation' – a key Francoist phrase – as a supreme political value, and voiced scepticism about decentralization.[39] While these were relatively small parties in Spain, they proved to be moderately successful in Galicia. At this point, the AP looked a rather unlikely contender for power. The majority of its members were middle- and low-ranking Francoist officials, divided into seven separate right-wing strands, each unclear about their future within a democratic Spain. None of them seemed likely to attract a mass membership.[40]

The PCG (Partido Comunista de Galicia – Communist Party of

Galicia) was the Galician branch of the Spanish Communist Party. Its principal support came from the working-class suburbs of A Coruña, Pontevedra and Vigo. Lastly, while the two Galician nationalist parties, the PSG and the UPG (campaigning as the BN-PG) did not perform well, their votes were increasing, particularly in Pontevedra province. The key difference between the two was the BN-PG's ability to win some support in rural areas, principally in Lugo, where the party campaigned hard on behalf of peasant farmers. The third Galician nationalist coalition in the 1977 election was formed by two small groups: PPG (Partido Popular Galego) and PGSD (Partido Galego Social Demócrata). Both represented attempts to break with the far-left politics of the BN-PG and PSG, with the PPG a centrist grouping and the PGSD a moderate-left alternative. Significantly, neither proved to be successful.

For the BN-PG and the PSG these results were disappointing, and triggered a long series of often bitter debates within both groups. There were differences in their tactics. The UPG was still committed to revolutionary Maoist politics, but – as part of this strategy – understood the first step as the formation of a broad coalition, represented by the BN-PG. In order to build this coalition, it was willing to appeal to different sections of Galician society, and it gradually began to win more votes than its rival. The PSG, however, did have a certain advantage in its urban base in Vigo. This concentration of votes did, on occasion, allow it to win more seats than the bigger BN-PG. Furthermore, the presence of several prominent university lecturers within its ranks pushed the PSG into producing clearer, more coherent programmes than those offered by the BN-PG. 'Its discourse was more rational and its politics more sophisticated,' notes Vilas, 'but these positive elements seemed to be less attractive to the electorate than the rhetorical irrationalism of the BN-PG.'[41]

One consequence of these poor electoral performances meant that Galician nationalism was not represented at the new Cortes in Madrid. This led to a curious situation in 1979 and 1980. Following the granting of autonomy to Catalonia and the Basque country, there was a debate on Galician autonomy, which was supported by the UCD. The move was intensely studied by the PSG and BN-PG. The PSG was sceptical about the measures proposed, the BN-PG bluntly hostile. At the regional referendum in December 1980 to ratify the Statute of Autonomy, the PSG called for abstention, while the BN-PG advised its supporters to vote against the bill.[42] In fact, of those who voted, 73.1 per cent were in favour of the Statute: but only 29 per cent of the electorate did vote.[43]

It is difficult to explain this extremely low participation rate. In 1936, there had been real enthusiasm for this cause: 74.5 per cent of the electorate voted in the 1936 referendum. In 1980, Galician voters were confused and sceptical. They did not feel involved in the debates concerning autonomy, and hence were unwilling either to support or oppose the measure.

Fraga's Galicia: the rise of the Partido Popular

The first test of the new arrangements came in October 1981, with the elections to the first parliament of the new autonomous authority, the Xunta, as it is called in Galego. Voters remained unenthusiastic about the institution: of the 2.17 million voters in Galicia, only just over a million – or 46.3 per cent – participated. However, this did represent a significant increase in participation, compared with 29 per cent who had voted in the previous referendum. The electoral distribution of seats was unsatisfactory, with a significant overrepresentation of Lugo province: here, each deputy represented 22,200 voters, while in A Coruña province each deputy represented 38,400 voters.[44]

The voting patterns resembled those identified above: a clear defeat for the left and for the Galician nationalists, and a convincing victory for the centre and right (see Table 5.6).

However, there was one important innovation in the 1981 election. Fraga's AP was now the biggest party in the Galician parliament, pushing the centre-right UCD back into the conservative eastern

Table 5.6. Seats in the Galician parliament, October 1981[45]

Party	A Coruña	Lugo	Ourense	Pontevedra	Galicia
AP	9	5	5	7	26
UCD	5	6	7	6	24
PSOE	6	3	3	4	16
BN-PG/PSG	1	1	0	1	3
EG	0	0	0	1	1
PCG	1	0	0	0	1

provinces. Fraga himself had led the election campaign, inspiring AP members to greater levels of activity, and organizing meetings in the smallest of villages. 'Cyclone Fraga', commented Gerardo Fernández Albor, the leader of the Galician branch of the AP, recalling the vigour of the 1981 campaign.[46] Curiously, it seems that the AP's *lack* of political principle served it well: Fraga was able to dictate a pragmatic programme to its members. As the leader of the biggest regional section of the AP, his words carried weight. The success of his initiatives, however, caused a long-term problem for the party: could it exist without him? On the other hand, the UCD had grown divided, its members uncertain about its role as a post-Francoist reformist party and split in their attitudes to Galician autonomy. This move continued over the next five years. The UCD split into warring factions, while Fraga's party continued to win ever-greater victories in the Galician parliament: 34 seats in 1985 and 38 in 1989. (Following this last contest, it acquired its definitive form as the Partido Popular in April 1990, with Fraga as its regional President.) The PP's victory in 1989 in Galicia gave the party an absolute majority in the 75-seat Galician parliament.[47] Fraga himself, then aged 67, became President of the Xunta. From 1989 to June 2005, the PP enjoyed an absolute majority in the Galician parliament.

In 1981, the BN-PG and the PSG had formed a coalition to fight this election, and had between them won 6.3 per cent of the vote. To their numbers could be added the votes for the EG (Esquerda Galega – Galician Left), a 'new left' split from the PSG, inspired by the ideas that developed out of the May 1968 uprising in Paris. The EG won 3.4 per cent of the vote, including a significant concentration of some eighteen thousand votes around Vigo, which brought the EG its one deputy. These two strands – the BN-PG / PSG and the EG – had quite different attitudes to the Galician parliament. Both currents criticized the autonomy statute as too limited, complaining that there had been little real consultation with the Galician people. But while the BN-PG / PSG was *on principle* opposed to the parliament, the EG argued that this imperfect body could still provide a start to a meaningful process of auto-determination.

The three BN-PG / PSG deputies refused to swear an oath of loyalty to the Galician parliament, for this would imply a recognition of the authority of the Spanish state. They boycotted the proceedings, which eventually led to their formal expulsion from the Galician parliament. Camilo Nogueira, the solitary EG deputy,

stayed. He proved to be a remarkably dogged and persistent partici-
pant, initiating by himself more legislation and motions than the
total produced by *all* the other 67 deputies in the parliament![48]

When considering the performance of the Xunta since 1981, it
should be remembered that this was a new body, without the historical precedents of some of the seventeen other 'autonomous
communities', as the Spanish constitution of 1978 termed the new
bodies representing the regions. A subtle cultural shift affected all
the parties in the Galician parliament during the 1980s, almost as if
Piñeiro's call for the 'galeguización' of all organizations in Galicia
was at last being realized (see chapter 4). All the parties began to
speak of the distinctive qualities of Galicia and the value of Galego:
it formed a 'master frame' for their different political discourses.[49]
One caustic review of the 2005 Xunta elections accurately noted that
all three main parties (the PP, PSOE and BNG) presented themselves
as reformists and *galeguistas* (Galician patriots), as democratic and
tolerant, and as progressive and very, very modern.[50] The most
radical change, however, was within the PP itself, which moved from
open scepticism about the value of the autonomy statute to a cele-
bration of Galicians' unique nature. One striking example of this
change in attitude was seen in 1993 and 1997, when massed bands of
some two thousand Galician bagpipers celebrated the PP victories in
the Galician parliamentary elections of those years.[51]

Another example of this commitment to Galician identity is the
speed with which the Xunta acted to establish Galego as a 'co-offi-
cial' language, alongside Castilian. A vital aspect of this task was the
difficult question of constructing a 'standard' form of Galego.
Readers should perhaps remember that in the case of the English
language, approximately five centuries was required from its thir-
teenth-century emergence as a sophisticated language used – on
occasion – by elites, to its eighteenth-century codification through
the first coherent grammar guides and dictionaries. Galician
linguists are attempting to produce an equally coherent form of
Galego within a far shorter time-frame.

Some preliminary linguistic research had been conducted by the
nineteenth-century cultural militants, and in the 1920s and 1930s the
first steps were taken towards the development of an orthodox
Galego. But all these initiatives were cut short by Franco. During the
1960s and 1970s the question of 'standard Galego' developed into a
highly politicized issue, with several competing forms circulating. J.

Kabatek summed up the confusion with the dry observation that Galicia possessed a thousand and one forms of standard Galego.[52]

The Xunta established a linguistics committee, which worked on the assumption that Galego was a separate language in its own right, with some strong resemblances to both Portuguese and Castilian. The committee devised an orthodox format in 1982, and in June 1983 the Xunta passed the Law of Linguistic Normalization, which formally enshrined the duty of Galicians to learn Galego, and their right to use it.[53] Galego was not simply *taught* in schools: it also became the normal teaching language for many academic subjects. I will return to this issue in the next chapter, but for the moment it should be noted that there were problems with the interpretation and implementation of this legislation.

The Xunta has been highly active in a number of other fields. It has developed new universities in Vigo and A Coruña, planned new motorways and railways, sponsored the modernization of Galicia's fishing industry, and established a separate, regional television network in 1985. Between 1981 and 1995 the Galician parliament enacted 146 laws, making it one of the most active autonomous communities in Spain.[54] While economists and sociologists will still argue that Galicia is a relatively deprived area within the EU, no one could doubt the extent to which Galicia has changed in recent decades, and, in most cases, this technological, social and cultural development has benefited from the Xunta's direction.

The success of the Xunta has been intertwined with the development of the PP and, more specifically, with Fraga's leadership of the PP. This is a more problematic area. The PP now presents itself as a forward-looking centre party. The PP programme from the Ponteareas section in 2004 described the party as of the 'reformist centre', a position which is defined by 'an absence of extremism', coupled with the values of 'liberty, toleration, dialogue' and 'authentic social solidarity'.[55] The PP's 2005 manifesto stressed how the party had grappled with the 'unavoidable task of modernizing this land'.[56] Fraga himself refers to his loyalty to 'an eternal Galicia', which is constantly improving under his programme of modernization and rationalization. His supporters have termed the absence of severe social conflicts the '*pax fraguiana*', a phrase which delights him.[57] However, this assertion of Galician values should not be understood as an acceptance of Galician nationalism. PP pronouncements regularly condemn the 'venom' of separatism, and Fraga himself has argued that the BNG's policies would encourage the development of ETA-style terrorism in Galicia.[58]

Examining some of the PP candidates' pronouncements before the October 2001 Xunta elections, one reads some similar themes.[59] For example, Cástor Gago, the seventh candidate on the PP list for Ourense province, stressed his formative experience in the Catholic, agricultural movement of that province. He stated that his first wish was to be a missionary, and his greatest aim was to 'contribute to the development of his people, so that my sons can live here'. Inmaculada Rodríguez, the first candidate on the PP list in Ourense, revealed another side of the party. Thirty-six years old, she was a divorced mother with a degree in biology, from a university in Madrid, and business experience working in multinational companies. Her CV shocked a section of the Catholic, conservative electorate, but demonstrated Fraga's determination to encourage the entry of women into the Galician parliament. However, her political attitudes seemed less than challenging. For her, the PP was 'the natural space of moderate nationalism and centre politics'.[60] She had found the multinationals an inhuman environment, not at all easy for a woman. The words of Rodríguez and Gago, who were both elected, suggest that the PP is a paternalistic, consensual grouping.

Some quite different themes emerge in further interviews. José Manuel Baltar Blanco, number four on the PP's Ourense list, tried hard to present himself as a fun-loving Beatles fan with a practical, no-nonsense approach to government. He defined politics as 'finding solutions'. What is more worrying is his attitude to *caciquismo*. Baltar comments: 'if we mean by *caciques* those people who go out of their way for their neighbours, then it could be said that they solve problems, although they are resented.' Curiously, this 'social' interpretation of *caciquismo* was echoed by Xosé Cuiña, a PP deputy in Pontevedra. 'The concept of the *cacique* has been twisted by time. The *cacique* was, properly speaking, someone who was always ready to aid those who needed assistance and this, in practice, gave the *cacique* a certain sort of influence.'[61] These are peculiar opinions: one does not normally find twenty-first-century politicians defending a nineteenth-century form of organized electoral corruption. For this reason they are worth discussing a little further.

Firstly, let us note that *caciquismo* was never a formally organized system: there is no *caciques*' manifesto to which we can refer to check the nature of the system. There is an element of truth in the statements by both deputies. *Caciquismo* was exercised by people of a certain status, and many may well have considered their actions a social duty: they guided the ignorant, and at the same time they integrated the poor into wider economic networks. The main purpose of such actions, however, was not to benefit their societies, but to resist the expansion of politically liberatory ideas – whether republicanism, socialism or anarchism. An integral part of *caciquismo* was always censorship: the suppression of the political freedom of an entire community. For this reason, it was often a source of considerable bitterness among ordinary voters. It is therefore extremely surprising and worrying to find experienced and powerful politicians defending such practices today.

Returning to the electoral pronouncements from 2001, one finds some other strands in the PP. Jaime Pita Varela, number two on the PP's list for A Coruña, launched into a diatribe against the BNG. Underneath their innocent appearance is the black paw of Marxism: they are barbarians and fundamentalists. On the other hand, Juan José Lucas Jiménez, a PP minister from central government, considered that the real enemy of the PP in Galicia is the Socialist party, not the Galician nationalists.

One last theme in their pronouncements is the reverence and admiration with which the PP members speak of Fraga. According to Lucas, he is 'a light' for all Spanish politicians who has attracted admiration from across Europe, marked by his 'personal honesty'. Following the PP's 2001 victory in the Xunta elections, the President of the Lugo PP analysed their success with a memorable description of Fraga's Galicia.

> The Galicia people in general, and those of Lugo province in particular, have voted for the Galicia of Manuel Fraga: the Galicia of motorways, fashion, the Xacobeo [a religious festival to celebrate Saint James], the ten million tourists, the high-speed trains, the 'world heritage' wall at Lugo, the dry dock at Monforte – in a word, they have chosen the Galicia of progress and stability which Fraga has built up, day by day, since he became president of the Xunta . . . Fraga is unquestionable and irreplaceable and, thanks be to God, Fraga still has much time.[62]

Such reverence for its leader creates problems within the Galician PP. In 2005, Fraga described himself as an 'eighty-two-year-old lad'.[63] Could he still lead the PP to another victory in the Galician parliament elections? Significantly, there was even a mini-crisis when

PSOE and BNG critics suggested that Fraga's 2005 campaign photograph had been doctored to remove the wrinkles from his face, a claim hotly denied by Fraga.

PP members in Galicia found it difficult to debate Fraga's position, for any suggestion that Fraga might not continue was interpreted as a form of disloyalty. Fraga restricted himself to making statements of Olympian ambiguity about his political intentions throughout the summer of 2004, but finally announced his intention to stand again at the end of August.[64] Significantly, he gave two reasons for this decision: firstly, to protect his legacy of reform and development, and, secondly, to prevent the PP from splitting. The latter point suggests the degree to which the party is dependent on Fraga. 'All division is bad', he commented.[65] The PSOE immediately stressed this point, suggesting that Fraga's decision demonstrated that the PP was 'weak, on the defensive, and bogged down'.[66] This was a surprising statement from the PSOE – which has lost every Galician parliamentary election since 1981 – but it showed a new mood of confidence on the left.

The reasons for this are not hard to see. Fraga was no longer an impressive figure but 'a dinosaur', in the eyes of many. In 2004 I asked one Galician for her opinion of Fraga's effectiveness as a speaker. She thought for a moment, and then stated that she found him slightly clearer than Pope John Paul II. Bearing in mind the frail, weak figure of the Pope at his last public appearances, this was a very cutting comment indeed. Once, Fraga was the master of *retranca*, a peculiarly Galician form of double-edged speech. By 2005 Fraga generally spoke poorly: he mumbled, to the point where many listeners could not understand his words.[67] He walked stiffly. He refused a television debate with the leaders of the BNG and the PSOE. Xosé Manuel Beiras, a speaker for the BNG, asked if Fraga would still be standing for election when he was blind and in a wheelchair.[68] His comments were cruel, and possibly unacceptably rude, but still pertinent: was Fraga still physically able to run a region of two and a half million people?

The opposition grew more critical of Fraga's reign. In the years since 1989, they have achieved little electoral success. The Galician nationalists united into a single core group, the BNG (to be discussed in the next chapter). Their vote gradually increased during the 1990s, but since 2001 has declined. With only 19.6 per cent of the vote and thirteen seats in the last Xunta elections (2005), they are further than ever from commanding a majority.[69] The PSOE saw its vote drop dramatically in the late 1990s, although the latest elections (2001, 2004 and 2005) suggest a substantial and sustained revival in support. On the other hand, the PP vote is steadily decreasing, election by election. The most important losses are in the western cities, to the point whom Fraga told urban voters in 2005 that they should learn to think 'like a Galician peasant'.[70]

The principal accusation made against the PP is that it has made use of the opportunities given to it by its electoral victories to build up its own power-base in Galicia, not to benefit Galicia. Economic development in the region is shaped by the public subsidies distributed from the Xunta, and these in turn are tied to support for the PP.[71] One example of this is the decision in the 1990s to cite a science park near Ourense. This small rural town, isolated from any major communications route or centres of industry, does not look like a suitable base for such an enterprise. Its one strength, in the eyes of the Xunta authorities, was that Ourense was a secure base for the PP. Sarah Batterbury interviewed an anonymous EU official about such practices. She recorded the following comments.

> Galicia's principal strength lies in the coastal area from Vigo to La Coruña: this is also where you find the voters for the Spanish Socialist Workers Party [PSOE]. Away from the coast, in the interior, you find a strong presence of the Partido Popular. Because of this, the Xunta does all it can to direct aid to small towns.[72]

Such practices not only distort important economic policies, they also have affected the running of the Xunta itself. In August 2004 the PSOE accused the PP regional government of nepotism: it found that between twenty and thirty close relations of regional ministers were employed in the Xunta. They included Fraga's sister, two of his nieces and one of his sons-in-law. In the eighty-nine institutions run by the Xunta, such as the Galician Consumers' Institute, salaries for some key employees had been doubled between 2001 and 2003, and many job contracts had been issued improperly.[73] As one writer commented to a French reporter in January 2003, for a young person planning a career, what mattered was not qualifications, but membership of the PP network.[74]

Such arguments reveal another side to the PP, and – once more – make us think again about their officials and candidates who defend *caciquismo*. Inevitably, it is difficult to find 'hard', incontrovertible evidence that will settle the debate. But what is clear is that among political scientists and regional activists, the accusation of PP corruption is made frequently.

Fraga's most eloquent opponent was Manuel Rivas, a novelist, poet and political commentator from A Coruña. He has written a string of articles in different newspapers which, taken together, form a type of counter-history of Fraga's reign.[75] Rivas has satirized and caricatured the pretensions of this neo-Francoist leader. A point which emerges clearly is Rivas's fury at Fraga's arrogance – this party boss who can proclaim that Galicia is 'the best country in the world', whose political model is JR from Dallas, who exploits Galician patriotism, who acts like an old-fashioned Galician hidalgo, who – most extraordinarily of all – exchanged visits with Fidel Castro. Rivas wrote a caricature of events, which has aged quickly and translates only with difficulty. But within this flood of astringent phrases, one forceful insight is repeated. Rivas notes Fraga's clumsy, calculating exploitation of Galician nationalist themes: the bagpipers at his victories, the publication of the massive *Gran Enciclopedia Gallega*, and the purposeful use of Galego at public occasions. In a sense, he is acknowledging Fraga's tactical genius: throughout the twentieth century, the Spanish right had nearly always been against Galician nationalism. Fraga had shown the right how to compromise with Galician culture, and therefore how to achieve power.

Fraga certainly has the knack of finding phrases to infuriate his opponents. For example, the 2002 Iraq war was a military campaign which was massively unpopular in Spain, with one opinion poll indicating that 96 per cent of the population were against the decision by Aznar, the PP Prime Minister, to support the American–British attack. Fraga listened to the protests, and then in April 2003 pointed out that more people were killed in traffic accidents in Spain than had then been killed by bombs in Iraq.[76]

A tourist's Galicia

Fraga's remaking of Galician identity, with its construction of a 'safe', integrated form of culture, is almost ideal for attracting tourists to the region. Since the 1990s, and particularly since 2000, there has been a concerted attempt to project Galicia as an appealing place for tourists. Such publicity usually plays on the theme of Galicia as different from the better-known and massively popular resorts in the south-east of Spain and the Balearics. This reflects, in part, a Spanish government acknowledgement that the southern and Mediterranean resorts have reached their maximum capacity, and will probably prove less attractive to tourists in the coming years.

A firm appealing to British tourists describes the region in the following terms.

> If you would like to shatter all the usual stereotypes of Spain, Galicia is the place to go. It is fresh and verdant, it has gushing rivers and a coastline more reminiscent of Scotland than Spain. The weather is cool, often misty, and the land is impregnated with an age-old magical atmosphere, which travellers can share in cathedrals, castles, dolmens and hill-forts. You may even hear the Galician bagpipes (*gaitas*) droning across the pasture.
>
> Galicia is in the north-western corner of Spain. It is the most forgotten of the seven Celtic nations. Even so, it has some of the oldest Celtic traditions, going back more than 2,000 years.[77]

The key point to gain here is how effortlessly the themes initiated and popularized by early Galician nationalists have been transformed into the easy clichés of tourist literature.

In 2003, Turgalicia, an agency of the Xunta, ran the 'Galicia Viva' ('Galicia alive') campaign. This made use of a number of striking images to represent Galicia's 'difference', stressing its greenness. One such advert, directed at Spanish tourists, showed the surreal juxtaposition of an enormous woman's head lying back among a forest of trees. It also made use of almost abstract, lyrical lines:

> Galicia is movement and rest. A break and a bite. A good soup and a good fire. Galicia is a walk, a market, a festival. Galicia is looking at a field, crossing a river. An open door and a meal. And everything is waiting for you. It is well worth finding, well worth living.[78]

Another advert in the same campaign made use of a striking image: a tall, good-looking black man, with a broad smile and trilby hat . . . holding a bagpipe. A small, inset picture in the bottom right-hand corner shows a rather more stereotypical picture of a march of male and female bagpipers (all white), wearing their 'traditional' black velvet and white cotton outfits.[79] At first sight, this is an extraordinary image. I have been to countless folk festivals, and heard many bagpipers and many black musicians – but I have never seen a black bagpiper.[80] How can this image represent Galicia? The answer comes in the near-untranslatable caption: 'touched by Galicia' or, perhaps, 'caught by Galicia'. The black man is presented not so much as representing the region as representing the effect of the region on its visitors: the message is that Galicia is such a laid-back, happy-go-lucky place, that *even* a black tourist will feel at home there, and so feel inspired to pick up a pair of bagpipes and join in.

There is some indication that these campaigns have been successful: there has been a significant growth in the numbers of tourists coming to Galicia (see Table 5.7).

Table 5.7. Number of tourists visiting Galicia in August 2000 and August 2003[81]

	August 2000	*August 2003*
Spanish tourists	357,343	423,226
Foreign tourists	72,870	88,046

Galicia does seem relatively popular among Spaniards: the 423,226 who visited in August 2003 represent 9.78 per cent of the total number of Spanish tourists on holiday in Spain. On the other hand, the quantity of foreign tourists is still small when compared with the total number who visit Spain: the 88,046 foreign tourists who visited Galicia in August 2003 represent only 2.6 per cent of the total number of foreign tourists who came to Spain in that month.

Throughout the whole of 2002, 474,049 foreign tourists visited Galicia (Table 5.8).

Table 5.8. Home nations of the most significant groups of foreign tourists in Galicia, 2002[82]

Country	*Number of tourists*
Portugal	156,362
France	47,249
Italy	44,860
Germany	43,368
United Kingdom	29,576
United States	27,072
Argentina	10,625

This distribution is easily explained. The Portuguese are, of course, the closest foreign nation. Germans, Italians and French people have to travel somewhat further to get to Galicia, people from the UK and USA still further. Lastly, the small, but significant, presence of Argentinians is a reminder of Galicia's continuing trans-Atlantic connections.

The most popular destinations for these tourists seem to be 'green' sites in rural areas, offering places to walk, plus a slower, more relaxed pace of life.[83] Here, we encounter once more a paradox that was mentioned at the end of chapter 2: lifestyles and settlements which might be described as backward, poverty-stricken, conservative or isolated, can be represented as natural, healthy, stress-free and relaxing. To a limited extent, the Galician tourist industry has been able to profit from this paradox.

In previous chapters I suggested that cultural exchanges, such as the pilgrimages to Santiago de Compostela and the migrations across the Atlantic, encouraged the process of identity formation in Galicia. Can tourism be seen in the same light? Certainly, posters such as those referred to above are important in fixing an identity for the region. However, in contrast with the two previous exchanges, tourism to Galicia does not actively involve the majority of the population: it is therefore difficult to see it as a process of exchange or a debate.

Conclusion

Despite appearances, Francoism has not disappeared from Galicia. Some eight months after the last public statute of Franco in Galicia had been dismantled, the PP municipal council of Ourense refused a motion from BNG councillors to change the names of streets which were named after Francoist military leaders. The council leaders explained that changing the names would confuse shoppers and traders.[84]

After Francoism, Fraga-ism. Fraga's PP represented a profound change in Galicia. For the first time, the region was run by a political party which accepted the idea that Galicia was distinct from other Spanish regions, and which worked to ensure that this difference was given a political form. The foundation of the Xunta, in 1981, was central to this. The PP's implementation of the new language-use policies, alongside the region's dramatic economic development, amounted to a radical transformation in the nature of Galicia. But this transformation left many dilemmas unsolved. Fraga-ism represented, at best, a stop-gap, a temporary political framework within which a set of processes continued to unfold. In the next chapter I will survey some of the most important challenges to Fraga's rule.

Notes

[1] Mónica Rodríguez, 'Franco se va de Ponteareas con la marcha del clan de los Castros', *La Voz de Galicia*, 9 July 2003.

[2] Beatriz López, *Hasta la Victoria siempre . . . testimonio de Carmen Cornes, emigrante gallega y militante de la vida* (Sada: O Castro, 1992), p. 117.

[3] See Sharon R. Roseman, '"Strong women" and "pretty girls": self-provisioning, gender and class identity in rural Galicia (Spain)', *American Anthropologist*, 104:1 (2002), 23–37.

[4] Susana de la Gala González, 'Day workers, main heirs: gender and class domination in the parishes of Mourisca and Beba', trans. Sharon R. Roseman, *Antropológica*, 41 (1999), 143–53.

[5] Information from Miguel M. Cuadrado, *Elecciones y partidos políticos de España (1868–1931), Vol II* (Madrid: Taurus, 1969), pp. 922–8; Edelmiro López Iglesias and Mar Pérez Fra, 'Axuste agrario e despoboamiento rural', *Grial*, 162 (2004), 36–43; and *www.ine.es*, consulted 18 July 2004.

[6] Information from 'Apéndice estadistico', *www.xunta.es*, consulted 18 July 2004.

[7] Juan Capeáns, 'En Santiago hay más de 41.000 solteros y cerca de 800 divorciados', *La Voz de Galicia*, 2 April 2004.

[8] Information from 'Apéndice estadistico', *www.xunta.es*, consulted 18 July 2004.

[9] Rafael Crecente, Carloz Alvarez and Urbana Fra, 'Economic, social and environmental impact of land consolidation in Galicia', *Land Use Policy*, 19 (2002), 135–47.

[10] www.ige.xunta.es, accessed 1 August 2004.

[11] José María Irujo, 'Marée blanche sur la côte espagnole', *Courrier international*, 720 (August 2004), 34–5. (This article originally appeared in *El País*.)

[12] *La Voz de Galicia*, 4 April 2004.

[13] *La Voz de Galicia*, 31 March 2004.

[14] 'Encuesta de ocupación hotelera 2002', *www.ine.es*, consulted 20 July 2004.

[15] Information from 'Apéndice estadistico', *www.xunta.es*, consulted 18 July 2004.

[16] *Galicia Hoxe*, 2 September 2004, and *La Voz de Galicia*, 31 August 2004.

[17] *La Voz de Galicia*, 1 April 2005.

[18] 'El entorno económico y social en 2003', *www.ine.es*, consulted 19 August 2004.

[19] Gala, 'Day workers, main heirs', p. 144.

[20] See Ramón Maíz and Antón Losada, 'Institutions, policies and nation-building: the Galician case', *Regional and Federal Studies*, 10:1 (2000), 62–91.

[21] Information from 'Apéndice estadistico', *www.xunta.es*, consulted 18 July 2004.

[22] Xosé M. Santos Solla, 'A población galega, algo máis ca unha crise demográfica', *Grial*, 162 (2004), 18–25 (20).

[23] Fernanda Amarelo de Castro, *A galeguidade: un sentimento común* (n.p.: Xunta de Galicia, 1995), p. 53; *Voz de Galicia*, 19 October 2001.

[24] Javier Sierra Rodríguez, 'Elecciones al Parlemento de Galicia 2001', www.monografías.com/trabajos10/gali/gali, consulted 1 August 2004.

[25] *El País*, 13 July 2003.

[26] *La Voz de Galicia*, 9 July 2003.

[27] *Galicia Hoxe*, 1 August 2004.

[28] Xoán Bouzada Fernández and Xesus A. Lage Picos, 'O retorno como culminación do ciclo da emigración galega', *Grial*, 162 (April 2004), 26–35.

[29] *El País*, 4 April 2005.

[30] 'Declaración de principios del Partido Socialista Galego', in José Luis de al Granja, Insto Beramendi and Pere Anguera, *La España*, pp. 402–3.

[31] Raymond Carr and Juan Pablo Fusi, *Spain: Dictatorship to Democracy* (London: George Allen and Unwin, 1981), p. 212.

[32] Ibid., pp. 203–4.

[33] Ibid., p. 224.

[34] Manuel Anxo Fernández Baz, *A formación do nacionalismo galego contemporáneo (1963–1984)* (Santiago de Compostela: Laiovento, 2003), p.67.

[35] Ibid., pp. 76–9.

[36] Sierra, 'Elecciones al Parlemento'.

[37] José Vilas Nogueira, *Las elecciones en Galicia (1976–1991)* (Barcelona: Working Paper 57, 1992), pp. 3–6, provides a useful analysis of the possible reasons for Galicia's high abstention rates.

[38] Information taken from Fernández, *Formación*, p.179; original source Pedro Arias and Miguel Cancio, *Las elecciones en Galicia, 1977–97* (Santiago de Compostela: Tórculo, 1999).

[39] Granja, Beramendi and Anguera, *La España*, p.199.

[40] Nieves Lagares Diez, *Génesis y Desarrollo del Partido Popular de Galicia* (Madrid: Tecnos, 1999), pp. 86, 96.

[41] Vilas, *Elecciones*, p. 17.

[42] Fernández, *Formación*, p. 92.

[43] Ibid., p. 183.

[44] Vilas, *Elecciones*, p. 1.

[45] Ibid., p. 39.

[46] *La Voz de Galicia*, undated (October 2001?), *www.lavozdegalicia.com*, consulted 1 August 2004.

[47] In fact, there were 71 seats in the Galician parliament in 1981. An electoral reform law following the 1985 elections created some new seats in the western provinces, resulting in a 75-seat parliament.

[48] Justo G. Beramendi and Xosé M. Núñez Seixas, *O Nacionalismo Galego* (Vigo: A Nosa Terra 1996), pp. 269–70.

[49] Maíz and Losada, 'The Galician case', p. 87.

[50] *Galice Hoxe: RDL*, 9 June 2005.

[51] Xelis de Toro Santos, 'Bagpipes and digital music: the re-mixing of Galician identity', in J. Labanyi (ed.), *Constructing Identity in Contemporary Spain* (Oxford: OUP, 2002), pp. 237–53 (p. 239).

[52] Cited in Xosé M. Núñez Seixas, 'Idioma y nacionalismo en Galicia en el siglo XX: un desencuentro histórico y diversos dilemas en el futuro', *Revista de Antropología Social*, 6 (1997), 165–91 (177). See also Manuel González González, 'La recuperación del Gallego', *Revista de Filogía Románica*, 3 (1985), 101–19.

[53] Núñez Seixas, 'Idioma y nacionalismo', 178–9.

[54] For more details, see Maíz and Losada, 'The Galician case', pp. 72–6, 80.

[55] *www.lanzadera.com/ppponteareas*, accessed on 18 August 2004.

[56] PP, *O Noso Compromiso con Galicia: Manifesto Electoral*, undated (2005?) *www.ppdegalicia.com/*, accessed 16 June 2005.

[57] *Correo Gallego*, 19 October 2001.

[58] *El País*, 2 October 2004.

[59] Information cited in the following paragraphs is taken from the *La Voz de Galicia* website, which has an 'especiale' archive section for the 2001 election, which collects some of the *Voz*'s most important articles for that election. Unfortunately, it does not provide dates for the original publication of these articles; one can guess, however, that they must have been published in September or October 2001. See *www.lavozdegalicia.com/especiales/elecciones_gallegas/entrevista/index*. Accessed 1 August 2004.

[60] *Correo Gallego*, 14 October 2001.

[61] *El País*, 10 December 2001.

[62] *Correo Gallego*, 23 October 2001.

[63] *Galice Hoxe*, 17 May 2005.

[64] *El País*, 21 August 2004; and *La Voz de Galicia*, 31 August 2004.

[65] *El País*, 12 September 2004.

[66] *Galicia Hoxe*, 1 September 2004.

[67] On *retranca*, see Marcial Gondar Portasany, *Crítica da Razón Galega* (Vigo: A Nosa Terra, 1995).

[68] 'Beiras compara a Fraga con Joaquín Balaguer', *Galicia Hoxe*, 1 September 2004.

[69] Anxo Lugilde, 'Cuarta mayoría de Fraga', *La Voz de Galicia*, 20 October 2001.

[70] Xornal.com, 23 May 2005 (*www.xornal.com/articale.php3?sid=20050523142817*, accessed 4 June 2005).

[71] Maíz and Losada, 'The Galician case', p. 81.

[72] Cited in Sarah C. E. Batterbury, 'Evaluating policy implementation: the European Union's small and medium-sized enterprise policies in Galicia and Sardinia', *Regional Studies*, 36:8 (2002), 861–76 (871).

[73] *La Voz de Galicia*, 18 August 2004.

[74] *Le Monde*, 3 January 2003.

[75] They are collected in *Galicia, Galicia* (Madrid: Santilla Ediciones Generales, 2002).

[76] *La Voz de Galicia*, 3 April 2003.

[77] 'Galicia', *www.hume-travel.com*, accessed 9 January 2003.

[78] This advert featured prominently in many quality papers. My copy comes from *El País*, 15 April 2003.

[79] My copy is from *Le Monde*, 24 September 2003, but, once again, this advert was distributed widely.

[80] There is something curious about the bagpipe's reputation as a quintessentially Celtic instrument: ethnomusicological research suggests that bagpipes originated in the Middle East.

[81] 'Encuesta de ocupación en alojamiento turísticos', *www.ine.es*, consulted 18 July 2004.

[82] 'Encuesta de ocupación hotelera, 2002', *www.ine.es*, consulted 18 July 2004.

[83] *La Voz de Galicia*, 6 February 2004.

[84] *La Voz de Galicia*, 2 April 2004.

6

Nunca Máis: The new Galicia?

In 1983, the thirteen-year-old Mercedes Peón went on holiday to the ominously named A Costa da Morte, or Death Coast, an area some forty kilometres south-west of A Coruña. (Its sinister name comes from the frequency of shipwrecks in this area.) Peón had grown up in A Coruña, and did not normally speak Galego. While on holiday she heard a group of women singing and – as she recorded many years later – was amazed by them.

> The first surprise was that I couldn't understand what they were saying . . . The second surprise was that it seemed as if we were in Algeria or Morocco . . . But how could this be? Only forty kilometres from my home? This question obsessed me and led me to question everything.[1]

Peón became a collector of such tunes and songs, travelling around rural Galicia with a cassette recorder; eventually she gathered two thousand. As will be seen, they inspired her to become a successful singer and songwriter.

This brief account of a simple summer holiday suggests a surprisingly complex itinerary: a journey in space, but also a voyage through cultures and history. One could say that Peón was discovering another Galicia, a land which lay hidden beneath the official repackaging of Galician culture implemented by the victorious Fraga and the PP. It is a journey which many Galicians have made in recent years. It could be described as a journey back to one's roots, if not for the qualification which Peón herself makes: these people in the villages were as foreign to her if they had been Moors. How can such communities be seen as providing the roots of modern Galicia? The route along which Peón and others are travelling is more complex.

The title of this chapter – Nunca Máis – is drawn from a remarkable protest movement that developed in Galicia late in 2002. The phrase means something like 'Never Again!' or 'No More!' As will be seen, this phrase was originally directed against a particular target, but it quickly became generalized, to the point where it resembled an expression of a new, post-Francoist generation, who refused the conformity and conservatism of their parents.

In this chapter we will follow Peón's journey, first surveying some issues which Fraga's PP has left unsolved, such as the status of Galego and the nature of 'traditional' Galician culture, and then consider the Nunca Máis movement in more detail. My intention here is to raise some questions about contemporary Galicia and – inevitably – some of them must remain unanswered.

The politics of the Galego language

Since 1975 there has been a protracted series of debates concerning Galician identity. Some simply aimed to uncover the 'real' Galicia: they argued, like Murguía, like Risco (see chapter 3), that a single Galician identity was created by vast anonymous historical forces centuries ago, and that the task of all true Galician patriots was to defend that legacy. For others – such as Fraga himself – the purpose of discussing Galician identity was to understand how best to use it, preferably with the PP directing the process. For a rather nebulous third strand, however, the question has been more awkward and more complex. Let us illustrate these different attitudes by examining the debates concerning the status of the Galego language in Galicia today.

During Franco's regime, using Galego was seen as a mark of social inferiority, and was frequently publicly condemned by the regime's officials. The creation of the Xunta in 1981 was supposed to end this sense of inferiority. Its laws of 1982 and 1983 were intended to develop Galego as a rich, subtle, modern language. Its programmes have clearly had an effect. For example, a survey in 2003 asked Galego-speakers how they had learnt the language (see Table 6.1).

Table 6.1. Methods for learning Galego, by age groups, in percentages[2]

	5–29 years old	30–49 years old	More than 50 years old
Family	17.19	31.23	52.23
School	96.14	55.96	20.36
Friends, neighbours	0.83	2.79	3.37
Work	0.18	4.06	3.94
Elsewhere	1.12	20.66	30.13

The difference between the respondents who were over fifty, and who therefore were born during Franco's dictatorship, and those under twenty-nine, and who therefore has spent most of their life within the Xunta's structures, is striking: the older people mainly learnt Galego in their families, the younger respondents mostly learnt it through the school programmes initiated by the Xunta's legislation. However, these measures have provoked much bitter controversy and there is now some real question about the long-term success of the legislation.

At first sight, Galego seems certain of a secure future – unlike many minority languages in Europe today. Any tourist or traveller will hear and see Galego everywhere in Galicia: it is present in the shops and cafés, on the streets and in the media. In schools it is used as a teaching language for many subjects, while in any bookshop in Galicia one finds works in Galego, not tucked away in a special section, but scattered across the shelves. Opinion polls seem to confirm these impressions. Data from 1994–6 suggests that 62.4 per cent of all Galicians considered Galego as their first language, 11.4% as their second language, and 68.6 per cent use it as their normal language of communication.[3] Similar research from 2003 even suggests a growth in the use of Galego, 80.95 per cent answering that they can understand it well, 16.25 per cent that they can get by in Galego, and only 2.80 per cent stating that they know little or no Galego.[4] (These figures are considerably higher than those revealed by similar studies of the proportion of people who can speak Catalan, Basque or Welsh in their respective communities.) Significantly, pressure groups which take a militant attitude to the conservation and/or development of Galego attract little support. This may well be a sign of confidence in the language's future, although – as will be seen – other explanations are possible.[5]

Some doubts creep in as one looks a little closer. Take, for example, the *Voz de Galicia*, Galicia's leading daily paper. Most of the *Voz* is in Castilian, although – fascinatingly – if someone speaking Galego is quoted, the paper will print their words in Galego, without a Castilian translation. Secondly, it does carry a handful of articles in Galego, often those written by BNG members or their sympathizers. Again, these are printed without translations. These points suggest a curious juxtaposition, quite unlike apparently similar situations else-where in the world. The *Voz* editors assume that *all* their readers will be able to understand both languages, and yet they also clearly consider it appropriate to publish predominantly in only one of these languages. In fact, among the couple of dozen daily papers printed in Galicia, there is only one which is written entirely in Galego: *Galicia Hoxe*, which started in 2003, developing from the *Correo Galego* daily, which began in 1994.

There are distinct constraints to publishing in Galego. Despite the potentially bigger market, fewer books are published in Galego than in Catalan or Basque.[6] Publishers are faced with an awkward dilemma: do they specialize in printing the works of a limited number of recognized 'classic' Galician authors, or do they try to innovate? Often, they are obliged to consider only titles which have some chance of reaching a mass audience – such as school textbooks – and, above all, works in Galego that might appeal to readers who normally buy Castilian works.[7] The BNG estimates that only about 10 per cent of the books sold in Galicia are written in Galego.[8]

Most importantly, one often finds invisible borders defining limits to the acceptable use of Galego. One Galician explained to me that normally Galicians use Castilian when they first meet, and then might switch to Galego when they feel they know each other. Revealingly, a Galician friend told me that she would always use Castilian when she applied for a job –a telling indication of the type of social prestige this language carries. The research by Henrique Monteagudo is more than twenty years old, but it still reveals much about these invisible barriers. Monteagudo found that 97 per cent of the people of Galicia *could* speak Galego, but he went on to ask the more important question: *did* they speak Galego? Two-thirds (65 per cent) replied that they normally used Galego within their home, 48 per cent with their friends and neighbours, and 39 per cent with school friends.[9] These figures are instructive. They suggest that the use of Galego is constrained in almost the same manner as that recorded by Emilio González López (see chapter 3). It remains largely a domestic language, for private use. The further one goes from home, the less one uses it.

Another study considered how officials in the Xunta used Galego: it uncovered a similar framework of hidden constraints within this milieu. Castilian was most frequently used in written communications, Galego in speech; Castilian was most used by senior officials, Galego by junior officials; and, lastly, Castilian was more frequently found in the towns, Galego in the rural offices.[10]

There are some counter-tendencies. Some students, particularly at the University of Vigo, are keen to use Galego on all social occasions. Predictably, BNG supporters usually speak Galego. A new generation of Galician musicians are rediscovering Galego songs – a point to which we will return. Overall, however, recent research suggests some significant problems for Galego: if it is identified with the poor, the less well-educated and the powerless, then it will become a language without prestige. On the other hand, Castilian possesses much social prestige: it is identified as the language of culture and modernity. If this trend continues, then slowly Castilian will become not simply the dominant language – one could argue that this is already the case – but actually the most commonly used language.

Furthermore, there are worrying indications that today's Galego-speakers increasingly use the language in a passive way: thus, in a 2003 study, 57.97 per cent of Galicians said that they understood written Galego well, but only 28.14 per cent that they wrote in it.[11] While 80.95 per cent said that they knew how to speak Galego well, only 42.62 per cent said that it was their normal language for speech, although another 18.38 per cent did say that they spoke Galego more than they did Castilian.[12] This 'passivication' of Galego appears more serious when the age of the respondent is considered: fairly consistently, it is the Galego speakers who are less than thirty years old who are least likely to make active use of the language, and those who are over fifty who are most likely to do so.

Another dimension to the issue is revealed when the figures are broken down according to province. The conservative eastern province of Lugo contains the largest proportion of monolingual Galego speakers (57.72 per cent), while the modernizing western province of Pontevedra contains the largest proportion of monolingual Castilian speakers (24.14 per cent).[13]

These points suggest an astonishing paradox. The young generation, those under thirty, are better educated in Galego and more confident in their ability to speak and write Galego correctly than any previous generation, and yet they are also more reluctant to speak or write Galego than any previous generation. And then, there is still another twist to this paradox: it is also precisely these young people who declare themselves the most optimistic about the language's future.[14]

Another contradiction in Galicia's linguistic profile emerges when we consider rural Galego-speakers, who often still live in a monolingual Galego environment. One might have expected that the Xunta's programmes would have given such people a sense of confidence in their language and culture, and thus stimulated a process of cultural empowerment. Instead, one often finds a sense of bewilderment, if not actual alienation, among them. The moves to standardize Galego have had an unexpected result. The rural speakers now often feel *more* inferior: not only are they unable to speak the more prestigious Castilian language correctly, but they have now learnt from schools and television that they do not even speak a 'proper' form of Galego.

Sharon Roseman, a Canadian anthropologist, researched this issue in a Galician village. Working through a standard list of questions, she first asked her interviewees which languages they spoke. She found that often the reply was a single, devastating sentence which speaks volumes about linguistic policy: 'You know, we don't speak anything, neither Galego nor Castilian.'[15] Roseman also records another telling example: when a well-known news announcer from the regional TV channel visited the village, he would always begin his conversations with the local people in Galego. Almost each time, they would automatically respond to him in Castilian, a reaction which would infuriate him. Either they simply did not recognize the form of Galego which he spoke as *their* Galego, or – more likely – they had learnt to address all public figures in Castilian.

The points made above suggest some of the complexities and contradictions in language-use policy in Galicia, and explain why the Xunta's 1982 and 1983 laws have not been universally welcomed. In fact, Galician nationalist commentators have been highly critical of these laws, but often react by producing some curious counter-arguments. This is now a politicized issue, and often both PP conservatives and BNG nationalists have analysed this issue in predominantly political terms. The easy dismissal of the new standard Galego by Galician nationalists as the 'PP version' is a telling example of such attitudes.[16] The nationalists' principal criticism is that this new, standard Galego had made the language into a mere sub-dialect of Castilian. By not making Galego sufficiently distinct, the Xunta's laws therefore fail to give it any sense of social or cultural prestige. The key to the language's revival and full development, they argue, lies in a radical reform of its structures. In most cases, these critics look to Portuguese as an alternative source of inspiration: firstly, to provide a distinct structure for Galego orthography, but also as a complete model for pronunciation and grammar.[17] Such commentators argue that Galego should join the family of some two hundred and ten million 'Lusitanians' – the speakers of the various forms of Portuguese in Portugal, Brazil and West Africa. Camilio Nogueira, a BNG Euro-deputy, even argues that Galego is closer to the languages of Brazil than is Portuguese.[18] There is also some cautious support for a limited restructuring of Galego along these lines from linguists and academics.[19]

However, even among these commentators there is much debate. The hardliners, termed 'reintegrationists', want a root-and-branch reform of Galego to make it significantly different from Castilian and far closer to Portuguese. More moderate critics – or 'moderate reintegrationists' – accept the premise that Galego resembles *both* Castilian and Portuguese, but consider that the Xunta's laws have not struck the correct balance between the two languages.[20]

These debates concerning Galego are fascinating, and also reveal some important aspects about the state of political culture in Galicia today. But, in many ways, the existing research is still inconclusive. The most fundamental question relates to the use of language by young people: current research indicates that this generation feels contradictory emotions. On the one hand, there is a deep affection for the presence of Galego in public life, correctly recognized as one of the clearest signs of post-Francoist freedom. One can even find families in which Galego-speaking children criticize their Castilian-speaking parents for not doing enough to preserve Galicia's cultural heritage. On the other hand, many young people associate Galego with the village and the parish: the old, conservative Galicia of their parents, and not the land in which they wish to grow up.[21] This point was nicely illustrated to me by a young Galician, who normally spoke Galego on all social occasions. She told me that one must *never* speak Galego in an A Coruña nightclub: in this context, Galego is simply not cool. The proposals made by radical critics of the Xunta's legislation seem to have little relevance to these young people's experiences. Within Galicia today, there is no strong sense of identification with Portugal, and making Galego more 'Lusitanian' in character will probably do little to raise its status.

Lastly, one wonders about the manner in which these enquiries are carried out. It is good to see that researchers have moved beyond the single, simplistic question, 'Can you speak . . .?' to the more important question, 'Do you speak . . .?', which, as it raises questions of daily activity, is clearly more revealing. But it is still unclear whether any research has actually grasped the real nature of the complex, daily interplay of Galego and Castilian – and between Galego variants of Castilian and Castilian forms of Galego. More studies are needed of the languages used by Galicians to tell jokes, to insult, to tease, to relate stories, to boast, to shout . . . It seems at least possible that such contextually sensitive studies might reveal that Galego is entrenched in daily life in a manner not revealed by a simple statistical counting.[22]

Music, gender and tradition

Let us return to the thirteen-year-old Mercedes Peón travelling to A Costa da Morte. One aspect of the shock she felt has now been debated: in 1983, there were few areas of A Coruña city in which Galego speakers were predominant. But the other surprise that she experienced was the musical culture in these villages. As will be seen in a few pages, no one could describe Peón as a typical Galician. However, there are aspects of her journey which illuminate broader themes within modern Galician society: in particular, concerning the presence of women in public life.

The Francoist regime was confused in its attitudes to Galician folk music. On the one hand, it was suspicious of any regionalist sympathies. On the other hand, the Catholic and conservative connotations of much traditional folk music, with its celebrations of northern rural values, seemed entirely in tune with Francoist political culture. Sometimes awkward compromises were reached: for example, people could play the traditional Galician *gaita* (bagpipes) at public events *if* their instruments were decorated with the red and yellow colours of the Spanish flag.[23]

After 1975, there was a brief period in which singing in Galego or playing bagpipes in public was seen as a type of rebel, anti-state activity. More importantly, debate recommenced on the nature and meaning of Galician traditional music. One important result has already been discussed: Fraga's use of mass *gaita* bands to celebrate his election victories in 1993 and 1997. Such occasions were not chance events. The Xunta set up an infrastructure of support and finance to encourage mass *gaita* groups, taking Scottish bands as their model. In the 1990s, this innovation led to much acrimonious debate, leading to a conflict which the press dubbed the 'bagpipe wars', in which some Galician traditionalists argued that the Scottish pipers were not an appropriate model for Galician bands.[24] Xelís de Toro Santos has studied these debates, and he distinguishes between three forms of post-Francoist Galician culture.[25]

1. Those who consider the priority to be adapting old forms to new circumstances, in particular to the new technical possibilities of the digital age. To an extent, the Xunta's initiatives could be classed in this category.
2. A strand of youth or urban culture, which deliberately promoted an ironic or satirical attitude to both Spanish nationalist pretensions and Galician traditionalism
3. An essentialist strand, that sought to preserve Galego and Galician culture within changing circumstances, and which was often sceptical about all innovation.

Inevitably, these currents often overlap. However, Toro's distinctions are useful in reminding us that there is no single, homogeneous form of Galician culture.

For many musicians, the years after 1975 were an exciting period that led to a radical questioning of the nature of the 'traditional'.[26] Xosé Manuel Budiño, a talented, innovative *gaita*-player, gives an evocative description of this period, in terms which recall Mercedes Peón's journey.

> At the beginning of the 1980s, young people, like me, kids, fifteen years old, had the possibility of working with the old instruments at the Universidade Popular [at Vigo]. Then we started to travel, to play at festivals, and at the same time, all these people who came from outside – from Brittany, from Ireland, from everywhere – it was almost compulsory to meet them at the Universidade Popular . . . And so we got to know all these people. One of our aims was to go out, to travel abroad, to get to know other cultures and express our own.
>
> In my case this meant that I needed to know more and more about my own culture in order to express it abroad. At the beginning one very much liked to find out about Irish music, Breton music, but later you got to the point when you returned to Galicia and you searched for the traditional music, because it's your music, your own culture that you want to express.
>
> We young people who were beginning to travel and also getting to know our own music have become professional, are making records, playing in festivals around the world, and in Galicia and Spain. And in Galicia, at every festival and concert where we're booked, very young people, fifteen- or sixteen-year-olds, hear the music, buy the records . . . And so there's *un boom*, because the culture and the music now in Galicia is very alive.[27]

Significantly, Budiño describes this process as an exchange, in a manner reminiscent of the processes identified around the pilgrimages to Santiago de Compostela (see chapter 1) or the emigrations to Latin America (see chapter 2).

Among the achievements from this period one could cite the following successful groups:

1. Milladoiro, an acoustic and traditional folk group who began in 1979, playing mainly instrumental material. They are proud of Galicia's Celtic identity. Their recent CDs demonstrate their technical ability to the point where, like the Irish band the Chieftains, their music can almost be categorized as classical music;
2. Berrogüetto, musically more innovative, drawing in jazz and fusion influences, using both electric instruments and electronically generated sounds, presenting a mixture of traditional material and their own compositions, and playing some songs as well as instrumental material;
3. Fuxan Os Ventos, rather conservative in their largely acoustic, traditional songs, but with an explicit commitment to the BNG and Galician nationalism;
4. Carlos Nuñez, a *gaita*-player, who has been important in developing 'Celtic' links between Galician and Breton musicians, particularly via the famous Festival Inter-Celtique at Lorient in Brittany.

These groups and artists share one point in common: they are largely male. Women appear on their CDs only as 'guest artists' or as singers: they rarely feature as writers or instrumentalists.

In the 1990s there were the first signs of women claiming the status of professional musicians. For example, one could consider Susana Seivane, a now-celebrated *gaita*-player, who has released three successful CDs. It is interesting to compare the illustrations from her *Alma de Buxo* ('the Soul of the Forest') released in 2001, with those used by Nuñez on his *Mayo longo* CD, released in 2000. Both are illustrated by pictures of the musicians, holding their *gaitas*, among the trees of a forest. This is not fortuitous: such pictures serve to demonstrate the 'authenticity' of – for example – Nuñez's music by, firstly, linking his status to the forests of Galicia, recalling the popular theme of the earth in sentimental nationalist works. Secondly, the illustration also refers to the wood from which the

bagpipes are made – from Galician trees, obviously! – thus rein-
forcing the status of his music as 'authentically' Galician. Seivane's
CD uses the same scenario, but with an important difference: she
appears almost naked, covered – in part – by her *gaita* and by some
careful photomontage of foliage on to her body. Her adoption of
this pose adds a third theme to it: the female body, source of fecun-
dity, is also equated with the earth and the trees of Galicia. The
difference between the portrayals of Seivane and Nuñez is indicative
of the extent to which female musicians stand in a different relationship to 'traditional' music from that of their male colleagues.

When the thirteen-year-old Peón went to listen to groups of
women singers in the summer of 1983, she was – unknowingly –
tapping into another, quite distinct Galician musical tradition: the
pandereteiras. These are all-female groups, singing in close harmony
and accompanied by *panderetas*, or tambourines. Such groups are
popular in Galicia, to the point that almost every town or village has
one. They usually sing in Galego: much of their material is
ephemeral and humorous. They sing about singing, dancing, love –
and usually about the disappointments that love brings – and sometimes about motherhood. Sometimes their material is more bawdy in
nature, rather like 'gossip set to music', as one Galician told me.

Such material is usually labelled 'traditional'. It is clear, however,
that this simple label often hides more than it reveals. Another
perceptive study by Sharon R. Roseman suggests a contrasting
perspective.[28] She has lived among Galicia's last peasant families,
who inhabit a curious borderland, with the men travelling out across
Spain, even across Europe, in search of unskilled labouring jobs,
while the women stay on the farms and preserve a base of agricultural self-sufficiency for their families. These are tough, multi-skilled
women, who have learnt to run their farms, and are proud of their
independence. They often sneer at those they term the *señoras finas*,
the 'pretty girls' of the cities. If anywhere in Galicia was going to be
the preserve of an autonomous, traditional, female musical tradition, then this should be it.

Yet Roseman mentions music only once in her study. Travelling
bands, playing a type of Galician variant on pop and rock 'n' roll,
tour the village halls. Their gender profile resembles that already
described: male musicians, often male lead singers, and glamorously
dressed women as backing singers and dancers, archetypical 'pretty
girls'. For one evening, the younger peasant women dress up and join

in, and then they go back to their farms the next morning. The key point here is that the term 'traditional' music is more problematic than it sounds. On the one hand, people like today's *pandereteiras* might be singing songs about peasant girls falling in love with Portuguese sailors, but this does not mean that they are peasant girls (or that they are in love with Portuguese sailors). On the other hand, the last peasants seem to be content to leave these 'traditional' Galician songs to the town-based *pandereteiras*, while they enjoy local sub-derivatives of Euro-pop. Which of these musical forms should be seen as the most authentically Galician?

In the last decade there have been several attempts to reclaim the *pandereteira* tradition. One of the most notable is being made by the group Faltriqueira, whose first CD was released in 2003. This five-girl group is from Pontedeume in A Coruña province.[29] They were all friends, and began to sing together just for fun. Today, they form a more sophisticated group than many of the amateur *pandereteiras*: their harmonies are more developed, the rhythms more complex, and the whole process has been tightened up, polished, professionalized. They learn their material from tapes of older singers. On their CD, male session musicians accompany them, but the girls' voices and the tambourines still predominate. They usually sing in Galego, and term their songs 'popular', rather than traditional. Their image, as seen in their publicity shots and CD covers, is 'girl next door': bright, cheerful, breezy; nothing too serious, nothing very challenging.

Peón's music is quite different. Her first CD, *Isué*, was released in 2000, followed by her second, *Arjú*, in 2003. Her originality lies in the fact that she has never tried to present an uncritical, smoothed-out pastiche of tradition. To start with, her appearance is deliberately shocking: she appears shaven-headed, a gesture which has considerable resonance in a country in which Francoists shaved the heads of female republicans as an act of public humiliation. Peón takes a quite ruthlessly revisionist approach to the *pandereteira* tradition. Her songs are mixed: some tracks are entitled 'traditional', others blend traditional tunes with Peón's words, and still others sample *pandereteira* songs from Peón's collection of recordings. Peón appears as singer, as backing singer, percussionist and *gaita*-player. One or two tracks feature her in six or eight different roles, multi-tracked. She frequently produces as well. The material is uneven: put simply, Peón presents two formats. There is one type of deliberately shocking, quasi-techno, head-on shout, in which Peón's strident voice is accompanied by a full rock drum-kit, techno-bass, electric guitars and screeching *gaitas*. This style contrasts with some slow, gentle ballads. Curiously, while Peón is a reasonably gifted singer, in the second CD her vocal style has often been stripped down to a mere chant. The subject matter is resolutely feminine: meeting boys at dances, romance and, curiously, given her 'punk' image, several lullabies, including one disastrous Galician reggae lullaby. On her first CD there is also a furious hymn of praise for the virtues of Galego, the language in which Peón normally sings.

Peón has an intriguing understanding of the relationship between her music and Galician traditional music. In an interview, she explained:

> For me tradition is the people like those *señoras* who were on stage last night. That's tradition, tradition, tradition. A *folklórico* group, that dances, sings like them, is imitating what they were – it isn't their own family, it doesn't come from transmission, it's a copy. The chain of transmission was broken thirty years ago. And I, as a musician, use the modulations, the ornamentation and so on from the tradition, in a music of creation, with a connection and with a feeling, it's not traditional music; it's Galician, but it's different.[30]

This is a quite subtle analysis of what constitutes 'the traditional'. Peón has no illusions about her ability to step into a cultural time-machine and magically recreate a legendary Galician past. She considers, probably correctly, that the past *is* past. Her task, instead, is to draw something living from it. For Peón, therefore, the traditional is synonymous with the new: a tradition has to evolve and to develop in order to survive. If it fails to do so, then it is no longer 'traditional', but merely a fossilized example of folklore. Peón also suggests a challenging assertion of what constitutes femininity, rejecting both the quasi-maternal images presented by Seivane and the wholesome 'girl-next-door' or 'pretty girl' look of Faltriqueira, and demands acceptance without these feminine stereotypes.

It is easy to dismiss these musical innovations and movements as 'just entertainment', with little lasting significance. However, when placed in their historical context, a more substantial meaning emerges. Firstly, it should not be forgotten that these discussions would never have been permitted during the Franco years. These singers and musicians are concrete evidence of a new cultural confidence in Galicia: for this reason alone, their debates about what constitutes the 'traditional' are worth considering. Secondly, one must also recall that they emerged during the Fraga years. While the BNG and the PSOE appeared to be stuck in permanent opposition to the unbeatable Fraga, these musicians and singers demonstrated an example of successful innovation which was, to some extent, critical of Xunta policies. Lastly, it should also be remembered that this area is one of the few in modern Galicia in which women have achieved some public prominence.[31]

The BNG and the PSOE

The 1980s and 1990s were difficult years for the opposition parties. There was some development: in 1983 a prominent and charismatic leader from the Galician nationalist PSG, Xosé Manuel Beiras, joined the BNG and renovated its policies, presenting the organization as a more inclusive, less intransigent grouping, willing to fight Galician parliamentary elections. (Part of this process was the dropping of the Maoist terminology implied in the old title BN-PG (Bloque Nacionalista-Popular Galego), and the adoption of the new acronym, BNG (Bloque Nacionalista Galego.) The organization grew more stable, with a core of some ten to twelve thousand members in the first years of the twenty-first century.[32] Its new identity is also growing clearer: it recruits from a relatively young, well-educated middle class, living in the cities and the big towns, open to libertarian and green politics, and clearly committed to left-wing causes.

While the cause of Galego and Galician culture is important to the BNG, it has never given these issues an overriding priority. Significantly, in the BNG's 256-page 2001 manifesto, Galego is not discussed until page 181. The bulk of the document is concerned with socio-economic proposals to develop Galicia's productive capacity: this is seen as the essential base for real autonomy.[33]

The typical BNG member is highly active, which can sometimes give a misleading impression of the breadth of the party's appeal. There are tensions, however, within the organization, which remains a coalition of different strands. Some frustration has been voiced with the strategy of an inclusive 'front', and – in 2001 – some concern emerged about Beiras's direction. Following the stagnation of the BNG's support in the 2001 Xunta election, Beiras resigned, to be replaced by Anxo Quintana, whose pleasant smiling face, with its neatly cropped beard, was replicated in electoral posters in 2005.

Quintana made a deliberate effort to tone down the BNG's style,
calculating that Beiras's firebrand nationalism probably scared
wavering PP voters. However, this new style did nothing to reverse
the decline in the BNG vote (Table 6.2).

Table 6.2. BNG votes in Xunta elections, 2001–5[34]

	Per cent vote	Seats
2001	23.3	17
2005	19.6	13

Despite its ability to represent about a fifth of the population, it
sometimes appears as if the BNG is caught within the trap set by the
famous 'three generations' rule, whereby the grandchild tries to
remember what the grandparent tried to forget. Núñez Seixas, one of
the most skilled analysts of Galician political cultures, alludes to this
by citing an extremely telling quotation from a 1993 edition of *A Nosa
Terra*, now the BNG weekly. The article begins by referring to the
respect that conservative cultural nationalists give to the wisdom of
the old.

> It is said that when each old man dies, a novel is lost. In Galicia, the death
> of an aged Galego-speaker is the death of someone who probably votes for
> the PP or the PSOE, of a pensioner, of someone who expects his *cacique* to
> find his grandson a job before he becomes a drug addict, of someone who
> never talks about the civil war but who carries in his memory the horrific
> sight of his cousin, shot and dying, lying in a ditch.
>   On the other hand, with every new birth in Galicia, a Castilian-speaker
> is born, someone who will spend three hours a day watching television, who
> knows nothing about the Catholic kings, but who has seen Santa Claus in a
> shopping centre, who will be a fan of Magic Johnson [a celebrated
> American baseball player] and Bebeto [a Brazilian footballer], someone
> heading for unemployment . . . probably set to be a BNG voter.[35]

While this passage is clearly meant to be ironic, it does raise some
serious questions about the BNG's support. I discussed this point
with one Galician activist, and was then told a joke about the mixing
of Galician politics and Galego. Readers should bear in mind that
BNG speakers nearly always use Galego, while PP speakers normally
use Castilian. However, to a Galician listener, BNG speakers sound
as if their first language is Castilian, and they are struggling to speak
well in Galego, while PP speakers sound like Galego speakers who
have difficulty expressing themselves correctly in Castilian.

Like Peón, the BNG's political culture suggests a complex dialectic with 'tradition': it is clearly a modern, forward-looking, leftist grouping, appealing to a relatively young audience, who retain a connection, if only indirectly and sentimentally, with some of the older themes of previous Galician nationalisms. While it successfully broadened its support in the 1980s, its votes still come principally from a relatively limited social milieu: the urban, radical young.

The socialist PSOE has some more reason to be confident. In 2004 there were about nine thousand three hundred PSOE members and a further sixteen thousand people classed as 'sympathizers' in Galicia: like the BNG supporters, they are strongest in the big cities.[36] The PSOE contains a number of divergent views concerning Galego and Galician identity. Francisco Vázquez, the PSOE mayor of A Coruña, has expressed some fervently anti-Galician statements in recent years, and such tensions prevented cooperation between PSOE and BNG councillors in Vigo in 2003 – thus allowing the minority PP to run the council. On the other hand, the PSOE certainly does not wish to challenge the existence of the Xunta: it accepts the principle of autonomy.

In recent years the rise of the PSOE and BNG has led to an apparent paradox, neatly expressed in a *Voz de Galicia* headline: 'The poorest parts of Galicia vote for the PP and the richest vote for the Left'.[37] Of the twenty-five poorest councils in Galicia in 2003, twenty-three voted in PP representatives, and only two for a PSOE majority. Of the twenty-five richest councils in Galicia, ten were held by the PSOE, three by the BNG, and two others by left-leaning independents. The paradox is resolved by looking at the data more closely: the poorest councils are all in rural Galicia, and contain large numbers of retired people. The young people of the richer cities are more likely to vote BNG, the middle-aged for the PSOE.

Galicia and the Prestige *disaster*

In November 2002 the oil-tanker *Prestige* sank 240 kilometres off the shores of Galicia. This event triggered a wide-ranging crisis in Galician society and even across Spanish society: obviously, it was an ecological crisis, but it was also an economic crisis and, in several different forms, a political crisis, most sharply symbolized by the rise of a new pressure group, Nunca Máis.[38] Nunca Máis represents something radically new in Galician history, and for this reason we will spend some time exploring the movement.

To the west of Galicia is one of the world's most important north–south sea routes, second only to the English Channel. Estimates of the number of ships that pass through vary from forty thousand a year to sixty thousand, but nobody denies the route's importance.[39] This point also has a fearsome reputation for ship-wrecks. During the winter months, in particular, the weather is often stormy, and there are strong and unpredictable currents in the seas. This is the part of the coast which Peón visited in 1983: Death Coast. In recent decades the most important shipping accidents have involved oil-tankers. There were seven serious incidents between 1970 and 2001, involving oil leaking from damaged ships, tankers sinking and – most bizarrely of all – the tanker *Aegean Sea* which caught fire off the coast near A Coruña in 1992.

The *Prestige* was built in 1976 in Japan, with the capacity to carry about eighty thousand tonnes: it was 243 metres long and 35.5 metres wide.[40] It was registered in the Bahamas, owned by Mare Shipping (Liberia), run by Universe Maritime (Athens), and hired by Crown Resources (Russia, UK and Switzerland) to carry oil from Latvia, via Gibraltar, to an unknown destination. Its crew consisted of a Greek captain, a Greek and a Romanian officer, and twenty-four Filipinos, each paid 400 euros a month. When the *Prestige* had been sent for repairs in China in 2001, it had been reported as suffering from rust, covering 10 per cent of its surfaces: it was still allowed to make the journey from Latvia.

On 13 November 2002, the *Prestige* was sailing southwards, fifty kilometres off Galicia. It was stormy: there were force nine gales, blowing at 75 to 87 k.m.p.h., and waves reaching eight metres high. The ship had already reduced its speed from 11.5 knots to 6.5.[41] At some point before 3 p.m. there was a loud bang, like an explosion, from the right side (starboard) of the ship: soon after, it began to list. Water began to leak in. Two of the ship's alarms sounded shortly afterwards, and its engines then cut out. At 3.15 p.m. an SOS call was put out by radio. The tanker was drifting, and the inexperienced and undertrained Filipino crew were terrified. Helicopters were called from Galicia, and the twenty-four Filipinos were lifted off at shortly after 6 p.m., while the captain and the two officers remained on board. Meanwhile, the captain had begun to take corrective action to correct the ship's angle: the interior of the boat was divided into compartments, and, by taking in water in those tanks opposite the leak, the angle was corrected.

At the same time the Spanish maritime authorities had ordered tugs out to pull the *Prestige* away from the coast. There then follows a confused episode: it appears that the captain was trying to contact the ship's owners (but which ones?) to get permission for the expensive process of being towed. Some three hours went by before he began to cooperate with the tug. Unfortunately, the heavy seas made it extremely difficult to attach a line securely to the *Prestige*. Sixteen attempts were made. It was not until 12.40 p.m., on the following day, that a line was finally attached. By this point, the *Prestige* could be seen from the port of Muxia, and oil was leaking from it. People could smell petrol on the sea. Even after a line had been attached, the Spanish tug was not powerful enough to pull the *Prestige* away: a second was needed. Later in the day, the ship's engines were reactivated. However, on the morning of 15 November, the captain shut down the engines, arguing that the vibrations were likely to damage the tanker.

Reports concerning the events of 14 and 15 November remain confused, but it appears that the captain and the Spanish authorities could not agree on the appropriate action to take, and so on 15 November, Wyste Huismans, a Dutch captain employed by Smit Salvaje, was sent to the ship by helicopter and given command of it. The captain was taken off the ship, and arrested as soon as he arrived in Galicia. At this point, the Spanish authorities needed to decide what to do. Francisco Alvarez-Cascos, the PP Minister for Public Works, gave clear instructions: they were to get the tanker as far away from the coast as possible.

At first sight, this seems to make sense. However, a number of criticisms can be made. Firstly, in which direction was the tanker to be pulled? Secondly, was it wise to pull the clearly damaged tanker? Expert opinion quickly expressed doubts, and recommended allowing the tanker to drift until the weather calmed, and then docking it in the port at A Coruña. Sixty-seven experts from the University of Vigo issued a public letter warning against the government's strategy.[42]

Government pronouncements remained resolutely confident at this point: the tanker was under control; only a small amount of oil had leaked out; the *Prestige* was too far away for its fuel to reach Galicia; and – above all – there was no danger of an oil slick hitting Galicia.

Galician public opinion was sceptical. Firstly, it was obvious that the authorities were not prepared for a disaster. The number of tugs available for such emergencies had been cut from twelve to five in 1997.[43] No anti-contamination ships were available; no barriers were being prepared in the coastal towns; and the army was not being mobilized. They also noted the differing opinions as to the best course of action.

It seems possible that the government's strategy was simply to get the *Prestige* out of Spanish waters. At 10.00 p.m. on 18 November, the Portuguese authorities warned the Spanish that they would not allow the *Prestige* to be towed into Portuguese territory. On the next day, 19 November, at 8.00 a.m. the tanker split into two. Its stern sank at 11.45 a.m., its prow at 1.22 p.m.

Even at this moment, the government remained optimistic. The *Prestige*'s wreck lay more than three kilometres under the sea: at that point the temperature was barely above freezing. Government officials argued that the oil would solidify and never leak. Above all, they gave out instructions that no one was to use the term '*marea negra*', meaning 'black tide' or 'oil slick'. The authorities seemed blindly ignorant of one simple point: the dominant currents from the position where the *Prestige* had sunk would send any leaking oil direct to the coast of Galicia.

These contradictions were becoming too obvious to ignore. For example, the Instituto Hidrográfico Portugués declared that the sunk ship would leak, flatly contradicting the Spanish government's analysis.[44] On 20 November, the government calculated that three to four thousand tonnes would leak from the ship, while the *Voz de Galicia* estimated eighteen thousand.[45] On 23 November, when French and Portuguese authorities warned that fuel was approaching the Galician coast, the Spanish authorities denied it.[46] On 29 November, when the Portuguese warned that an oil slick was thirty-five kilometres from the coast, the Spanish authorities estimated that it was sixty kilometres away.[47]

To make matters worse, Fraga was away from Galicia, on a hunting trip. His first reaction to the disaster was to visit the government in Madrid, and he did not return to Galicia until 28 November.

The dispute was growing political. On 24 November the Galician section of the PSOE declared that it would issue a motion of censure against Fraga. Commentators noted with interest that the PSOE was considering cooperation with the BNG on this matter, an innovation in Galician politics.[48] The response by Aznar, the PP Prime Minister of Spain, was swift and angry. He declared that anyone seeking to make political points concerning the crisis was 'a vulture'.[49]

To summarize: both the Xunta and the Madrid Government had underestimated the dangers represented by the *Prestige*. Both had sought to minimize the implications, and both had been reluctant to talk to the media or to local experts.

Galicians quickly realized that they could get more accurate information on the *Prestige* from Portuguese or French media than they could from the largely state-controlled Spanish television channels. Local journalists in the press, radio and television were extremely concerned, and issued a number of open letters condemning the government's 'irrational strategy of concealment'.[50]

There were some exceptions to this silence. The *Voz de Galicia*, normally apolitical and consensual in tone, was surprisingly outspoken, from the first news of the *Prestige* on 13 November. The left-of-centre *El País*, a national daily, picked up the story. And, lastly, the Galician nationalist writer Suso de Turo published a series of articles in the national daily *La Vanguardia*, which were at once quite furious in their tone and surprisingly prescient. His almost daily articles gave voice to a sense of the region's abandonment, and he criticized a government which showed arrogance and incompetence in equal measure.[51]

The oil slick reached the Galician coast in the last days of November. In the absence of any official provisions, local fishers made frantic efforts to hold it back. When it arrived, there was an astonishing mobilization of volunteers to clean the beaches: local students, ecologists, even tourists, coming from Spain, France and Germany. Almost ten thousand appeared, to the point where some coastal towns had to issue declarations that they were full, and could not accommodate any more.[52] The work that they were doing was difficult and dangerous: the oil is toxic, and should not be touched or inhaled. It may even be carcinogenic. For this reason, the volunteers wore cumbersome white overalls.

Approximately thirty-five thousand tonnes seeped out of the *Prestige*; much of it spilled on to the Galician coast, but it also drifted on northwards and eastwards to Asturias, the Basque country, and to the French coastline, between Bordeaux and Brittany.

Nunca Máis

The arrival of the oil slick produced an immediate, massive protest. As the PP was the party in government in both the Xunta and Madrid, it was the clear focus for the Galician protests.

Many factors were important in shaping a new mood. It was based on a fairly widespread and well-informed public scepticism, and on the example given by the heroic mobilization of the volunteers, including the many sympathetic foreigners, all wearing their distinctive white overalls. While officials spoke of hydrocarbon, petroleum derivatives or fuel, the volunteers spoke of *chapopote* (a Mexican term), *piche* (that is, pitch, English), *galipote* (French) and *mierda* (international). A bitter, ironic humour shaped the way they described the tar on the beaches: they would identify *galletas* (pancakes), *tortas* (biscuits), pizzas and lasagne. Manuel Rivas comments that they devised a cosmopolitan language of their own, drawn from the speech of migrants and sailors.[53] In itself, this semantic point may seem of little importance. In context, however, it is an indication of the growing separation of much of the Galician population from their regional and national governments.

The first real signs of protest came from outside established political parties. The open letter by scientists from the University of Vigo has already been cited. On 19 November, a group of writers and artists met in a bar in A Coruña to plan another initiative. They took the name 'Burla Negra', or black joke, which was also the name of a ship sailed by an infamous eighteenth-century Galician pirate.[54] On 27 November they issued a call for a mass demonstration in Santiago de Compostela. At this point, they were represented by Manuel Rivas and Uxía Senlle, a female singer. They created a new umbrella organization, Nunca Máis, which was supported by forty different groups, including political parties, trade unions, fishermen's associations and ecologists. (The slogan 'Nunca Máis' had previously been taken up by demonstrators during the *Aegean Sea* disaster in 1992. It is a Galego phrase; the Castilian equivalent would be 'Nunca Más'.) Nunca Máis of 2002 quickly devised a logo of its own: they took the Galician flag – white with a diagonal blue stripe – then painted its white background black, symbolizing the oil slick, and superimposed the slogan Nunca Máis on it.

It should be remembered that this movement grew up in the shadow of Fraga's fourth successive election victory in the Galician parliament, in 2001. This record seemed to demonstrate that Galicia was a conservative land, in which the PSOE and BNG had been outwitted for the best part of two decades. It was reasonably expected that, at most, some ten thousand might gather to protest on 1 December, and even these estimates declined when heavy rain began on the morning.

The final figure is still 'subject to debate'. Estimates range from one hundred and fifty thousand to three hundred thousand – the latter figure would be the equivalent of one-tenth of the region's population. In a sense, it could be compared with the massive anti-Iraq war protest in London in February 2003: both protests reached out far beyond the usual spectrum of politicized militants. The same comment circulated: 'I've never been on a demonstration before, but this time . . .' Often whole families turned up, carrying a surreal variety of homemade posters. Songs and slogans flowed through rain-sodden crowds. One point is indisputable about the December 2002 protest: this was the biggest demonstration in Galicia's history. Rivas had intended to read out a manifesto at the end of the demonstration. He finally had to read out his text four times, as more and more demonstrators crammed into the Obradeiro square, in front of Santiago's cathedral.

Following the success of this event, Nunca Máis organized a series of imaginative, well-planned protests across Galicia, and even into Spain. Some of the most important are listed below.

1. 1 December 2002, about 200,000 in Santiago
2. 6 December 2002, the 'Sea of Bagpipers', about 20,000 in Santiago
3. 28 December 2002, funeral wake at A Coruña
4. 25 January 2003, human chain along the coast of Galicia
5. 9 February 2003, 'Nós non emigramos' (we didn't emigrate) suitcase demonstration at A Coruña
6. 23 February 2003, the 'Dignity March', at least 100,000 in Madrid

In every case, these events benefited from massive public sympathy, expressing a widespread feeling that Fraga's government was patronizing, uncaring, incompetent and – above all – dishonest.

Let us look at two protests in a little more detail. The 'Sea of Bagpipers' event was organized by musicians: Peón and Seivane were among the first to contribute, and they made use of their contacts and networks to mobilize others. It was addressed by Xurxo Souto, a prominent Galego musician, who castigated the government's laxity and its contempt for the Galicians. Slightly unusually, Souto also referred to the defence of Galician culture, language and agriculture: by and large, Nunca Máis speakers avoided such explicit cultural nationalism. Most interesting of all, however, was the commentary by Toro, who spoke of how 'Our happy, free bagpipers have blocked, forever, the images of that pompous, obscene coronation of some local monarch, who was aided by a thousand hired bagpipers.'[55] Toro is contrasting the 'Sea of Bagpipers' with the spectacle of Fraga's investitures in 1993 and 1997. But, more significantly, he is also contrasting two visions of cultural nationalism. Fraga has created a type of 'theme park' national identity for Galicians, in which they are largely passive spectators in the repackaging of their own culture. Nunca Máis is suggesting a different type of Galician identity, certainly making use of Galego and rooted in their region, but open to contacts and interchanges from outside. Significantly, the Nunca Máis events celebrate the sea and the Atlantic ports. The organization is clearly based in the most modern and most open sectors of Galician society.

The 'suitcase' demonstration at A Coruña in February 2003 was a powerfully eloquent and imaginative use of peculiarly Galician symbols. It referred back to the comment by Castelao, the exiled Galician nationalist (see chapter 4), that Galicians don't protest, they emigrate. The slogan of the demonstration was a refusal of this logic: the protesters were not going to emigrate, they would stay in Galicia and protest. The site of the protest – the dockyards of A Coruña, from where so many Galicians had emigrated – gave an added poignancy to the protest. Each protester brought a suitcase (or a homemade replica of a suitcase), decorated with their individual slogans and pictures. They ranged from ferocious caricatures of Fraga, through images of oil-sodden seagulls, repeated representations of the Nunca Máis logo, to slogans: 'Arise Galicia! No more caciques!'

The Nunca Máis logo became ubiquitous. The pretty girls of Faltriquera placed Nunca Máis stickers on their tambourines. It could also be seen on car bumpers, on the balconies of high-rise flats, on graffiti on walls, at concerts, on T-shirts and on badges throughout 2003. Nunca Máis inspired at least two CDs and a dozen or so books. To give one further example, when I flew out from Santiago de Compostela airport in June 2003, I had some time to spare. I bought a CD at a kiosk: when the shop assistant wrapped it, she used 'Nunca Máis' sticky tape.

One observer has claimed recently that Nunca Máis is the most important social movement in Galicia since the Civil War.[56] Putting it mildly, this is a provocative claim: a challenge to the record of the leftist trade union federations of the early twentieth century (the UGT and the CNT), to the agrarians, the Partido Galeguista in the 1930s, the BN-PG and PSG in the 1980s and the PSOE in the 1990s. Nonetheless, it is a claim worth taking seriously.

There is, however, some difficulty in evaluating Nunca Máis's influence. As an umbrella organization, Nunca Máis does not, strictly speaking, have members: it merely federates existing groups. In 2003 it was supported by approximately three hundred other organizations. Perhaps predictably, its active support certainly seemed to decline during the last months of 2003. A demonstration was organized in November 2003 in Santiago de Compostela, with the explicit aim of celebrating the 'memory' and 'dignity' of the movement. The march on 1 December 2002 had assembled between one hundred and fifty thousand and three hundred thousand people: eleven months later, between forty and a hundred thousand gathered in Santiago de Compostela. This latter figure still represents a substantial number, far higher than the numbers that supported any of the demonstrations called by Galicia's political groups, but – also – undoubtedly far fewer than in the original demonstration.[57] Whom did the movement represent?

At first sight, one might say that Nunca Máis was extremely unusual, quite atypical of this conservative and conformist region, dominated by Fraga's PP. Examining it more closely, it seems more accurate to classify Nunca Máis as the expression of a new generation of Galician opposition, which should be seen as the direct descendant of the historic radical initiatives from A Coruña, such as its republicans and its Irmandade. One of the real innovations of this new movement is that it is so solidly rooted in the new urban west of Galicia. Previous movements had either originated elsewhere in Spain (such as the UGT and the CNT, or the republicans), or were, at least in part, a product of the eastern towns of Galicia. One recalls that the base for Risco and the conservative elements of the Partido Galeguista was in Ourense. Nunca Máis takes the urban west as its norm, and proclaims that the fishers and workers of the western coast *represent* Galicia. There are some problems with this: while the sea is tremendously important for the Galician economy, the fishers constitute only a small minority of the population.

After the protests

The right-wing press constantly claimed that Nunca Máis was merely a cover for the BNG. The first opportunity to test this claim came in May 2003, with the municipal elections. There was some expectation that the excitement of Nunca Máis would produce a decisive swing away from Fraga's PP. Beiras, speaking for the BNG, certainly seemed hopeful. He declared that 'Nunca Máis expressed a growing sense of Galician patriotism and the only political expression which represents such sentiments in a nationalist group like the BNG'. On the other hand, the PSOE was rather more reluctant to claim such close affinity to the protests.[58] Finally, the PP leaders attempted to discount the effects of the *Prestige*, with Mariano Rajoy commenting that it was 'history', and Fraga then qualifying that comment with the phrase 'prehistory'.[59]

The votes at the May 2003 elections showed surprisingly little change in the region's political profile. The PP clearly remained the largest party in the region, winning the largest share of the vote in all four provinces. Most surprising, it even kept its councils along the coast, sometimes even improving its score: it appears that voters were persuaded by the argument that PP councillors would be most effective in lobbying for compensation payments.[60]

On the other hand, all was not good news for the PP. Its overall vote was in decline: only in Ourense did it retain the absolute majority of votes. In A Coruña and Pontevedra provinces, the combined votes of the BNG and the PSOE exceeded the votes won by the PP. Most surprising of all, the PSOE was making steady progress in Lugo province. But the most serious lesson for the PP was that it was losing the urban vote. Of Galicia's seven big cities, the PP held only two (Ourense and Ferrol), while the PSOE held three (Lugo, Santiago de Compostela and A Coruña), and Pontevedra was won by the BNG. In Vigo, a split vote eventually resulted in the PP as the nominal head of the council, but in without a majority of seats.

The latest voting figures, from the March 2004 general elections and the June 2005 Xunta elections, suggest that these slow processes are continuing (see Table 6.3). There has been no dramatic break-through, but the PSOE continues to rise steadily, the BNG to stagnate, and the PP to fall, election by election. The 2005 Xunta election seemed to suggest that Galicia was divided almost equally into pro- and anti-Fraga sections.

Table 6.3. Voting results in the June 2005 Xunta elections[61]

	PP	PSOE	BNG
Votes (%)	44.9	32.5	19.6
Seats	37	25	13

The results in Pontevedra province were so close that a meticulous, eight-day check on postal votes was run: many expected that this conservative sector would vote mainly for the PP. However, on 27 June 2005, the results were confirmed: 37 seats for the PP, 38 for the newly formed BNG-PSOE coalition. Fraga's rule had ended.

Conclusions

In chapter 5, we surveyed the legacy of Fraga's four successive victories in Galician parliamentary elections. This chapter has demonstrated the incomplete nature of Fraga's success, to the point where – at last – some mass scepticism about his rule seems to be emerging.

It is hard to be sure how deep-rooted Nunca Máis is in Galician society, and equally difficult to demonstrate that Nunca Máis had any decisive influence over election results. What remains is an inter-esting, original and significant reworking of some of the classic themes of nationalism. Nunca Máis defends a certain Galician cultural legacy, but often twists this in a new way. One finds in its activities the classic nationalist pairing of intellectuals and people, and the passionate denunciation of an illegitimate ruling class. Here it is significant, however, that many of its most prominent intellec-tuals are non-party people: scientific experts, writers and musicians.

Nunca Máis's defence of Galician identity is clearly non-ethnic and avoids any essentialism. Speakers in Castilian are accepted at

Nunca Máis rallies, without resentment; manifestos and texts in Castilian are included, untranslated, in Nunca Máis writings. Instead, its politics are closer to the 'constitutional patriotism' proposed by Jürgen Habermas, within which the nation is valued as a framework for human rights.[62] In this case, the particular right that is being demanded is a right to ecological – and therefore economic – security. In terms of the classic categorization of sub-state nationalisms – regional, autonomist, separatist – Nunca Máis simply does not fit. Its first demand is for an *effective* autonomy, which does not necessarily equate with any particular constitutional arrangement. The significant rallying to the PSOE by Galician voters in 2004 may well be an expression of this.

After 1983, Mercedes Peón may have thought that she had discovered the true Galicia on A Costa da Morte. Her perceptive thinking on the nature of tradition followed, and it could be argued that the protest movement of Nunca Máis has actually demonstrated the truth of what she argued. A new Galicia is emerging: internationally orientated, open-minded, largely Galego-speaking, activist, confident and angry.

Notes

[1] Marta Malda, 'Mercedes Peón: un reino de contrastes', *Fusion: revista mensual* (December 2000).

[2] Instituto Galego de Estadística, *Enquisa de condicións de vida das familias: Coñecemento e uso do Galego* (Santiago de Compostela: IGE, 2004), p. 16. NB: interviewees could tick more than one box, therefore the column totals are all greater than 100.

[3] Cited in Bernadette O'Rourke, 'Conflicting values in contemporary Galicia: attitudes to "O Galego"', *International Journal of Iberian Studies*, 16:1 (2003), 33–48.

[4] Instituto, *Enquisa*, p. 5.

[5] Xosé M. Núñez Seixas, 'Idioma y nacionalismo en Galicia en el siglo XX: un desencuentro histórico y diversos dilemas en el futuro', *Revista de Antropología Social*, 6 (1997), 165–91.

[6] Ibid., p. 169.

[7] Xoán González-Millan, 'Publishing and selling Galician literature', *Galician Review*, 1 (1997), 83–97.

[8] BNG, Programa *de Governo Bloque Nacionalista Galego, 2001–05* (n.p.: no publisher, 2001), p.202.

[9] Cited in Manuel González González, 'La recuperación del Gallego', *Revista de Filogía Románica*, 3 (1985), 101–19.

[10] Ibid., p. 111.

[11] Instituto, *Enquisa*, pp. 12–14.

[12] Ibid., p. 19.

[13] Ibid., p. 20.

[14] O'Rourke, 'Conflicting values', pp. 39–40.

[15] Sharon R. Roseman, '"Falamos como Falamos": linguistic revitalization and the maintenance of local vernaculars in Galicia', *Journal of Linguistic Anthropology*, 5:1 (1995), 3–32.

[16] Núñez Seixas, 'Idioma y nacionalismo', p. 186.

[17] See Tracy Henderson, 'Language and identity in Galicia: the current orthographic debate', in C. Mar-Molinero and A. Smith (eds), *Nationalism and the Nation in the Iberian Peninsula* (Oxford: Berg, 1996), pp. 237–53.

[18] *La Voz de Galicia*, 9 July 2003.

[19] See *Voz de Galicia*, 12 July 2003.

[20] Núñez Seixas, 'Idioma y nacionalismo', p.180.

[21] O'Rourke, 'Conflicting values', pp. 40–5.

[22] In making this point, I am thinking of the thoughtful arguments by Joshua A. Fishman, 'Making good boundaries; interview by Xavier Erize', *Planet*, 140 (2000), 66–75.

[23] Xelís de Toro Santos, 'Bagpipes and digital music: the remixing of Galician identity', in J. Labanyi (ed), *Constructing Identity in Contemporary Spain* (Oxford: OUP, 2002), pp. 237–53.

[24] See ibid.

[25] *Idem*, 'Negotiating Galician cultural identity', in H. Graham and J. Labanyi (eds), *Spanish Cultural Studies* (Oxford: OUP, 1995), pp. 346–50.

[26] Andrew Cronshaw, 'Celtic Iberia', in K. Mathieson (ed.), *Celtic Music* (San Francisco: Backbeat, 2001), pp. 140–75, provides a useful survey of the contemporary Galicia music scene.

[27] Interviewed in Andrew Cronshaw, 'Stars and gaitas', *Folk-Roots*, 201 (2000), 20–5.

[28] Sharon R. Roseman, '"Strong women" and "pretty girls": self-provisioning, gender and class identity in rural Galicia (Spain)', *American Anthropologist*, 104:1 (2002), 22–37.

[29] Andrew Cronshaw, 'Tambourine queens', *Folk-Roots*, 242 (2003), 20–5.

[30] Interview in Andrew Cronshaw, 'After Isué', *Folk-Roots*, 214 (2001), 20–5.

[31] However, see also Sharon R. Roseman's study of the rather more limited revival of literary feminism in post-Francoist Galicia: 'Celebrating silenced words: the "re-imagining" of a feminist nation in late twentieth-century Galicia', *Feminist Studies*, 23:1 (1997), 43–72.

[32] See the informative study by Sydney A. van Atta, 'Regional nationalist parties and "new politics": the Bloque Nacionalista Galego and Plaid Cymru', *Regional and Federal Studies*, 13:2 (2003), 30–56.

[33] BNG, *Programa de Governo*.

[34] *El País*, 23 June 2005.

[35] This passage was so interesting that Núñez Seixas has cited it twice, once in English in his 'National reawakening within a changing society: the Galician movement in Spain', *Nationalism and Ethnic Politics*, 3:2 (1997), 29–56 (53), and once in Castilian in his 'Idioma y nacionalismo' (168). The version here is my own translation of the original Galego text.

[36] *La Voz de Galicia*, 6 April 2004.

[37] undated article from *Voz de Galicia* website on municipal elections of May 2003, *www.lavozdegalicia.es/especiales/municipales03*, consulted on 25 August 2004.

[38] For useful English-language analyses of the disaster, see J. D. García Perez, 'Early socio-political and environmental consequences of the *Prestige* oil spill in Galicia', *Disasters*, 27:3 (2003), 207–23; Gabriel Rei-Doval, 'Realpolitik, Galician style: the aftermath of the *Prestige* disaster', *Planet*, 163 (2004), 6–14.

[39] Luis Gómez and Pablo Ordaz, *Crónica negra del Prestige* (Madrid: Ediciones El

País, 2003), p.11 cite 60,000; Suso de Toro, *Nunca Máis* (Barcelona: Ediciones Península, 2003), p. 27, cites 40,000.

[40] Information from Gómez and Ordaz, *Crónica negra*, pp. 12–18, and *La Voz de Galicia*, 14 November 2002.

[41] Gómez and Ordaz, *Crónica negra*, pp. 12–18.

[42] Ibid., p. 149.

[43] Ibid., p. 140.

[44] *La Voz de Galicia*, 22 November 2002.

[45] Ibid., 20 November 2002.

[46] Ibid.,, 23 November 2002.

[47] Ibid.,, 29 November 2003.

[48] Ibid.,, 25 November 2003.

[49] Ibid.,, 26 November 2003.

[50] 'O colexío profesional de xornalistas de Galicia denuncia e condena . . .', in A. Paz (ed.), *Nunca Máis I* (Ourense: Difusora, 2003), p. 69.

[51] Toro's articles are collected in his *Nunca Máis* (Barcelona: Ediciones Península, 2003).

[52] *Voz de Galicia*, 14 December 2002.

[53] *El País Semenal*, 10 August 2003, 36–45.

[54] Gómez and Ordaz, *Crónica negra*, p. 144.

[55] Toro, *Nunca Máis*, pp. 53–4.

[56] Paz, introductory text to his edited collection, *Nunca Máis I*, p. 15.

[57] *El Mundo*, 17 November 2003.

[58] *Voz de Galicia*, 19 May 2003.

[59] *El País*, 27 December 2003.

[60] *La Voz de Galicia*, 26 May 2003.

[61] *El País*, 23 June 2005.

[62] See his *Après l'état-nation; une nouvelle constellation politique*, trans. Rainer Rochlitz (Paris: Fayard, 2000).

7

Conclusion: Galicia and nationhood

Galicia is a land marked by a unique history. Over the past three millennia, invaders have occupied this land to exploit its mines, pilgrims have visited its shrines, peasants have farmed its land, naval engineers have built up its ports, migrants have left from its docks, submarines have reprovisioned from its harbours, musicians have visited its universities, tourists have relaxed in its villages and oil tankers have sailed past its shores.

All of these factors have left their mark on Galician society, although none of them defines it in any obvious or complete manner. To understand contemporary Galician identities, we need to consider how feelings of nationhood have evolved in this land.

At first sight, nationhood appears to be an obvious topic: so many people feel, instinctively and with a blinding certainty, that they belong, body and soul, to a particular nation. However, as one looks more deeply, contradictions and inconsistencies begin to emerge in such simple assertions of belonging. For example, one finds families in which the son says he is Welsh, but the daughter calls herself British. Academics and researchers have attempted to study and to clarify such debates in recent decades, but, it must be acknowledged, their studies have been inconclusive.

Galicia provides some intriguing examples of how such debates have developed. Firstly, it must be stressed once more that medieval Galicians, like all the medieval peoples, simply did not have access to the concept of 'nationhood', for the obvious reasons that they did not have access to the necessary technologies of nationhood: no mass literacy, no mass media, no press, no radio, no television. At best, in the Middle Ages, one finds that structures which define ethnic, religious and cultural identities are based on non-national movements, such as Islam or Christianity, or on the more spontaneous, unplanned developments of folk culture – its tales, songs and riddles. Perhaps one can find a 'proto-nationalism' here, but such phrases suggest too strict a path for the unpredictable manner in which identities develop.

One of the first attempts to define national identities was developed by German Romantic nationalists, such as Johann Herder (1744–1803), who in turn influenced Murguía and Risco in Galicia. Such philosophers attempted to establish objective criteria by which nationhood could be identified: they argued that if, for example, a particular people possessed a distinct language, a separate culture and a specific set of political institutions, *then* such people constituted a nation. One could illustrate this attitude by citing the example of Risco, in the early 1930s, who argued that there was no need for a referendum on Galician autonomy, as it was clear that Galicia already constituted a nation – in other words, the wishes of the people of Galicia did not matter. Here, the weakness of this interpretation is revealed: how can a nation exist if the majority of the people in that land do not recognize it?

The second great and influential attempt to understand nationhood came from French political thinkers. It stressed the *subjective* nature of nation-building: nationhood required active popular assent. This is exemplified in the dictum by Ernest Renan (1823–92) that a nation is like a daily referendum: it is *as if* the entire population was being asked each day whether they considered that they were French, German or Galician. The weakness of this interpretation is that often such referendums are fixed: having experienced schooling and conscription, and having been issued with a passport, did the population really have any choice but to say 'yes' to their nationhood?

In practice, the nineteenth- and early twentieth-century Spanish state tended to present its citizens with a rather weak amalgam of the two forms of nationhood, stressing imagined racial and cultural traditions, but also accepting the need for representative political forms, which eventually extended to adult male suffrage in 1891 and adult suffrage in 1931. Its attempts to integrate the population were, of course, ruined by *caciquismo*, which alienated most Spanish people from modern mass politics.

In Galicia, this debate on nationhood remains unfinished. Post-Franco, most mainstream Spanish politicians have argued against any form of nationalism, citing the terrorism of ETA as an example of what happens when national passions catch alight. Spain is now understood as a federation of seventeen autonomous communities, and Galicia, along with the Basque country and Catalonia, must remain part of this new entity. 'Objective' nationalists, such as Murguía, and more 'subjective' nationalists, like Castelao or Beiras, have replied that Galicia is clearly separate from Spain, but none of these strands has ever convincingly persuaded the mass of the Galician people. Indeed, one notes the growing social and cultural fractures within contemporary Galicia, making it harder to demonstrate that any single factor unites them: the divisions between the emigrants and those who remain, between republicans and monarchists, left and right, Galician autonomists and Spanish patriots, city-dwellers and villagers, those who live along the coast and those who live inland, eastern conservatives and western modernists, Galego speakers, Castilian speakers and speakers of a range of usually unacknowledged sub-variants.

Something constant remains, however: not an unchanging core, but a shared situation. This is the key point revealed by Nunca Máis. The movement was based on a demand for a political structure which would serve the people of Galicia, which would guarantee them their civic rights. It presents a highly original interpretation of nationhood, and it is no coincidence that it has emerged in this land, so bereft of the ordinary features of nationalism. Of course, one cannot claim that Nunca Máis *is* Galicia: the movement reached its peak early in 2003, and then declined. It never commanded the loyalty of the majority of Galicians. Its ideals and practices were firmly opposed by Fraga, the old fox of Galician politics, whose conservative values still retain the respect of many.

This, then, is the key lesson from Galicia. Fraga's PP gives an extraordinary example of how Francoist politicians can adapt to and change to fit the context set by parliamentary democracy. Galicia's history even shows how easily the techniques of democracy can be turned against the spirit of democracy. Fraga's PP works efficiently as a mechanism for the distribution of jobs, subsidies and favours. In return, it guarantees a certain degree of economic development and social progress. An integral part of this process has been the construction of a new type of conservative Galician identity. Nunca Máis demands something else: it speaks a language of passionate idealism and activism; it demands that individual Galicians take steps to seize control of their environment and their land. This is a challenging appeal which suggests a radically new type of Galician political culture: different from the deterministic certainties of Murguía and Risco, from the passive idealism of Piñeiro and from the hypermilitancy of the neo-Maoist nationalists of the 1970s. I hope that ideals like those of Nunca Máis will continue to inspire new generations of Galicians.

Bibliography

Further reading

English-language readers are at a disadvantage. While there are some excellent detailed studies of specific aspects of Galician history, there are no wide-ranging syntheses. I would recommend the following (see secondary sources for full details): Sydney Atta's provocative and well-researched comparison between the BNG and Plaid Cymru; Manuel Artaza's study of early modern political structures, which deserves an award for lucidity; the studies by Tracy Henderson and Bernadette O'Rourke, both remarkably clear expositions of the political implications of Galego language policy; Ramón Maíz and Antón Losada's analysis of Galicia under Fraga; Xosé M. Núñez Seixas's two English-language studies (Núñez Seixas is a remarkable Galician scholar whose work is always provocative, well-informed and coherent); and Sharon B. Roseman's studies – Roseman seems to be a latter-day Rosalía de Castro, documenting the life of Galicia's peasant women.

Readers who can understand Galego and Castilian have an advantage. The second edition of Ramón Villares's history is strongly recommended as an introduction: a more imaginative, better written and better researched version of his first work. Alongside that, Beramendi and Núñez, *O Nacionalismo Galego*, is an excellent work on Galician nationalism. Carlos Casares's collection of three biographies considers a wide range of issues and questions. Granja, Beramendi and Anguera present an imaginative and original project to outline the history of Spain as a collective history of different nationalities. Márquez Villanueva has written an excellent and incisive analysis of the myth of Saint James. Santos Solla's essay on the effects of the Galician demographic crisis is one of the most incisive analyses of contemporary Galician society available.

Primary sources

Blanco Torres, Roberto, *Xornalismo Irmandiño* (Vigo: A Nosa Terra, 1999).

BNG, *Programa de Governo Bloque Nacionalista Galego, 2001–5* (n.p.: no publisher, 2001).

Borrow, George, *The Bible in Spain* (London: Dent, 1961).

Buechler, Hans C., and Judith-Maria Buechler, *Carmen: The Autobiography of a Spanish Galician Woman* (Cambridge, Mass.: Schenkman, 1981).

Casas, Victor, *Escritos Políticos* (Vigo: A Nosa Terra, 1996).

Casares, Carlos, *Wounded Wind*, trans. Rosa Rutherford (Aberystwyth: Planet, 2004).

Castelao, Alfonso R., *Sempre en Galicia* (Buenos Aires: Galicia, 1976).

Castro Rosalía de, *Antología poética*, ed. Ernesto Sábado (Buenos Aires: Losada, 1998).

—— *Beside the River Sar*, trans. and ed. S. Griswold Morley (Berkeley, Calif.: University of California Press, 1937).

Chaucer, Geoffrey, *The General Prologue to the Canterbury Tales*, ed. James Winny (Cambridge: Cambridge University Press, 1965).

Cunqueiro, Alvaro, *El pasajero en Galicia* (Barcelona: Tusquets, 2002).

Fernán, M. A., and F. Pillado Mayor, *Conversas en Compostela con Carballo Calero* (Barcelona: Sotelo Blanco, 1986).

González López, Emilio, *Memorias de un estudiante liberal (1903–1931)* (Sada: O Castro, 1987).

—— *Memorias de un diputado de la Cortes de la República* (Sada: O Castro, 1988).

—— *Memorias de un diputado republicano en la Guerra civil española* (Sada: O Castro, 1990).

Hutchinson, John, and Anthony D. Smith (eds), *Nationalism* (Oxford: OUP, 1994).

López, Beatriz, *Hasta la Victoria siempre . . . testimonio de Carmen, Emigrante gallega y militante de la vida Cornes* (Sada: O Castro, 1992).

Martinez-López, Francisco, *Guérillero contre Franco: la guérilla antifranquiste du Léon (1936–1951)* (Paris: Syllepse, 2000).

Mellado, Francisco Paulo, *Recuerdos de un viaje por Galicia en 1850* (A Coruña: Arenas, 1999 [1850]).

Murguía, Manuel, *Historia de Galicia* edited selections in Justo G. Beramendi, 'Pensamiento Político Galleguista (*c.*1840–*c.*1950)' in J. Antón and M. Caminal (eds), *Pensamiento Político en la España Contemporánea, 1800–1950* (Barcelona: Teide, 1992), pp. 751–85.

Otero Pedrayo, Ramón, *Prosa Miúda: Artigos non coleccionadas (1927–1934)* (Sada: Ediciós do Castro, 1988).

Paz, A. (ed.), *Nunca Máis I* (Ourense: Difusora, 2003).

Pardo, Bazán, Emilia, *La Tribuna* (Madrid: Alianza Editorial, 2002).

Pérez Lugín, Alejandro, *La Casa de la Troya* (Santiago de Compostela: Galí, 1985).

Risco, Vicente, *Obra completa, I: Teoría nacionalista* (Madrid: Akal, 1981).

Rivas, Manuel, *Galicia, Galicia* (Madrid: Santilla Ediciones Generales, 2002).

—— 'La rebelión del mar', *El País Semenal* 10 August 2003, 36–45.

Sánchez, Pedro Antonio, *La economía gallego*, ed. Xosé M. Beiras (Vigo: Galaxia, 1973).

Newspapers (Articles of particular interest have been listed in the bibliography of secondary sources below)

Galicia Hoxe
Guardian
El Mundo
El País
La Voz de Galicia

Secondary sources

Alted Vigil, Alicia, 'La oposición republicana, 1939–1977' in Nigel Townson (ed.), *El republicanismo en España (1830–1977)* (Madrid: Alianza Editorial, 1994).

Alvarez-Junco, José, *The Emergence of Mass Politics in Spain: Populist Demagoguery and Republican Culture, 1890–1910* (Brighton: Sussex Academic Press, 2002).

Amarelo de Castro, Fernanda, *A galeguidade: un sentimento común* (n.p.: Xunta de Galicia, 1995).

Arias, Pedro and Cancio, Miguel, *Las elecciones en Galicia, 1977–1997* (Santiago de Compostela: Tórculo, 1999).

Artaza, Manuel María de, 'Regional political representation in the Spanish monarchy during the *Ancien Régime*: the *Junta General* of the kingdom of Galicia', *Parliaments, Estates and Representations*, 18 (1998), 15–26.

Atta, Sydney A. van, 'Regional nationalist parties and "new politics": the Bloque Nacionalista Galego and Plaid Cymru', *Regional and Federal Studies*, 13:2 (2003), 30–56.

Balcells, Albert, *Catalan Nationalism, Past and Present*, trans. Jacqueline Hall (Houndsmill: Macmillan, 1996).

Baliñas Pérez, Carlos, *Gallegos del año mil* (A Coruña: Fundación Pedro Barrié de la Maza, 1998).

Barret, Pierre, and Gurgand, Jean-Noël, *Priez pour nous à Compostelle* (Paris: Hachette, 1978).

Batterbury, Sarah C. E., 'Evaluating policy implementation: the European Union's small and medium-sized enterprise policies in Galicia and Sardinia', *Regional Studies*, 36:8 (2002), 861–76.

Beramendi, Justo G., 'Pensamiento Político Galleguista (*c*.1840–*c*.1950)', in J. Antón and M. Caminal (eds), *Pensamiento Político en la España Contemporánea, 1800–1950* (Barcelona: Teide, 1992), pp. 751–85.

Beramendi, Justo G., and Xosé M. Núñez Seixas, *O Nacionalismo Galego* (Vigo: A Nosa Terra, 1996).

Blinkhorn, Martin, 'Spain, the "Spanish problem" and the Imperial myth', *Journal of Contemporary History*, 15 (1980), 5–25.

Bobillo, Francisco, *Nacionalismo Gallego: La Ideologia de Vicente Risco* (Madrid: Akal, 1981).

Bonnassie, Pierre, 'La época de los visigodos', in P. Bonnassie, P. Guichard and M.-C. Gerbet (eds), *Las Españas medievales*, trans. B. Hervàs (Barcelona: Crítica, 2001), pp. 9–48. .

Bouzada Fernández, Xoán, and A. Lage Picos, Xesus, 'O retorno como culminación do ciclo da emigración galega', *Grial*, 162 (April 2004), 26–35.

Braudel, Fernand, *The Mediterranean and the Mediterranean World in the Age of Philip II*, trans. Siân Reynolds (London: Collins, 1973).

—— *Civilization and Capitalism, 15th–18th Century, Vol III: The Perspective of the World*, trans. Siân Reynolds (London: Fontana, 1984).

Brenan, Gerald, *The Spanish Labyrinth* (Cambridge, CUP: 1978),.

Cabrera Varela, Julio, 'Las precondiciones sociales de la identidad colectiva en Galicia', *Historia y Crítica*, 4 (1994), 209–38.

Cagiao Vila, Pilar 'Género y emigración: las mujeres immigrantes gallegas en la Argentina', in Xosé M. Núñez Seixas (ed.), *La Galicia Austral* (Buenos Aires: Biblios, 2001).

Callahan, William J., 'Crown, nobility and industry in eighteenth-century Spain', *International Review of Social History*, 11 (1966), 444–64.

Carbayo-Abengózar, Mercedes, 'Shaping women: national identity through the use of language in Franco's Spain', *Nations and Nationalism*, 7:1 (2001), 75–92.

Cardesin Díaz, José Maria, 'Paysannerie, Marché et Etat: la structure sociale de la Galice rurale au 19e siècle', *Annales HSS*, 6 (1996), 1325–46.

Cardona, Gabriel, *El Problema militar en España* (Madrid: Historia 16, 1990).

Carr, Raymond, and Juan Pablo Fusi, *Spain: Dictatorship to Democracy* (London: George Allen and Unwin, 1981).

Casares, Carlos, *Conciencia de Galicia: Risco, Otero, Curros; Tres Biografías* (Vigo: Galaxia, 2004).

Castelao, Rey, 'Los Gallegos en el Río de la Plata durante la época colonial' in X. Núñez Seixas (ed.), *La Galicia Austral* (Buenos Aires: Biblios, 2001), pp. 23–52.

Castro Pérez, Xavier, 'Las bases sociales del nacionalismo gallego', in Justo G. Beramendi and Ramón Maíz (eds), *Los nacionalismos en la España de la II Republica* (Madrid: Siglo XXI, 1991), pp. 255–73.

Champeney, Anna, 'Ethnography in north-west Spain: peasant crafts in Galicia: present and future', *Folklife*, 34 (1998), 83–99.

Charter, Christine, 'Susana Seivane', *Folk-Roots*, 254/55 (2004), 69.

Collins, Roger, *The Arab Conquest of Spain, 710–797* (Oxford: Blackwell, 1994).

Cores Trasmonte, Baldomero, *Ramón Suárez Picallo: Socialismo, Galleguismo y Acción des masas en Galicia* (Sada: O Castro, 1983).

Crecente, Rafael, Carloz Alvarez and Urbana Fra, 'Economic, social and environmental impact of land consolidation in Galicia', *Land Use Policy*, 19 (2002), 135–47.

Cronshaw, Andrew, 'Stars and gaitas', *Folk-Roots*, 201 (2000), 20–5.

—— 'Celtic Iberia', in K. Mathieson (ed.), *Celtic Music* (San Francisco: Backbeat, 2001), pp. 140–75.

—— 'After Isué', *Folk-Roots*, 214 (2001), 20–5.

—— 'Tambourine queens', *Folk-Roots*, 242 (2003), 20–5.

Cruz, Roberto, *El Partido Comunista de España en la II Republica* (Madrid: Alianza Universidad, 1987).

Cuadrado, Miguel M., *Elecciones y Partidos Políticos de España (1868–1931), Vol. II* (Madrid: Taurus, 1969).

Cunliffe, Barry, *Facing the Ocean: The Atlantic and its Peoples, 8000BC–AD 1500* (Oxford: OUP, 2001).

Davies, Norman, *The Isles: A History* (London: Macmillan, 1999).

Díaz Santana, Beatriz, *Os Celtos en Galicia: arqueología e política na creación de identidade galega* trans. Rosa María Guerrero (A Coruña: Toxosoutos, 2002).

Dubert, Isidro, 'Domestic service and social modernization in urban Galicia, 1752–1920', *Continuity and Change*, 14:2 (1999), 207–26.

—— *Del Campo a la ciudad: migraciones, familia y espacio urbano en la historia de Galicia, 1708–1924* (Vigo: Nigra Imaxe/Consorcio de Santiago, 2001).

Duran, J. A., *Agrarismo y Movilización Campesina en el país gallego (1875–1912)*, (Madrid: Siglo Veintiuno, 1977).

Estévez, Xerardo, 'Xacobeo 2004', *El País*, 15 May 2004.

Fernández, Alejandro E., 'Los Gallegos dentro de la colectividad y las asociaciones españolas en el primer tercio del siglo XX', Xosé M. Núñez Seixas (ed.), *La Galicia Austral* (Buenos Aires: Biblios, 2001), pp. 139–60.

Fernández Baz, Manuel Anxo, *A formación do nacionalismo galego contemporáneo (1963–1984)* (Santiago de Compostela: Laiovento, 2003).

Fernández Prieto, L., and X. M. Núñez Seixas, A. Artiga Rego and Xesús Balbao (eds), *Poder local, elites e cambio social na Galicia* (Santiago de Compostela: Universidade de Santiago de Compostela, 1997).

Fernández, Santiago, Marcelino X., 'Asociacionismo Gallego en Buenos Aires (1936–60)' in X. Núñez Seixas (ed.), *La Galicia Austral* (Buenos Aires: Biblios, 2001), pp. 181–201.

Fishman, Joshua A., 'Making good boundaries; interview by Xavier Erize', *Planet*, 140 (2000), 66–75.

Flitter, Derek, 'Icons and imperatives in the construction of Galician identity: the "Xeración *Nós*"', *Forum for Modern Language Studies*, 36:3 (2002), 296–309.

Freixanes, Victor F., 'Conversa con Francisco Fernández e Xaime Isla Conto', *Grial*, 157 (2003), 50–7.

Gala González, Susana de la, 'Day workers, main heirs: gender and class domination in the parishes of Mourisca and Beba', trans. Sharon R. Roseman, *Antropológica*, 41 (1999), 143–53.

Galdo, Xosé Rodríguez, and Fausto Dopico, *Crisis Agrarias y Crecimiento Económico en Galicia en el siglo XIX* (A Coruña: O Castro, 1981).

García-Lombardero, Jaime, 'Economic transformations in Galicia in the nineteenth and twentieth Centuries', in N. Sánchez-Albornoz (ed.), *The Economic Modernization of Spain, 1830–1930*, trans. K. Powers and M. Sañudo (New York: New York University Press, 1987), pp. 223–40.

García Perez, J. D., 'Early socio-political and environmental consequences of the *Prestige* oil spill in Galicia', *Disasters*, 27:3 (2003), 207–23.

Geary, Patrick, *The Myth of Nations: The Medieval Origins of Europe* (Princeton: Princeton University Press, 2002).

Gerbet, Marie-Claude, 'Los Espanoles de la "Frontera"', in P. Bonnassie, P. Guichard and M.-C. Gerbet (eds), *Las Españas medievales*, trans. B. Hervàs (Barcelona: Crítica, 2001), pp. 189–247.

Gómez, Luis, and Pablo Ordaz, *Crónica negra del Prestige* (Madrid: Ediciones El País, 2003).

Gondar Portasany, Marcial, *Crítica da Razón Galega* (Vigo: A Nosa Terra, 1995).

González Jiménez, Manuel, 'Frontier and settlement in the kingdom of Castile (1085–1350)', in R. Bartlett and A. McKay (eds), *Medieval Frontier Societies* (Oxford: Clarendon, 1989), pp. 49–74. .

González González, Manuel, 'La recuperación del gallego', *Revista de Filogía Románica*, 3 (1985), 101–19.

González-Millan, Xoán, 'Publishing and selling Galician literature', *Galician Review*, 1 (1997), 83–97.

Grandío Seoane, Emilio, 'O pader local na provincia da Coruña durante a II República' in L. Fernández Prieto, X. M. Núñez Seixas, A. Artiga Rego and Xesús Balbao (eds), *Poder local, elites e cambio social na Galicia* (Santiago de Compostela: Universidade de Santiago de Compostela, 1997), pp. 243–74.

Grandío Seone, Emilio, *Caciquismo e eleccións na Galiza da II Republica* (Vigo: A Nosa Terra, 1999).

Granja, José Luis de la, Justo Beramendi and Pere Anguera, *La España de los nacionalismos y las autonomías* (Madrid: Editorial Síntesis, 2001).

Habermas, Jürgen, *Après l'état-nation; une nouvelle constellation politique*, trans. Rainer Rochlitz (Paris: Fayard, 2000).

Harrison, Joseph, 'Big business and the failure of right-wing Catalan nationalism, 1901–1923', *Historical Journal*, 19:4 (1976), 910–18.

Henderson, Tracy, 'Language and identity in Galicia: the current orthographic debate', in C. Mar-Molinero and A. Smith (eds), *Nationalism and the Nation in the Iberian Peninsula* (Oxford: Berg, 1996), pp. 237–53.

Henn, David, 'Looking for scapegoats: Pardo Bazán and the war of 1898', in A. H. Clarke (ed.), *A Further Range* (Exeter: University of Exeter Press, 1999), pp. 44–60.

Hermida García, Modesto, *As revistas literarias en Galicia na Segunda Republica* (Sada: O Castro, 1997).

Heywood, Paul, *Marxism and the Failure of Organised Socialism in Spain, 1879–1936* (Cambridge: CUP, 1990).

Iglesias, María Antonia, 'Manuel Fraga: "Los buenos toreros mueren en la plaza"', *El País*, 12 September 2004.

Instituto Galego de Estadística, *Enquisa de condicións de vida das familias: Coñecemento e uso do Galego* (Santiago de Compostela: IGE, 2004).

Irujo, José María, 'Marée blanche sur la côte espagnole', *Courrier international* 720 (August 2004), 34–5.

Jaspe, Alvaro, 'The military uprising of 1936 and the repression in Galicia', *Galician Review*, 3–4 (1999–2000), 77–102.

Jones, R. F. J., 'The Roman occupation of north-west Spain', *Journal of Roman Studies* 66 (1976), 45–66.

Julía, Santos (ed.), *Víctimas de la Guerra civil* (Madrid: Historia, 1999).

Kamen, Henry, *Spain, 1469–1714: A Society of Conflict*, second edn (London: Longman, 1991).

—— *Spain's Road to Empire: The Making of a World Power, 1492–1763* (London: Penguin, 2003).

Kuethe, Allan J., and G. Douglas Inglis, 'Absolutism and enlightened reform: Charles III, the establishment of the *Alcabala* and commercial reorganization in Cuba', *Past and Present*, 109 (1985), 118–43.

Lagares Diez, Nieves, *Génesis y Desarrollo del Partido Popular de Galicia* (Madrid: Tecnos, 1999).

Lamela García, Luis, *'Foucellas': el riguroso relato de una lucha antifranquista (1936–52)* (Sada: O Castro, 1993).

Lenerz-De Wilde, Majolie, 'The Celts in Spain', in Miranda J. Green (ed.), *The Celtic World* (London: Routledge, 1995), pp. 533–51.

López Iglesias, Edelmiro and Mar, Pérez Fra, 'Axuste agrario e despoboamiento rural', *Grial*, 162 (2004), 36–43.

Maíz, Ramón, 'El galleguismo de Castelao: Nacionalismo Organicista y democracia política', in J. Antón and M. Caminal (eds), *Pensamiento*

Político en la España Contemporánea, 1880–1950 (Barcelona: Teide, 1992), pp. 787–809.

Maíz Ramón, and Antón Losada, 'Institutions, policies and nation-building: the Galician case', *Regional and Federal Studies*, 10:1 (2000), 62–91.

Malda, Marta, 'Mercedes Peón: un reino de contrastes', *Fusion: revista mensual* (December 2000).

Malefakis, Edward E., *Agrarian Reform and Peasant Revolution in Spain* (New Haven and London: Yale University Press, 1970).

Manzano Moreno, Eduardo, 'The creation of a medieval frontier: Islam and Christianity in the Iberian peninsula, eighth to eleventh century', in D. Power and N. Standen (eds), *Frontiers in Question* (Houndsmill: Macmillan, 1999), pp. 32–54.

Márquez Villanueva, Francisco, *Santiago: tragectoria de un mito* (Barcelona: Bellaterra 2004).

Martín Najera, Aurelio, *Segunda Republica: El Grupo Parlamentario Socialista* (Madrid: Fundación Pablo Iglesias, 2000).

Martínez Barreiro, Enrique, *La Coruña y el Comercio colonial gallego en el siglo XVIII* (A Coruña: O Castro, 1981).

Martinez Cuadrado, Miguel, *Elecciones y Partidos Políticos de España (1868–1931), Vol. II* (Madrid: Taurus, 1969).

Martínez García, X. Antonio, *A Igrexa antifranquista en Galicia (1965–1975)* (Sada: O Castro, 1995).

Mirás, Jorge and Chico, 'A campaña en fotos', *Galice Hoxe: RDL*, 9 June 2005.

Moradiellos, Enrique, 'The Potsdam Conference and the Spanish problem', *Contemporary European History*, 10:1 (2001), 73–90.

Moreno, Francisco, 'La represión en la posguerra', in Santos Juliá (ed.), *Victimas de la guerra civil* (Madrid: Historia, 1999), pp. 275–406.

Moya, José C., *Cousins and Strangers: Spanish Migrants in Buenos Aires, 1850–1930* (Berkeley, Calif.: University of California Press, 1998).

Mullins, Edwin, *The Pilgrimage to Santiago* (Oxford: Signal Books, 2001).

Neale, Sara T., 'Literacy and culture in early modern Castile', *Past and Present*, 125 (1989), 65–96.

Núñez Seixas, Xosé M. (ed.), *La Galicia Austral* (Buenos Aires: Biblios, 2001).

Núñez Seixas, Xosé M., 'Emigración y nacionalismo Gallego en Argentina, 1879–1936', *Estudios Migratorios Latinoamericanas*, 5:15/16 (1990).

—— 'National reawakening within a changing society: the Galician movement in Spain', *Nationalism and Ethnic Politics*, 3:2 (1997), 29–56.

—— 'Idioma y nacionalismo en Galicia en el siglo XX: un desencuentro histórico y diversos dilemas en el futuro', *Revista de Antropología Social*, 6 (1997), 165–91.

—— 'The region as essence of the Fatherland: regionalist variants of

Spanish nationalism (1840–1936)', *European History Quarterly*, 31:4 (2001), 483–518.

O'Neill, Mary, 'Oral and literate processes in Galician–Portuguese song', *Galician Review*, 3–4 (1999–2000), 8–18.

O'Rourke, Bernadette, 'Conflicting values in contemporary Galicia: attitudes to "O Galego"', *International Journal of Iberian Studies*, 16:1 (2003), 33–48.

Ortega Villodres, Carmen, 'Participación y abstención Electoral: la Segunda República en perspectiva comparada', *www.ciere.org/CUADERNOS/Art%2049*, accessed on 23 July 2004.

Pagden, Anthony, *Peoples and Empires* (London: Weidenfeld and Nicolson, 2001).

Pallares, Carmen, and Portela, E., 'Les revueltas compostelanas del siglo XII: un episodio en el nacimiento de la sociedad feudal', in Ramon Villares Paz (ed.), *La Ciudad y el mundo urbano en la historia de Galicia* (Santiago de Compostela: Torculo, n.d.), pp. 89–105.

Partido Popular, *O Noso Compromiso con Galicia: Manifesto Electoral*, undated (2005?) *http://www.ppdegalicia.com/*, accessed 16 June 2005.

Payne, Stanley G., *Spanish Catholicism: An Historical Overview* (Madison, Wisc.: University of Wisconsin Press, 1984).

—— *Spain's First Democracy: The Second Republic, 1931–1936* (Madison, Wisc.: University of Wisconsin Press, 1993).

Pereira, Dionisio, *A CNT na Galicia, 1922–1936* (Santiago de Compostela: Laiovento, 1994).

Pérez de Tudela y Velasco, María Isabel, 'Guerra, violencia y terror: la destrucción de Santiago de Compostela', *La España medieval*, 21 (1998), 9–28.

Poase Antelo, José Manuel and Pernas Orozo, Herminia, 'O desenvolvemento da política local no marco dun concello rural: A Baña, 1900–1936', in L. Fernández Prieto, X. M. Núñez Seixas, A. Artiga Rego and Xesús Balbao (eds), *Poder local, elites e cambio social en Galicia* (Santiago de Compostela: Universidade de Santiago de Compostela, 1997), pp. 373–92.

Preston, Paul, *Franco; A Biography* (London: HarperCollins, 1993).

Rei-Doval, Gabriel, 'Realpolitik, Galician style: the aftermath of the *Prestige* Disaster', *Planet*, 163 (2004), 6–14.

Rodríguez Lago, José Ramón, 'Sociología y Comportamientos politicos del clero parroquial en la Galicia rural (1898–1936)', in L. Fernández Prieto, X. M. Núñez Seixas, A. Artiga Rego and Xesús Balbao (eds), *Poder local, elites e cambio social na Galicia* (Santiago de Compostela: Universidade de Santiago de Compostela, 1997), pp. 287–325.

Romasanta, Alberto, 'Víctor Casas: O compromiso galeguista', in Casas, *Escritos*, pp. 7–60.

Roseman, Sharon R., '"Falamos como Falamos": linguistic revitalization and the maintenance of local vernaculars in Galicia', *Journal of Linguistic Anthropology*, 5:1 (1995), 3–32.

—— 'Celebrating silenced words: the "re-imagining" of a feminist nation in late-twentieth-century Galicia', *Feminist Studies*, 23:1 (1997), 43–72.

—— '"Strong women" and "pretty girls": self-provisioning, gender and class identity in rural Galicia (Spain)', *American Anthropologist*, 104:1 (2002), 23–37.

Rosende, Anxel M., *O Agrarismo na Comerca do Ortegal (1893–1936): a loita pola modernización da agricultura* (A Coruña: Ediciós do Castro, 1988).

Ruiz, Juan Pro, 'Fraude, statistique et pouvoir dans l'Espagne libérale (1840–1868)', *Revue d'histoire moderne et contemporaine*, 41:2 (1994), 253–68.

Saavedra, Pegerto, *La vida cotidiana en la Galicia del Antiguo Régimen* (Barcelona: Crítica, 1994).

Sallmann, Jean-Michel, *Géopolitique du XVIe siècle, 1490–1618* (Paris: Seuil, 2003).

Santos Solla, Xosé M., 'A población galega, algo máis ca unha crise demográfica', *Grial*, 162 (2004), 18–25.

Schmidt-Nowara, Christopher, '"La España Ultramarina": colonialism and nation-building in nineteenth-century Spain', *European History Quarterly*, 34:2 (2004), 191–214. .

Shaver-Crandell, Annie and Paula Gerson, 'Introduction', *Pilgrim's Guide to Santiago de Compostela: A Gazetteer* (London: Harvey-Miller, 1995).

Sierra Rodríguez, Javier, 'Elecciones al Parlemento de Galicia 2001', www.monografias.com, accessed 1 August 2004.

Siguan, Miquel, *España plurilingüe* (Madrid: Alianza Universidad, 1992).

Tojo Ramolla, José Antonion, *Testimonios de una represión: Santiago de Compostela, julio 1936 – marzo 1937* (Sada: O Castro, 1990).

Toro, Suso de, *Nunca Máis* (Barcelona: Ediciones Península, 2003).

Toro Santos, Xelís de, 'Negotiating Galician cultural identity' in H. Graham and J. Labanyi (eds), *Spanish Cultural Studies* (Oxford: OUP, 1995), pp. 346–50.

—— 'Bagpipes and digital music: the re-mixing of Galician identity', in J. Labanyi (ed.), *Constructing Identity in Contemporary Spain* (Oxford: OUP, 2002), pp. 237–53.

Townson, Nigel (ed.), *El Republicanismo en España (1830–1977)* (Madrid: Alianza Editorial, 1994).

Tuñón de Lara, Manuel, *Poder y Sociedad en España, 1900–1931* (Madrid: Colección Austral, 1992).

Varela Ortega, José, 'Aftermath of splendid disaster: Spanish politics before and after the Spanish–American War of 1898', *Journal of Contemporary History*, 15 (1980), 317–44.

Vásquez González, Alejandro, 'Factores de empuje y condiciones de trans-porte de Galicia hacia el Ríon de la Plata (1850–1930)', in Xosé M. Núñez Seixas (ed.), *La Galicia Austral* (Buenos Aires: Biblios, 2001), pp. 53–68.

Velasco Souto, Carlos F., 'Repensado o caciquismo: algunhas reflexións e preguntas . . .', in L. Fernández Prieto, X. M. Núñez Seixas, A. Artiga Rego and Xesús Balbao (eds), *Poder local, elites e cambio social na Galicia* (Santiago de Compostela: Universidade de Santiago de Compostela, 1997), pp. 275–86.

Vieites Torreiro, Dolores, 'La participación de los Gallegos en el movimiento obrero argentino (1880–1930)', in Xosé M. Núñez Seixas (ed.), *La Galicia Austral* (Buenos Aires: Biblios, 2001), pp. 161–80.

Vilas Nogueira, José, *Las elecciones en Galicia (1976–1991)* (Barcelona: Working Paper 57, 1992).

Villares, Ramón, *Historia de Galicia* trans. Ezequiel Méndez (Madrid: Alianza Editorial, 1999).

—— *Historia de Galicia*, second edn (Vigo: Galaxia, 2004).

Wilde, Majolie Lenerz-De, 'The Celts in Spain', in Miranda J. Green (ed.), *The Celtic World* (London: Routledge, 1995), pp. 533–51.

Williams, Derek, *The Reach of Rome* (London: Constable, 1996).

Wolf, Philippe, *Western Languages AD 100–1500*, trans. Frances Partridge (London: Phoenix, 2003).

Wulff, Fernando, *Las esencias patrias: historiografía e historia antigua en la construcción de la identidad española* (Barcelona: Crítica, 2003).

Compact Discs

Carlos Núñez, *Mayo Longo* (BMG Music Spain, 74321 770572).

Mercedes Peón, *Isué* (Resistencia 106).

—— *Arjú* (Trompo, DM 838-02).

Resonet, *¡Santiago!* (Boanerges, 2022).

Susana Seivane, *Alma de Buxo* (BOA 10002028).

Sequentia, *Vox Iberica I: Donnersöhne* (Deutsche Harmonia Mundi 77199).

Websites

Centro de Investigaciones y Estudios Republicanos, *www.ciere.org*

Hume Travel, *www.hume-travel.com*

Instituto Galego de Estatistica, *www.ige.xunta.es*

Instituto Nacional de Estadística, *www.ine.es*

Partido Popular de Galicia, *www.ppdegalicia.com*

Partido Popular de Ponteareas, *www.lanzadera.com/ppponteareas*
La Voz de Galicia, *www.lavozdegalicia.com*
Xornal: el primer diario electrónica de Galicia, *www.xornal.com*
Xunta de Galicia, *www.xunta.es*

Index